PHILLY SPECIAL

THE INSIDE STORY OF HOW THE PHILADELPHIA EAGLES WON THEIR FIRST SUPER BOWL CHAMPIONSHIP

Sal Paolantonio
ESPN National Correspondent

30 YEARS®

TRIUMPH
BOOKS

Library of Congress Cataloging-in-Publication Data is available upon request

This book is available in quantity at special discounts for your group or organization. For further information, contact:

Triumph Books LLC
814 North Franklin
Chicago, Illinois 60610
(312) 337-0747
www.triumphbooks.com

Printed in U.S.A.
ISBN 978-1-62937-741-4
Design by Sue Knopf
Page production by Patricia Frey

Photos courtesy of AP Images unless otherwise indicated

Contents

Prologue

The 2017 Philadelphia Eagles were a great team. But they were an even better story.

It's the story of how a star-crossed NFL franchise defied the critics and the oddsmakers, won its first Super Bowl title, and became America's team. Several days after it happened, former NFL wide receiver Nate Burleson said on NFL Network, "It's a movie." Yes, you could say that. But it was all too real. I saw it with my own eyes. I had a front row seat the whole way. In short, I lived it. What follows is the inside story of how it really happened.

For me, the highlight of the story came just minutes after Tom Brady's Hail Mary pass to tight end Rob Gronkowski fell harmlessly to earth at U.S. Bank Stadium in Minneapolis on Sunday, February 4. NFL commissioner Roger Goodell handed Eagles owner Jeffrey Lurie the Lombardi Trophy. Green and white confetti were shot into the air with hydraulic cannons and cascaded onto the players and coaches and their families.

Doug Pederson slowly descended from the national television riser and found me waiting at the bottom of the steps.

Here we were, two guys who live just a mile or so from one another in the small town of Moorestown, New Jersey, which is about 15 miles from the Eagles' home stadium, Lincoln Financial Field in South Philadelphia. At that moment, we seemed to be suspended at the confluence of our careers and history, with hundreds of cameras and reporters from all over the world surrounding us, talking to one another about how the Eagles did it—beat the mighty New England Patriots and won their first Super Bowl title.

We looked at each other, the camera rolling—a moment frozen in time and bright lights. Then my instincts just took over. I knew I had just a few minutes before Pederson's NFL escort was going to yank him away from me, so I discarded the pleasantries and just did my job: I asked him a question.

"Doug," I began, "you said all along this would be a 60-minute game, it would come down to the end, how did you do it?"

"It's just a resilient group, Sal," he said. "They battled all year long. I just made my mind up to stay aggressive all the way throughout the game. Trust our players. Trust our quarterback. Trust our players to make plays."

* * *

Oh, boy, was he aggressive. In the annals of Super Bowl head coaches, Pederson may go down as the greatest gambler ever. And I know exactly where that came from.

I remember talking with Doug Pederson the morning of his first regular season game, Sunday, September 11, 2016. His father, Gordon, who was his mentor and taught him the game of football, had passed away in Monroe, Louisiana, just nine days earlier. It was a tough nine days for Doug; his wife, Jeannie; and their family, burying the patriarch of the Pederson family. The man who infused family, church, and football into the fabric of their lives was not going to be there when his son put on the headset on an NFL sideline as the head coach of a pro football team for the first time. In fact, Pederson had missed part of the week of preparation to attend the funeral and be with his mom, Teri; brother, David; and sister, Cathy, in Louisiana. So Pederson was about to take the field in his professional debut with a hole in his heart.

That morning, the Eagles' public relations staff had warned me that I only had time for three questions. Talking to an NFL head coach before the game at the stadium is pretty rare. It happens maybe once or twice a season. Got to be a coach who's pretty comfortable dealing with the media. Let's put it this way, it's not something Patriots coach Bill Belichick would ever agree to do. Pederson is the polar opposite. But still, it was his first game. I can tell you for a fact, having covered the NFL for 25 years, that just doesn't happen.

I asked Doug about the game, then his talking points to the team. But I had to ask him about his father's passing. I knew it was touchy, but if I didn't ask it I would be derelict in the basic duty of journalism. He was ready for it. "Doug," I said, "what advice do you think your dad would give you this morning?"

"He would say, 'Son, be yourself, but stay aggressive. Always stay aggressive,'" Pederson replied.

Covering his tenure for two years, I always came back to that interview as a guidepost to understanding Pederson's go-for-it mentality in his first year as the Eagles' head coach, an approach that was perfectly suited for his rookie quarterback, Carson Wentz, the young buck from North Dakota who took the franchise and the NFL by storm in 2016.

Pederson was often criticized for going for it too often on fourth down in 2016. The chorus of complaints on Philadelphia's two vibrant sports talk radio stations was brutal. He was called misguided and foolhardy, and worse, much much worse.

But, in retrospect, he was setting the foundation that would allow him to remain aggressive throughout the championship season of 2017, including going 2-of-2 on fourth down in Super Bowl LII.

The night before Super Bowl Sunday, I was the only reporter invited into the Eagles' team hotel, the Radisson Blu, on the south end of the Mall of America. The layers of security were brutal. The feds were concerned about terrorists. The local cops were deathly afraid of a renegade local gunman. The Eagles' security staff was worried about one thing: Belichick stealing a look, a hint, a tendency—anything that gave the Patriots an edge. (But there's time for a full examination of that later in this book.)

Pederson and I met in the lobby for a long interview for *SportsCenter*. As a small gift of appreciation for his time and candor all year long, I brought him his favorite dessert: A pint of Häagen-Dazs vanilla ice cream. I asked him if he would be channeling his father on Super Bowl Sunday. "I'll definitely be thinking about him," he said. "I'll be thinking about what he told me."

* * *

Which brings us to the most famous and successful fourth-down play in Super Bowl history: The Philly Special.

Now, I want you to think about this for a minute. NFL coaches, by nature, are conservative. They rarely go for it on fourth down. But going for it on fourth down on the one-yard line in the Super Bowl—running a play that's never been tried in the 52-year history of the Super Bowl, a play that your team has never tried before in a game—that's being aggressive. In the streets, in the locker room, they have another nickname for that brand of hutzpah. Let's just say on Super Bowl Sunday, Doug Pederson decided to wear his big boy pants.

The Philly Special was a reverse toss to a tight end who throws a pass to the quarterback leaking out of the line of scrimmage into the end zone. And it starts with a direct snap to an undrafted rookie running back, Wisconsin's Corey Clement, who went to Glassboro High School, which is South Jersey rival to Moorestown, where Pederson's kids go to school.

Now, that's a wow.

So, here are the particulars: 38 seconds left in the half, the Eagles had fourth-and-one. Even though the Patriots had just scored, Philadelphia had the lead, 15–12. So, Pederson could've kicked a field goal, gone up 18–12, and nobody would have questioned him. But Pederson's defense was failing him and he knew it. They could not stop Tom Brady, and would not stop him until late in the game, which Pederson had no way of knowing.

During a timeout, quarterback Nick Foles came to the sideline and looked at Pederson, who held the laminated play sheet over his mouth. Foles said, "Philly, Philly?" Pederson knew what he meant: Philly Special—a play that the Eagles had practiced for four weeks and were going to run against the Minnesota Vikings in the NFC Championship Game before deciding the Vikings might sniff it out because the Chicago Bears, their division rival, had run it. This time, Pederson just said, "Yes, let's do it." That simple.

Foles went to the huddle and said just two words: "Philly Special." At the line of scrimmage, he yelled, "Kill, kill!" and moved slightly to his right, right behind right tackle Lane Johnson. Clement took the direct snap, ran to his left, and tossed the football like a loaf of bread to tight end Trey Burton, who had been a high school quarterback in Florida.

Burton threw a perfect spiral to Foles, who crept into the end zone like a thief disappearing into the night. Foles, who played high school basketball in Texas, has big, soft hands—he's caught many passes in the low post.

"It seemed like the ball would never get there," Foles told me. "All I kept telling myself is, focus on the ball. I knew I was already in the end zone and all alone."

"That's who I am," said Pederson. "That's my alter ego. That's my evil twin, I guess. I learned that from my dad, his aggressiveness with us growing up. I want every play scoring touchdowns and every defensive play losing five yards. I may come off as soft-spoken to you guys, but inside, I want to win the game. Not at an all-cost expense, but pretty close. When you're playing the Patriots, Bill Belichick, Tom Brady, if you're not playing aggressive, you're going to lose those games. I made up my mind after the Vikings game, I knew we were playing the Patriots, I was going to have to maintain that aggressiveness in the football game. The pressure of the game was not going to change who I am."

* * *

The touchdown shocked the world. Burton became the first tight end in NFL history to throw a touchdown pass in a Super Bowl. And Foles became the first quarterback to catch a touchdown pass in a Super Bowl. More important, the call and its execution announced to the Patriots they were in a fight and it proclaimed to the Eagles players standing with Pederson that he entrusted them to win the most important game of any of their lives.

Particularly Foles. Remember, this is the guy who replaced a player who had reached mythical, Paul Bunyanesque status in just 29 NFL starts—Carson Wentz. Foles needed to know that Pederson trusted him—make no mistake about that. Since December 10, when Wentz blew out his knee in Los Angeles, Pederson's trust in Foles never publicly wavered—even while Foles' game went through the natural ebb and flow of a late, in-season replacement quarterback.

A little history here: Since the Super Bowl era began in 1970, this kind of thing had only happened once before. In 1990, New York Giants quarterback Phil Simms suffered a freak foot injury after his team had accumulated 11 wins. He was replaced by Jeff Hostetler, who won three postseason games, including Super Bowl XXV in Tampa, when Scott Norwood's kick sailed wide right and the Buffalo Bills lost their best chance at a world title.

The Giants, an NFC East team, beat the Bills, an AFC East team—just like the Eagles over the Patriots. But that's where the comparison breaks down. Remember, that Giants team was coached by Bill Parcells, who had already won a Super Bowl title with New York and was on his way to the Hall of Fame. His defensive coordinator that day was Bill Belichick, who would go on to win five more Super Bowl titles with the Patriots and is on his way to Canton. And that team had Hall of Famer Lawrence Taylor and the best defense of its time.

No one is prepared to say that Pederson will end up a Hall of Famer—yet. Remember, when Pederson was brought on to replace Chip Kelly in 2016, *USA Today* ranked him dead last of the seven NFL head coaching hires that year. Dead. Last. (Three of those coaches have since been fired. The other three had losing records in 2017.)

And the 2017 Eagles' defense was good, but not historically good. So what Foles did was far more difficult than what Hostetler accomplished. Indeed, you could say it was unprecedented.

By making that Philly Special call, Pederson told everybody—the team, 100 million television viewers, and the Patriots' defense—that he believed in Foles. "That play-call said to all of us, 'We got this—to the bitter end,'" safety Malcolm Jenkins said.

Foles, the MVP of Super Bowl LII, had done what many quarterbacks had tried to do for the Eagles franchise and its fan base: Bring home the Lombardi Trophy.

* * *

Four days after the game, the day before the biggest championship parade in the city's history, I had a quiet moment with Foles outside the Eagles' locker room at the team's NovaCare Complex practice facility in South Philly.

"Nick," I said to him, "I hope you know what you've done. You've erased three generations of doubt and disappointment and disrespect—not only for this team and franchise, but for a community of people, millions of fans around this area and all over the country who have waited for this moment."

He just looked at me, soaked it all in. I knew he got it.

I continued: "Just from my perspective, I've covered this team for 25 years—trying to tell the story of this quest. That's a lot of road trips. A lot of Sundays away from my family. A lot of sacrifice that my family made for me to be with this team. So, for my family there is certainly elation and closure. You did it for all those families out there who I can tell you are feeling the same thing."

He reached out and hugged me, and said, "That's awesome."

"Yes, it is," I said. "Thank you."

And then, literally 30 minutes later in an auditorium on the other side of the building, Pederson ruined that touchy-feely moment. Pederson proclaimed that the team was not done. The story was not over—that we were all not going anywhere.

"Get used to this," Pederson said. "Get used to playing football in February. This is the new norm. This is just the beginning."

So, that's where we shall start this Eagles championship story, at the beginning.

PART I

WELCOME TO WENTZYLVANIA

Chapter 1

The Wentz Wagon Hits the Road

The Eagles at the Redskins
Sunday, September 10, 2017 • Landover, Maryland

"The dude is a stud."

That's what Nick Foles said about Carson Wentz.

On Sunday, September 10, 2017, before he would transform himself into a full-blown NFL stud, before he would become the leading candidate for league MVP in just his second year in the league, before he would lead the Philadelphia Eagles on the most implausible nine-game winning streak anybody could contemplate, Carson Wentz would have to do something he did not do once his entire rookie season: Win a division game on the road.

It was one of those swampy, humid early September mornings in the suburbs of the nation's capital and Wentz was wearing big designer headphones, listening to gospel music, running along the sidelines of FedEx Field, getting ready for a game that his head coach, Doug Pederson, was about to tell his team was vitally important if the Eagles were going to make any kind of trouble in the always volatile NFC East. The Eagles, Washington Redskins, New York Giants, and Dallas Cowboys have traded division titles off and on for the last 13 seasons. Indeed, the NFC East has been the only division in the NFL without a repeat title winner during that time. In short, the division is the dictionary definition of dog eat dog in professional football. And step one to winning a division title, to making the playoffs: Win on the road Week 1 in Washington.

Wentz, who has the bow-legged gallop of a wild mare, finished the individual and team drills and sprinted with his teammates and the coaching staff to the visitors' locker room. The chief of Eagles security Dom DiSandro—known as "Big Dom" because he looks like he could be the bouncer at any high-end Manhattan nightclub—closed the door behind them.

And that's when Doug Pederson began laying down the law. His speech was passionate, but to the point. He gave the 2017 Eagles three marching orders:

"OK," he said, "we got to do something we didn't do very well last year. We got to start fast. We talked about it all summer. Start fast, finish strong."

In 2016, Pederson and Wentz stormed onto the scene with three straight wins to start the season, but then tailed off badly, losing six of eight games in November and December that doomed the promise of both their rookie campaigns. The Eagles made a habit of getting off to dismal starts and playing from behind. That forced the team to rely more and more on

Wentz—as a passer and a runner—and it was clearly too much for him. Remember, he had last played at North Dakota State, a notch below Division I college football. He had never before been tested like this physically and mentally. The city, the team, the league had fallen in love with No. 11—his jersey was near the top of all sellers in the NFL, alongside Tom Brady, Aaron Rodgers, and J.J. Watt. But he couldn't carry the team alone. Indeed, after the season was over, Pederson had told Wentz to "put down the football and get away from the game for a while," to rest his mind and body.

Wentz had heard about the all-consuming nature of the football fans in Philadelphia. He thought he was ready for it. He was not. At times, it overwhelmed him, especially when he thought it was time to get re-dedicated to the only task that mattered: Winning the city's first Super Bowl title.

"It's cool," he said. He said he and his teammates and family have talked about it a lot. "You've read about it. And everyone's talking about it non-stop. And then playing for a full season, it was real. I was a part of it. I told the story last year when Nelson [Agholor] dropped the ball in practice and they booed him at open practice. I was like, 'All right, this is real. The real deal.'"

But Wentz also remembers the last game of 2016, on New Year's Day. The Cowboys were in town. Both teams were out of the playoffs. "The place was packed," said Wentz. "I'll always remember that. Are they hard?" referring to the fans. "Sometimes. That's part of it. But I wouldn't have it any other way."

Pederson's advice after the 2016 season had worked. But now the head coach was asking Wentz to re-ignite that early 2016 fire and propel this team to another fast start.

"And we got to play with passion," Pederson continued in his team meeting. "We got to want it for 60 minutes. Especially when the other team gets tired in the fourth quarter. We got to bring the passion."

Pederson finished with a warning: "I want to see how we respond when a little adversity comes."

Looking back on how the 2017 season played out, it's quite amazing that Pederson's first three talking points to what would become a championship team were exactly what needed to be said and would carry through all 16 games of the regular season, the playoffs, and Super Bowl LII.

His teams would start fast, play with passion, and be challenged by a historical level of adversity—beginning with the first game of the year against a gnarly Redskins team that had just as much to prove.

* * *

Not everybody was all in on Carson Wentz, Year 2. Not by a long shot. There were three major unresolved issues: Mechanics, a lack of accuracy on his long ball, and durability. Wentz was exposing his body too much, taking too many hits.

All of those question marks were raised during one single play against the Redskins, who were on a five-game winning streak against the Eagles. Philadelphia had not beaten Washington since September 21, 2014, 37–34. And the last win *in* Washington was the September before that: 33–27. These games were always one-score battles of attrition.

And I had a ground level view. As luck would have it, I got the last-minute assignment to be the ESPN radio sideline reporter for this game. My broadcast partners were the incomparable Adam Amin and the Hall of Famer Bill Polian, a former six-time NFL Executive of the Year.

When you're on the sideline, you get to hear, feel, see, and smell the game in a completely different way. An NFL game is a carnival of color and anger, an often-confusing collision of bumper cars—without the cars. It's a fully engaged symphony— an orchestration that requires instant improvisation based on what the coaches and players see and experience. It's a chess match with one important difference: The other guy is trying to knock you out.

The American game of football, especially at the NFL level, is the last team sport on earth where it is legislatively okay to commit a violent act. "Your job is to take the other man down," said former Baltimore Ravens linebacker Ray Lewis, who was inducted into the Hall of Fame in the summer of 2018. "Take him down to the ground. Take him down violently. And take away the football violently. It's an act of violence. And in an act of violence, a man will eventually get hurt."

But football is also a game of specifically designed movements, a syncopation of timed events within clearly delineated spaces. It's not a mass movement game like soccer or basketball or rugby. Timing is critical. Until it's not. That's when a player just has to go out and make a play. It's a cliché. But it's true. The team with the best players almost always wins.

And there is nothing more important in the game of improvisation than what happens between a quarterback and a wide receiver on a deep pass down the field.

The quarterback has to have the right technique—footwork and release of the ball. The ball has to have the right trajectory. The wide receiver has to have the right release off the snap— the slightest hesitation or interference from a defensive back can ruin the timing. A second lost here or there and the connection is doomed.

NFL teams such as the Eagles practice throwing the ball deep hundreds of times in spring practices, in training camp, in preseason games, practice during the week, pregame warm- ups—until it all becomes second nature, until the muscle memory is so familiar it's like taking the dog for a walk or eating a bowl of Cheerios. And even then, it's often a miracle if it all works seamlessly in the game.

* * *

It was the Eagles' first offensive play from scrimmage, first-and-10 from their own 44-yard line. Wide receiver Torrey Smith—a brilliant off-season acquisition by vice president for football operations Howie Roseman who had already won a Super Bowl in Baltimore—had beaten the loud-mouthed Redskins cornerback Josh Norman right down the middle of the field, a seam route that had given Wentz fits the previous year. With Smith screaming toward the end zone wide open, Wentz had a clear shot. He took it. But the ball never got there and Smith never had a chance.

The same deep ball mechanics that he had spent all off-season to correct and looked polished in training camp and the preseason did not come back to the Eagles' second-year quarterback. Pederson would later say that Wentz's foot "slipped." His foot does slip a little. But not enough, from my vantage point, and then watching it on tape, to justify such an underthrown pass.

Wentz simply did not drive the football where it needed to be. Even though he established the team's all-time rookie record with 379 completions in 2016, routinely hitting the deep ball was something that plagued him, especially as the year wore on. There were questions about whether he had developed elbow soreness, which was never established. He did clearly seem tired. And why not? Wentz had thrown 607 passes in his rookie year, the second-most attempts of any rookie quarterback in league history. Only Andrew Luck threw more in his rookie year (627 in 2012). And look what happened to Luck: He was beaten and battered and wound up with his shoulder shredded, needing surgery that kept him out of football in 2017.

In the off-season, to adjust his mechanics, Wentz worked out with Adam Dedeaux, the quarterback whisperer and Motion Mechanics Instructor at 3DQB on the West Coast. From what I saw in spring practices, the fine-tuning worked. The ball came out more quickly and he seemed to be opening

Week 1 at FedEx Field, Carson Wentz talks to me about winning divisional road games, which he had failed to do in his rookie season. (Brian Franey)

up his front foot so that he could push off with more power and authority with the back foot. "I like what I see," Pederson told me at the time. "He's driving the deep ball better."

Dick Vermeil, the former Eagles head coach who took the team to its first Super Bowl appearance in 1980 and watched Wentz all summer, told me this: "Carson Wentz has the potential to be one of the truly great ones. I mean truly great. Number one area of improvement I want to see this year is his accuracy downfield. And he needs receivers who make all the catches, even the tough ones."

Well, Roseman provided two of those: Smith and Alshon Jeffery, a veteran free agent from Chicago. But if the pass was going to be that inaccurate, there was no way the receivers could make up the difference.

After the ball got away from him against Washington, Wentz was visibly upset and Pederson could sense it immediately. On the very next play, the Redskins beat the Eagles' offensive line and Wentz took a nasty hit and sack.

Pederson told me he had a decision to make: Call a running play on third-and-12 and hope for the best, then punt. Or, stay aggressive. He chose option two. Wentz slid into the shotgun. He eluded the rush—this is what would be both his signature move and drive everybody crazy. On this play, he bought just the right amount of time and threw a laser at wide receiver Nelson Agholor, who had been plagued by drops in 2016, when the Eagles led the league with 31 dropped passes. Agholor snagged the pass and pirouetted and found his way to the end zone. In all, 58 yards and a touchdown. Eagles 7, Redskins 0.

Start fast, play with passion, respond to adversity—all three boxes checked. In one play. On the first offensive possession of the first quarter of the first game.

And it was sweet redemption for Agholor, whose heart and commitment to the game had been severely criticized and questioned in 2016, leading Pederson to wonder whether Agholor was worth saving. But new wide receivers coach Mike Groh, the son of legendary Bill Parcells acolyte Al Groh, worked him hard over the summer and built his confidence.

After the game, Pederson would tell me: "You've got to take these shots. If you're struggling offensively or you're just not moving the ball and the defense sees that and they start crowding the box with eight or nine guys, then you're sunk. You got to take shots to loosen everybody up, the defense and your own team. Give them a scare. Give us some confidence that no matter what happens, we're going to play football."

* * *

And a lot did happen in this game. But the Eagles kept playing football.

I was on the sideline, wearing ESPN radio headphones, standing about 15 yards from Pederson when Ronald Darby—right in front of the Eagles' bench—crumpled to the turf. Initially, my view of the play and the player was blocked. But I could hear Darby's agony and I could see the stunned faces of his teammates. Darby's right ankle was a twisted mess.

Safety Malcolm Jenkins, the leader of the defense, kneeled. On the sideline, there was shock and disgust—the look that said, "Is this how this season is going to go?"

Darby was making his first start in an Eagles uniform. And he looked fluid and quick—just what Roseman wanted when he traded with his old nemesis, Buffalo Bills head coach Sean McDermott, to obtain Darby, shipping wide receiver Jordan Matthews to the Bills in a risky swap. Matthews was Wentz's best friend on the team. On the day of the trade, just before the season started, Wentz and several other teammates—tight end Zach Ertz, safety Chris Maragos, and linebacker Jordan

Hicks—drove Matthews to Philadelphia International Airport to say good-bye. There were no tears, just a lot of prayers. The four of them attend services and Bible study in the same church in Cherry Hill, New Jersey, where the motto is "God's vision for each of us is unique"—a sentiment that would help Matthews cope with leaving the team that drafted him and his closest friends in the world.

So, there was tremendous pressure on Darby. Good thing he had talent. Bad luck that he got hurt in a non-contact injury. Later, it would become official: Darby out for months.

But even before that realization, just moments after Darby was carted off the field, I could see one player urging his teammates on the sideline to rally to the cause, to close the deal, to get a road win at FedEx Field. It was veteran defensive end Chris Long, also in his first year with the team—the son of Hall of Fame pass rusher Howie Long who had won a Super Bowl title in 2016 with the New England Patriots. Long and Patriots teammate LeGarrette Blount were brought in as Sunday mercenaries by Roseman to teach the Patriot Way—do your job, find a way to win. No matter what the cost, no matter what the adversity.

"We got a game to play, let's go," said Long, running onto the field. "Let's go make a play."

* * *

And, foreshadowing what would happen five months later in Minneapolis, that's exactly what defensive end Brandon Graham did.

With just one minute and 38 seconds left in the game, the Eagles led by less than a touchdown, 22–17. Redskins quarterback Kirk Cousins had just hit tight end Jordan Reed for a seven-yard gain. It was second-and-three and Cousins again dropped back to pass. He'd already been sacked three times in the game. Here came another one. Graham bull-rushed the pocket and swiped at the football—a strip sack. The football landed gently in the lap of defensive tackle Fletcher Cox, who looked like Baloo in *The Jungle Book* as he danced happily to the end zone for a touchdown. There was a referee review. The play was upheld and the Eagles erupted in joy, culminating in a Gatorade bath for Pederson.

Mission accomplished: Road win in the division. And they had found something that would become imperative to building a championship team: A fourth-quarter pass rush. Defensive coordinator Jim Schwartz, the diabolic genius who doesn't mind you thinking he's a genius, had devised the perfect storm at exactly the right time with the right set of chess pieces.

Graham had two sacks, two tackles for a loss against the run, and forced an offensive holding call.

"That goes below the radar," Schwartz said. "You force a quarterback into intentional grounding. You force an offensive lineman into a hold. Good players can do those kinds of things. And Brandon is a good player."

Who sealed an important win.

But the cost was high. Darby gone. Future Hall of Fame left tackle Jason Peters, who left the game early complaining of a groin injury, had an uncertain season ahead. And kicker Caleb Sturgis was done with some kind of mysterious hip injury.

Nothing worse than having to look for a new kicker before you have to take on your old boss. Next up, Doug Pederson's mentor and confidante, Andy Reid, the Eagles' old head coach. On his turf.

One important statistical note: Wentz attempted six passes that traveled at least 25 yards downfield against the Redskins, his career high for a game. The only other quarterback to attempt six such passes in Week 1? Tom Brady. Wentz completed just one of those passes. So did Brady. The Patriots lost their game. The Eagles somehow won. But for both teams and both quarterbacks it was the beginning of a year of throwing deep, a year when the two franchises were on parallel tracks that would turn into a collision course at the Super Bowl.

Final score: Eagles 30, Redskins 17

Postscript: The day after the game, Doug Pederson made a comment that got very little attention. He said that early in the game the Redskins did some stunts and games with their defensive line that were "unscouted blitzes" that resulted in a free pass rusher getting a clear shot at Wentz. "Carson's got to see it," said Pederson. It was a rare example of the head coach publicly saying anything about Wentz that was critical in any way, shape, or form.

Chapter 2

Exposing Big Red

The Eagles at the Chiefs
Sunday, September 17, 2017 • Kansas City, Missouri

After beating the Patriots in Foxboro in the NFL opener, the Kansas City Chiefs under Andy Reid—known as "Big Red" for obvious reasons—were installed by Las Vegas as the favorite to win the Super Bowl.

Just like that: Tom Brady was out. Alex Smith was in.

But none of that concerned Doug Pederson. As he boarded the team flight for Kansas City, with the biggest road win of his young head coaching career now firmly planted at the top of his résumé, the truth is that Pederson was under siege. You wouldn't know it by looking at him or hearing him in public. But that's just Pederson's personality and approach in life. He learned it at a very early age from his football coach, his father, Gordon. There is an old saying in the military: "Never let the troops see on your face how hard your ass is getting kicked." Same goes for the head coach or quarterback of a football team. "You're the leader," Gordon would tell his son. "You always will be the leader. Never let them see you sweat."

There was no sweat, but there was plenty of seething anger. Once again, Pederson's credentials were being examined and dismissed. As a former player, he had seen it and heard it all before: "Oh, he's just a career backup." In Green Bay: "He's just Brett Favre's caddy." In Philadelphia, Pederson was there just to keep the seat warm until Reid's first draft pick, quarterback Donovan McNabb, was ready to take over as the starter. After his playing career was over, no NFL owner took him seriously. He went back to high school, Calvary Baptist Academy, in Shreveport, Louisiana, to become the head coach. Total enrollment: 800 students. He toiled there four years before Reid brought him back to Philadelphia in 2009 as an offensive quality control coach. In Kansas City, he was again labeled a clipboard holder for Reid, who called the plays. He held the title of offensive coordinator for three years, but Pederson was dismissed. People said he had very little input into the Chiefs' offense and the success of the underrated quarterback Alex Smith.

Pederson shrugged most of that off. But he heard it all. "He doesn't care about that stuff," said a long-time friend. "He just doesn't." He was happy in his marriage to his wife, Jeannie. They were raising three healthy sons, Drew, Josh, and Joel. And now he had one of the 32 most prestigious jobs in America: NFL head coach.

But on the doorstep of his second season, it all got too personal.

It started even before the season got underway. One name that would echo throughout the NovaCare building, throughout the city: Mike Lombardi. Lombardi, the former general manager of the Cleveland Browns—hired by owner Jimmy Haslam after receiving the highest possible recommendation from Lombardi's friend and mentor Bill Belichick—had been out of the NFL, trying to remain relevant in the ongoing pro football conversation in the mainstream media.

Here's what Lombardi said about Pederson in a theringer.com video, in all its glory:

> My beloved 76ers once hired a guy by the name of Roy Rubin from Long Island University. Poor Roy. He finished 4–47 before the Sixers canned him. 4–47! Years later, Fred Carter said, "Letting Rubin coach was like letting a teenager run a big corporation."
>
> Hey Fred, meet the Eagles' head coach, Doug Pederson! Now, everybody knows Pederson isn't a head coach. He might be less qualified to coach a team than anyone I've ever seen in my 30-plus years in the NFL.
>
> Pederson was barely a coordinator before he became head coach. Can you imagine if we elected a United States president who didn't have any real training? Sorry, don't answer that.
>
> Look, the Eagles looked increasingly sloppy and unprepared as the 2016 season limped along. That ain't changing in '17.
>
> Only Carson Wentz can save Pederson's job, and Wentz actually got worse during his rookie year, not better.
>
> When will the Eagles admit their mistake? Will they throw away 2017 by stubbornly sticking to the Pederson Principle?
>
> The immortal Roy Rubin lasted 51 games. I bet Doug Pederson lasts way less than that.

That is a full throttle put-down. And it came on the eve of the season opener. The timing and the comparison to the lowly Philadelphia 76ers, who had been insulting Philly fans for years by deliberately tanking with little to show for it, was undoubtedly intentional. The next day, Pederson got a flood of outraged texts from friends and family. Privately, he tried to explain it away, justify it as a non-factor in the totality of his life. But of course it hurt. It hurt because he had heard the same thing for years.

Still, he was determined to ignore it by pretending that he didn't know anything about it.

"I haven't seen the article, I'm not sure what you're talking about, so I don't pay attention to that," Pederson said six days before the team played the Redskins in the opener. Then he revealed that it clearly bothered him. "He's not in the building," Pederson added, referring to Lombardi. "I coach our coaches and coach our players. I haven't read the article."

A reporter filled him in. "How do you respond to that notion about your qualifications?"

"Someone here thought I was qualified," he responded. "That's good enough for me. Ask the guys in the locker room."

The locker room was a boiling cauldron of disgust. The players, most of whom live non-stop on Instagram and Twitter, had circulated the Lombardi comments and were exchanging expletive-laden responses to each other, the coaching staff, and Pederson.

"This dude takes so much crap," one player said to me in the locker room, only he didn't say "crap." "It's bull. That guy Lombardi ought to show his face around here."

All year, center Jason Kelce would simply say to people who asked, "That clown Lombardi." Someone suggested they make T-shirts, just like the one Patriots defensive coordinator Matt Patricia wore of Roger Goodell wearing a red clown nose after the Deflategate fiasco. But it was shot down. "We're not the Patriots," one player said. "They hate on people. We don't." At least in public.

The following week, it got worse. This time, the insinuation of Pederson's incompetence was incubated from within the team's practice facility. And it would start a Cold War with the Philly media that would linger all season.

* * *

Jim Schwartz played linebacker at Georgetown University. Not a football powerhouse. It's a basketball school synonymous with names like Iverson, Ewing, and Thompson. Not Schwartz playing linebacker. But you don't get into Georgetown unless you've got some seriously killer SAT scores. And while he was playing football, Jim Schwartz got a degree in economics. He was an academic All-American. He could have joined a major think tank or put on a military uniform and made a fine officer. Noted author Mike Freeman, who went to high school with Schwartz in Maryland, said, "He'd kick your ass and outthink you while doing it."

Schwartz thought about going to law school. But his passion was football, especially the angles and instantaneous reactions needed to play defense against an NFL quarterback.

Problem was his style was the opposite of Pederson's. He was smarter than you and he didn't have to tell you he was. You figured out the minute he walked into the room. His face and walk said it all: Swagger. Pederson wanted to show you how much he cared before he told you what he knew. Schwartz cared. But it took a while for you to figure that out.

It's easy to see why Schwartz—former defensive coordinator in Tennessee and head coach in Detroit—was in NFL exile for a year when Pederson hired him 2016. He's an acquired taste. But, boy, can he coach defense. He learned from the best, maybe the best ever: Bill Belichick.

Belichick gave him his first NFL job, evaluating players with the Cleveland Browns in the mid-1990s.

Are you connecting the dots here? Browns, Lombardi, Schwartz?

Just as the controversy over Lombardi subsided, the *Philadelphia Inquirer* published a story that insinuated that Schwartz was quietly positioning himself behind the scenes to be the next head coach of the Eagles if Pederson failed.

Without comment from Pederson or Schwartz—a fact that angered the Eagles organization—the story, which came out the day before the Eagles took the field in Washington, said Schwartz was walking around the NovaCare Complex like he owned the place. The story said:

> At the very least, the optics aren't favorable. One Eagles staffer said the only coach who probably doesn't think Schwartz is trying to undercut Pederson is Pederson. Three players, who requested anonymity, said that it has become well-known in the locker room that Schwartz is waiting to usurp power.

Interestingly, at three successive press conferences, Pederson was never asked for a reaction—even by the reporter who wrote it. The guy who worked more closely with Pederson than anyone in the building, offensive coordinator Frank Reich, wasn't asked about it either.

Only Schwartz—he was asked to confirm or deny a report he had nothing to do with—and after the story came out. He was guilty of being arrogant, sure. But that's always been the rap on him. But "undercutting" Pederson? No way.

In fact, just a few minutes before he talked to the media on September 12, 2017, Schwartz was in the cafeteria at NovaCare having lunch and he saw a player in violation of Pederson's dress code. Pederson was not around. So, Schwartz stepped in.

"Coach Pederson has a rule in the cafeteria that you can't wear tank tops or no sleeves," he said. "He wasn't in the cafeteria when I was. There was an offensive player that had no sleeves on, so I tapped him and said, 'You've got to get out. You've got to get sleeves on.'

"I know that when I was head coach, I wanted people around the building that were enforcing my rules. I did that for him. I respect that position. I'm going to execute the job the way that he outlined it for me. I think anything else, we can't really worry about."

Bad optics or not, the players again reacted to the story and were motivated by it. They all say they don't listen to talk radio or pay attention to social media. But most of them do. Tight end Zach Ertz was clear they heard about the article and were annoyed—twice in one week.

"There was a lot of hoopla with the article that came out before the game, which was very unfortunate, that it came out the day before the game like that," he said.

* * *

Getting ready to play his old boss, Pederson told his team in a meeting on Wednesday before the game to tune out the "outside noise." That was five days before kickoff at Arrowhead Stadium.

The night before, in the team hotel in Kansas City, Pederson stood before his players and warned them what was coming. The Chiefs, he reminded them, had just waltzed into the home of the world champs, the Patriots, and beat them, spoiled their opener before their home fans at Gillette Stadium, where the hopes and dreams of an AFC title normally go to die.

So, he said he had two clear, easy messages:

"On offense, we need to protect the football better, and on defense, we need to take it away."

In the first half against the Chiefs, the Eagles did not do either one. Philadelphia fumbled twice, punt returner Darren Sproles losing one. But Schwartz's defense had confounded Reid's play-calling: Alex Smith was sacked three times in just 18 pass attempts in the first half.

Pederson's crew was on a mission: To prove they belonged with the big boys of the NFL. In the halftime locker room, not much was said, except safety Malcolm Jenkins going around

Old friends, new adversaries: Andy Reid and Doug Pederson on the field at Arrowhead Stadium, Week 2 of the 2017 NFL season.

preaching the same thing over and over: "We got this, we got this." The defense had held the Chiefs' high-flying offense—with rookie speedster Kareem Hunt, the running back out of Toledo, and the pyrotechnic wide receiver Tyreek Hill—to just two field goals. It was 6–3, Chiefs.

Pederson told Wentz one thing: We're gonna keep firing. And that's what he did to open the second half. Five of the next six plays were passes. Nothing doing. Eagles had to punt. But the defense held.

And when the Eagles got the ball back, Pederson just flat-out refused to run the football. He smelled blood. He wanted to beat his old boss, he wanted to prove to his critics and the doubters that his team was totally legit—right now.

He called four more pass plays in a row: gains of 18, 11, 11, and 14 yards. Wentz, who had quietly asked Pederson for more autonomy at the line of scrimmage getting in and out of plays, was just letting it fly—without regard for his body, taking shot after shot. He had the Eagles on the Chiefs' 16-yard line. Reid's defense was on the ropes.

One more pass play: Wentz to Alshon Jeffery, 16 yards, touchdown.

The Eagles finally had the lead. But not for long. Five plays later, Hunt gashed the Eagles right up the middle, a majestic sprint of 53 yards and a touchdown.

The Eagles tied the score when the new kicker, Jake Elliott, hit a 40-yarder. Here it was, 13–13, 11 minutes and 57 seconds left in the game, and this upstart team had laid bare for all to see that the Chiefs could be beat. The Eagles were on the cusp of taking out the team that Vegas had annointed the new NFL darlings.

And that's when it all came apart. When the Eagles got the ball back, Pederson went back to the passing game, back to his second-year quarterback. But without a reliable running game—

running backs coach Duce Staley was inexplicably determined to stick with second-year back Wendell Smallwood—the Chiefs kept coming after No. 11 and he was intercepted at the Eagles' 28-yard line.

Smith hit Jason Kelce's brother, the mercurial tight end Travis Kelce, for a 15-yard touchdown, and that was it. One more score and the Chiefs walked away with a win. And all the questions about Pederson and his ability to call a game and be an NFL head coach were left wide open for another painful week.

The day after the game, back in Philadelphia, in the huge auditorium the Eagles use for team meetings and press conferences, adorned with wall-sized photographs of four legends—Chuck Bednarik, Tommy McDonald, Reggie White, and Steve Van Buren—Doug Pederson was treated like a washed-up middleweight by the Philly media. In short, he was interrogated.

In a foreshadowing of things to come, Pederson talked about run-pass options (RPOs) and whether they represented a good approach for Wentz.

"A lot of Carson's runs came on scrambles," Pederson said. "One of the things we did with Alex [Smith] obviously was more RPOs where he could utilize that athleticism. We haven't done it as much with Carson at this time." It wasn't because Wentz wasn't as athletic as Smith. Quite the opposite. Pederson didn't want to introduce RPOs to Wentz—he was already running too much, and taking as many hits as he was taking was not sustainable. That was the decision made privately among the coaches. It was something Pederson would later introduce for Nick Foles as a way of loosening up the defenses against him in the final four weeks of the season after Wentz blew out his knee.

But the first three rapid-fire questions put to Pederson were all about how and why Pederson thought he could possibly win on the road by throwing the ball so much, ignoring the running game and relying on Smallwood and Sproles while making LeGarrette Blount such an afterthought.

No answer Pederson gave was going to repel the attacks. He gave it a try. But the truth is he'd had enough of the press corps already—after the Lombardi and Schwartz stories. And it was only Week 2. So, he began to sort of sleepwalk through some shopworn responses—coachspeak.

"My aggressive play-calling was down the field and to attack down the field," he explained.

Later that night, he would admit to me, "We've got to get the run game fixed. We all know that. Too many third-and-longs. We had seven third-and-10-plus downs in this game. If that happens, they're going to tee-off on our quarterback all game." As the late, great Hall of Fame quarterback Ken "The Snake" Stabler of the Oakland Raiders and the University of Alabama used to say, with that gentle southern drawl and a grin, "Too many third-and-longs will make you sleep on your side of the bed."

One important statistical note: After two games, 74.4 percent of the Eagles' offensive snaps were designed pass plays, the second-highest rate in the NFL. Under Pederson, Philadelphia was 6–2 when it ran the ball on at least 40 percent of drop backs, but 2–8 when it didn't.

Time to find balance—or Pederson would squander what was clearly developing into a championship-level defense. And Wentz would not survive.

On the plane ride back to Philadelphia, Pederson sat alone for most of the flight, watching the game over and over on his iPad. Despite the loss, he was actually encouraged by several trends that he thought showed the offense was getting better. The Wentz connection with Jeffery showed better timing. Ertz was filling in for the absence of Jordan Matthews. Nelson Agholor was getting open.

So, while he was talking about balance, Pederson was trying to figure out how to unleash the power of a special group that he thought had the potential to win a lot of football games.

Which is exactly what was about to happen.

Final score: Chiefs 27, Eagles 20

Postscript: Before the season started, Carson Wentz said the toughest part of adjusting to the professional game from North Dakota State was only really difficult in one area. It was not the speed of the game, which is something all rookies say. No, he said, it was the exotic looks and pressures of different defensive coordinators. The Chiefs' defensive coordinator, Bob Sutton, had just confounded Wentz, who held his own to a certain extent. Next up was the first guy to beat Brady and Belichick in a Super Bowl: New York Giants defensive coordinator Steve Spagnuolo, who began his NFL coaching career with the Eagles.

Chapter 3

Malcolm in the Middle

The Giants at the Eagles
Sunday, September 24, 2017 • South Philadelphia

Two days before the Eagles' home opener, the NFL season was hijacked by the president of the United States.

And, right away, Doug Pederson knew he had to stay out of it. Let the players decide what to do. After all, it was the players who felt that they had been insulted by Donald Trump. They didn't need anybody else telling them how to respond.

There was another critical reason why Pederson didn't need to lead here. He had Malcolm Jenkins.

It would not be the first time Malcolm Jenkins showed the way. And it would not be the last. You've all heard the cliché: "This guy is the heart and soul of this football team."

Well, in this case, it was not a cliché. It was just fact. In the first Super Bowl championship season of the long, star-crossed history of a franchise dating back to 1933, Malcolm Jenkins was the heart and soul of the Philadelphia Eagles.

He was the leader of Doug Pederson's players council. He was the leader of Jim Schwartz's defense. He was the spokesman for the team—on the field, in the locker room, and in the Philadelphia community. He met with the city's police chief, spoke at schools, and cared for distressed children. He was a philanthropist and a businessman. And when the mood struck him, Malcolm Jenkins could knock the snot out of you. Just ask Brandin Cooks.

So, when the president of the United States decided to flex his political muscle and inject himself into the roiling debate over whether NFL players should be forced to stand for the national anthem, there was only one guy who had the moral authority to lead: Malcolm Jenkins.

What Bob Dylan said about Frank Sinatra is true of Malcolm Jenkins: "Right from the beginning, he was there with the truth of things in this voice."

* * *

Here's what the president did and said:

Donald Trump was campaigning down in Huntsville, Alabama, the deepest red of the red states, trying to convince voters there that Luther Strange, a Republican, deserved to be re-elected, which is, of course, like trying to convince your grandchild it's fun to eat ice cream. In essence, you're preaching to the choir. But if the president's advisers have learned anything about him it's that he delights in going off script, and that's exactly what Trump did, excoriating the NFL players who had been kneeling or sitting or raising their fists on the sideline during the national anthem as a way to bring voice to the urban voiceless, to shine a little light on what they perceived was social injustice after a series of confrontations between police and African Americans in Missouri, New York, and Florida. For well over a year, Jenkins had been raising his fist in the air. No one on the Eagles kneeled or sat during the anthem—no one followed the very public lead of former San Francisco 49ers quarterback Colin Kaepernick, who started the movement.

"We're proud of our country and we're proud of our flag," the president said, with the crowd hollering in a frenzy. And then there was this, which lit up the Twitterverse:

> Wouldn't you love to see one of these NFL owners, when somebody disrespects our flag, to say, "Get that son of a bitch off the field right now. Out! He's fired! He's fired!"

It was the SOB reference that ignited a visceral backlash. All across the NFL, team meetings were held. Players reacted on social media, denouncing the president. "It's just sad," tweeted running back LeSean McCoy, a former Eagle then with the Buffalo Bills. Some players suggested a boycott. Others vowed to sit or kneel in unison.

NFL commissioner Roger Goodell had a big problem. All the polls showed that the anthem protests were driving fans from the game. Ratings were down. Advertisers were angry. But the league is more than two-thirds African American and Trump had just called them a nasty name. Goodell, the son of the late liberal New York senator Charles Goodell, who once stood up to President Richard Nixon over the Vietnam War (it cost him his congressional seat after less than two years in office), had to stand with his players.

Most of the NFL owners demanded it, specifically Eagles team owner Jeffrey Lurie, who bought the team in 1994 and never met a liberal cause he didn't embrace.

"Divisive comments like these demonstrate an unfortunate lack of respect for the NFL, our great game, and all of our players," Goodell said. Players union president DeMaurice Smith went further: "We will never back down. We can no longer afford to stick to just sports. We will defend the players' civil rights." It was this type of rhetoric that alienated fans across the country. Many of them turned in their season tickets. Some just watched other sports. The NBA has a rule: Players and coaches must stand for the anthem. Why can't the NFL do the same thing? Now, the president was involved and emotions were running hot—in the NFL board rooms, locker rooms, and stadiums. And the Eagles' opener in South Philly was center stage.

I texted Doug Pederson on Saturday night before the home opener and asked him what he said to the players about the brewing controversy. He didn't get back to me until very early Sunday morning.

"I didn't have any discussions with them about his remarks," Pederson said to me. "However, as a team, along with military personnel and Philly police officers, we will stand together in a display of unity during the national anthem today."

While other teams were divided—the San Francisco 49ers, the Pittsburgh Steelers, the Baltimore Ravens, and the Seattle Seahawks, among others—with some players sitting, others kneeling, some reacting bitterly on social media, the Eagles held together with a display of unity.

And Malcolm Jenkins was the reason. As the leader of Pederson's council, Jenkins got together with other veterans and suggested that they all stand together with the police officers and members of the military. He had been telling them for months about his deepening relationship with Philadelphia police commissioner Richard Ross Jr., who leads the fourth-largest police department in the nation, how he went on a ride-along with a police officer to get a better prospective of how cops struggled to do their jobs right in the inner city, of how during his ride-along there was a shooting in North Philly.

"My father's best advice was, 'You don't know what you don't know,'" Jenkins told his teammates. "Meaning you constantly need to learn more."

* * *

The national anthem played. The Eagles players and coaches all stood, many of them arm in arm with each other and with men and women in uniform—Philly cops and firefighters, members of the U.S. Armed Forces.

And then there was a football game: Dating back to The Great Depression, the 171st meeting of the New York Giants

(from right to left) Malcolm Jenkins, team owner Jeffrey Lurie, and Brandon Graham, linking arms with a member of the Philadelphia Police Department at Lincoln Financial Field at the Eagles' home opener, Week 3.

and the Philadelphia Eagles for a Sunday afternoon of blocking and tackling.

And in the previous 170 games between these two teams, the Giants had won 86, the Eagles 82, and there were two ties. That's how close it's been. The two teams practice 99 miles from each other—I know the mileage by heart because I make the drive all the time from my home in South Jersey. No two division rivals are that close in proximity.

But, in terms of accomplishments and prestige and influence in the league, there's a huge gap between the two franchises— as wide as any comparison between New York and Philadelphia could be on any cultural, financial, or political level.

You walk into the Giants' practice facility and there are four gleaming Tiffany-designed silver Lombardi Trophies staring at you. The Eagles had none.

In fact, the NFC East has 12 Super Bowl titles in all—more than any other division in the NFL. Cowboys, five. Giants, four. Redskins, three. The Eagles had been shut out.

Tom Landry, Bill Parcells, Joe Gibbs—all those head coaches are in Canton. The Eagles have none in the Hall of Fame.

Wellington Mara, the patriarch of the New York Giants, is one of the original NFL owners, and his son John has enormous influence across the Hudson River in the league offices on Park Avenue in Manhattan. Goodell leans on Mara for advice on a near daily basis. Not so with Jeffrey Lurie.

And when Lurie wanted to replace the nascent Chip Kelly regime, he was in direct competition with Mara for Ben McAdoo, the former Green Bay Packers offensive guru. Lurie interviewed him, but McAdoo walked out without a deal and drove the 99 miles to the Giants and signed there. The Eagles hired Pederson instead. (Pederson and McAdoo are represented by the same uber agent, Bob LaMonte, a former history teacher who parlayed his friendship with former Packers head coach

Mike Holmgren into the most lucrative and powerful company representing coaches and front office executives the league has ever known. LaMonte also represents Andy Reid and Howie Roseman. And Frank Reich...and the list goes on.)

McAdoo and Pederson were hired in January 2016. The *USA Today* headline blared: SORRY, EAGLES FANS. The national consensus was that Philly had once again gotten the short end of the stick.

And with Eli Manning, who already had two Super Bowl titles, McAdoo won the NFC East in 2016. And just like that, the Giants had pole-vaulted ahead of the Eagles—again.

But recently the Eagles had been giving Eli Manning fits: Philly had won 14 of its last 18 games against the Giants (a .778 winning percentage), including the playoffs, as well as five wins in the last six meetings.

In the team meeting on Saturday night, Pederson kept his message to the team short and sweet.

"I want you to get ready for a physical football game for four quarters," Pederson said, reminding his team how the games against the Giants seemed to always come down to a field goal late in the fourth quarter.

"And I want disciplined football," he said. "We've been way too sloppy with the football. Tomorrow, I'm not going to let anything slide."

Think about all the distractions that had been dumped into Pederson's lap in the first three weeks:

The Lombardi takedown.

The Schwartz drive-by story.

Losing kicker Caleb Sturgis and Ronald Darby, the starting cornerback the team acquired on the doorstep of the season and desperately needed.

The national anthem protest debate that went all the way to the White House.

He reminded his team again: "It's all in how you respond to adversity."

And you must have a willingness to adjust: Your attitude, your game plan, your play-calling.

As former Eagles quarterback Ron Jaworski says, "It's an update league."

And against the Giants, Pederson did some serious updating. But, as he predicted, it still came down to a field goal in the fourth quarter. What he could not foresee, what no one could possible predict, is that the game would come down to the longest walkoff field goal in Eagles history—by a kicker playing in his first game in the city of Philadelphia.

* * *

The truth is that Malcolm Jenkins—whether he was bothered by the presidential distraction or befuddled by the Giants' wildly talented wide receiver Odell Beckham Jr.—had a mediocre game against the Giants.

Jenkins plays free safety. It's his job to patrol and protect the middle of the field. The free safety is the center fielder, the Willie Mays. But also the last line of defense. Nothing is supposed to fool the free safety. Jenkins, an eight-year veteran who has been to the Pro Bowl, was given full control over his movements, within the structure of the defense. But no matter what happened it was his job not to let the other team score. Nobody gets through. In military terms, the free safety is the last guy holding the fort.

Defensive coordinator Jim Schwartz always wanted a guy like Jenkins, who grew up in Piscataway, New Jersey, and went to Ohio State for track and football. Jenkins could run and he loved contact—invited it, looked for it. And he was pre-eminently coachable. A real yes sir, no sir guy. But, as everybody knows, you want the soldier who can take orders but also think on his feet, make quick decisions in the heat of the battle. That's Jenkins. But this day, he could not solve the puzzle of the Giants' passing game, particularly No. 13.

From the opening kick, Beckham ate their lunch. Game time temperature was 89 degrees. It was suffocatingly humid at the confluence of I-95 and the South Philly asphalt jungle and Beckham was nine steps ahead of everybody on defense—like he was Carl Lewis and they were all were wearing ski boots.

Making matters worse, pre-occupied with Beckham—in fact, overwhelmed by him—the Eagles lost sight of the rest of the Giants' receiving corps.

"With Beckham on the field, you have to defend every blade of grass," said Jim Schwartz.

Beckham lined up in the slot. He went in motion. He got lost outside the numbers, across the middle, and wiggled free deep down the middle. Manning threw him the ball a whopping 13 times—if he didn't, he would hear about it when Beckham got back to the huddle. The OBJ Rule was simple: He's always open. And he was. Manning only missed four times. Beckham finished with nine catches, two of them for touchdowns.

One member of the Eagles secondary came back to the sideline and said to defensive backs coach, Cory Undlin: "No. 13 is a monstrous pain in the ass. We can't handle him."

The Eagles tried double-teams and bracket coverage, using Jenkins and backup safety Chris Maragos (starter Rodney McLeod was hurt) as help. But Maragos, a gamer who was special teams captain, just didn't have the speed.

And the pre-occupation with No. 13 opened up the entire field for the Giants' other two beasts at wide receiver: Veteran Brandon Marshall and second-year speedster Sterling Shepard.

In fact, this is what was supposed to propel the Giants to back-to-back division titles: The play-calling of McAdoo, the experience of Manning, the embarrassment of riches at wide receiver.

In the off-season, with the additions of Torrey Smith and Alshon Jeffery and the development of Carson Wentz, Howie Roseman thought he was going to be able to keep up. It wasn't happening.

Pederson recognized quickly the only way to beat the Giants was to play small ball with a big back. It was time to give the league a taste of LeGarrette Blount, Version 2.0.

* * *

Just about everybody on the team was wondering what Pederson was waiting for. Outside the NovaCare Complex, the complaints were deafening on sports talk radio:

"They got this guy, they gonna use him?" said Bobby V. from A.C.

"Pederson's just like Andy—stubborn. And all he wants to do is throw the football," said Billy from Philly.

"They don't run the ball, Carson's gonna get killed!" said Tony from Hammonton.

Pederson wasn't listening to the callers. But he clearly listened to the input from his consigliere, offensive coordinator Frank Reich. Reich had a full-blown doctorate in the Buffalo Bills' K-gun offense, and in that offense quarterback Jim Kelly had running back Thurman Thomas, who—when he was paying attention—kept the offense on schedule and the quarterback whole. Wentz needed a reliable, veteran presence in the backfield to do just that, someone who didn't need an instruction manual every time he was five yards deep behind the line of scrimmage. Someone who could figure out where to go, who to block, and what to do—all the time. Blount was that guy.

In all, Blount carried the ball 12 times for 67 yards and a touchdown against the Giants—just enough of a taste. And Clement got the first six carries of his career, rambling for 22 yards and another touchdown.

Pederson dialed up 39 rushing plays for 193 yards, throwing off the stubborn tendency of his mentor, Andy Reid, who refused to recognize the importance of running early, often, and late—creating an enmity with the fans and a roadblock to his ultimate success.

Wentz threw the ball 31 times, completing 21, but for only 176 yards. He was sacked three times—the hits kept coming. But no interceptions. He was quickly getting the reputation—as Jon Gruden would call him—of being "North Dakota tough," the perfect fit for working class Philly.

If Eli Manning was NFL royalty for one of the league's blue chip franchises, Eagles would take the Wentz grit and grind in South Philly all day, all night.

As long as Pederson ran the ball.

* * *

Without Reid or Kelly hovering over his every move, Howie Roseman was free to maneuver, plug holes, and find fixes (quick and long-term) that he thought could sustain success. And Pederson was in lock-step. Finally, after buying the team in 1994, Lurie had a football operations team that worked in harmony—he found that "emotional intelligence" he was looking for.

But the job on this Sunday was still not done.

The "monstrous pain in the ass" would not go away.

In the fourth quarter alone, the two teams traded a remarkable seven scoring drives. Manning to Beckham: Touchdown. Manning to Beckham again: Touchdown. Manning to Shepard: Touchdown. Twenty-one unanswered points. Clement scored his first touchdown: Tie score, 21–21.

Both defenses were running on fumes. Manning put together a seven-play drive and had the Giants on the doorstep of another touchdown. But with young corner Jalen Mills covering Beckman, Manning misfired. Field goal: Giants had a three-point lead.

Pederson had proven prophetic, again: The Eagles needed to be prepared for a physical game for four quarters. But no one could've possibly predicted this kind of dizzying display of back-and-forth football in the unforgiving humidity of South Philly in the fourth quarter of the 171st meeting of the Eagles and Giants.

Wentz answered. The Eagles assembled an eight-play drive ending in a 46-yard field goal by Jake Elliott. Tied again, 24–24.

Then the Giants broke down. Two penalties on left tackle Ereck Flowers forced New York to punt, a 28-yard floater by Brad Wing that gave Wentz all he needed: Momentum and field position.

First-and-10, Eagles' 38-yard line. Wentz throws incomplete. Giants call timeout—why?

Wentz hits Alshon Jeffery: 19-yard gain. Giants call another T.O. Has McAdoo lost his mind in the hot South Philly afternoon?

Pederson sent his young kicker onto the field to try a 61-yarder to win it.

A word about Jake Elliott. He's just 22 years old. His bio says he's 5-foot-9, 167 pounds. If he's 167 pounds, I'm Santa Claus. There is nothing in his history or his bio that says he's got the mental or physical makeup to nail a 61-yard field goal with time expiring to win the Eagles' home opener, beat the dreaded New York Giants, and propel the Eagles onto a nine-game winning streak.

But that's exactly what happened.

61 yards: Longest field goal in Eagles franchise history.

61 yards: Third-longest game-ending field goal in NFL history.

61 yards: Longest field goal by a rookie kicker in NFL history.

That's a lot to happen on one Sunday of pro football. Fasten your seatbelt, we got a long way to go.

One important statistical note: Beckham caught both of his targets in the end zone against the Eagles. He caught 4-of-15 end-zone targets last season. Improvement, yes. But no improvement in attitude. Beckham was flagged with an unsportsmanlike conduct penalty following his first touchdown for pantomiming urinating like a dog—an obvious reference to the president's remarks. It was his fifth career unsportsmanlike or taunting penalty. Remarkably, he was not fined by the league for his actions.

Final score: Eagles 27, Giants 24

Postscript: Two days after the game, Malcolm Jenkins joined a group of players to meet with Roger Goodell and several NFL owners at the league offices to begin hammering out an agreement that would eventually put an end to the anthem protests. Several Sundays later, Jenkins brought down his raised fist. In May 2018, the NFL announced a new policy requiring players to stand for the national anthem or wait in the locker room.

Chapter 4

The Wentz Wagon
in La-La Land

The Eagles at the Chargers
Sunday, October 1, 2017 • Carson, California

LeGarrette Blount runs like his last name suggests. At 6-foot, 250 pounds, Blount is looking to punch holes in the defense and, if they're not there, make some of his own—violently.

"He will give you a mouthful of his facemask," said former Steelers running back Merrill Hoge.

The Wentz Wagon landed in Los Angeles on the last day of the first month of the season, getting ready to play a team now being called the Los Angeles Chargers. After the franchise had to sort of half-move from San Diego north up the West Coast to play temporarily in a soccer stadium called the StubHub Center in Carson City, the Chargers had very little identity.

The Eagles were in no mood to feel sorry for anybody else at this point. So, Doug Pederson's plan was simple enough. He would give this underachieving AFC West team something they were not ready for: A big, fat mouthful of LeGarrette Blount.

"When we saw the game plan, we were all like, 'Hell yeah!'" said one offensive lineman. Another player said, simply, "Finally."

Blount, born and raised in the Florida Panhandle town of Perry, was only two months and five days shy of his 31st birthday, ancient for an NFL running back, who has an average career span of 2.3 years. Blount was in his eighth year. But he proved to the Eagles' brain trust that he had a lot of spring left in his powerful thighs. And, more important, he proved that they could trust him—and that was important.

* * *

He was the perfect pickup at the perfect time for the Eagles. In the 2017 draft, which was held on the steps of the Art Museum in Philadelphia, a spectacle that had never been witnessed before in the NFL, the Eagles had missed out on drafting a running back. Truth was they needed more pass rushers and another cornerback. And Howie Roseman was convinced he could get Blount later in free agency.

And, of course, luck is the residue of design. When the draft was over, the football gods handed the Eagles a gift. No one had drafted Wisconsin running back Corey Clement, who grew up an Eagles fan in Glassboro, New Jersey, about 10 miles from Lincoln Financial Field. Roseman quickly signed him to a rookie free agent deal. And then, once the spring practices were over, Roseman waited and waited and waited until he could get Blount at the right price. It was not until May 17 that Roseman signed the star-crossed running back.

But the Blount signing was greeted with plenty of odd looks from the press corps and skepticism on sports talk radio. He had just won a Super Bowl with the Patriots—what's his motivation? He's had problems everywhere—not reliable. He'll upset the delicate balance in the locker room.

And when you look at the book on him, most everybody thought the Eagles were crazy. They needed a running back, but not *this* one:

February 2009: Blount was suspended indefinitely by the University of Oregon for "failure to fulfill team obligations" by head coach Mike Bellotti (reportedly for missing off-season meetings), was reinstated by new coach Chip Kelly before spring practice.

September 3, 2009: Punched Boise State LB Byron Hout following Oregon's 19-8 loss, was restrained by police from fans heckling him—suspended rest of season.

November 9, 2009: Reinstated by Oregon—played in two games, including bowl game against Ohio State.

April 25, 2010: Signs with the Tennessee Titans as undrafted free agent.

August 18, 2010: Punched teammate Eric Bakhtiari in the helmet after having his own helmet ripped off—he apologized to coach Jeff Fisher. Fisher said, "He didn't have to apologize. It's football. It's training camp."

September 6, 2010: Claimed by Tampa Bay Buccaneers off waivers.

April 27, 2013: Traded by the Buccaneers to the New England Patriots for Jeff Demps and seventh-round pick.

March 28, 2014: Signs two-year contract with the Pittsburgh Steelers.

August 20, 2014: Arrested for marijuana possession following traffic stop (with Le'Veon Bell)—suspended for Week 1 of 2015 regular season. Charges were dropped after he completed 50 hours of community service.

November 17, 2014: Leaves field before end of the Steelers' *Monday Night Football* win over the Titans.

November 18, 2014: Released by the Steelers.

November 20, 2014: Signs with Patriots. Wins Super Bowl.

So, why did Blount survive eight years in the NFL? Because he's actually a good dude. Ask his teammates. One guy who convinced the Eagles to sign Blount was his ex-teammate in 2016 in New England. "He'd do anything for you," said Chris Long. "Heart of gold."

And, to borrow the words of Bill Belichick, he could do his job.

Blount, with a big smile on his face, carried all that excess baggage into Philly, dropped it off, and didn't look back. And in the home opener of the team's first Super Bowl winning season, his head coach finally told him to unpack his suitcase. Against the Chargers, Pederson took it one big, important step further: He asked Blount to carry the team.

* * *

He had a lot of help. A wagon train of Eagles fans put down stakes in Southern California.

The StubHub Center only holds 27,000 people, making it the smallest NFL venue in the Super Bowl era. It is named for a company that exchanges and sells tickets to any event, anywhere, specializing in sports and people who want to crash other peoples' parties. Hello, Eagles fans. When the Chargers moved in there, they probably had no idea that the name on their building would mean this: On Sunday, October 1, it might as well have been Lincoln Financial West. The sky was a beautiful Southern California blue and the stadium was a sea of Eagles green. And every one of those fans was all they needed.

At one point, Eagles tight Brent Celek, with the team 11 years, said simply, "This is like a home game."

Only worse, much, much worse. StubHub is a soccer stadium, so the sidelines were about 10 yards narrower. The field was on top of the bench, which was on top of the fans, who were in your face. And you don't want Philly fans in your face all day. They will wear you out, which is what they did to Philip Rivers & Co. With Blount getting carry after carry and racking up big yards and giving the Chargers a mouthful of facemask, helmet, forearm, and football, the Eagles fans were an unrelenting chorus of mayhem and hate—spewing expletives at the Chargers that I won't even put in this book.

"Now, I get it. Now, I know what it's like to play in Philly," Blount said. "That was truly beautiful."

Beautiful for the Eagles, bad for the Chargers.

And great for Carson Wentz. "Honestly, it was unbelievable," he said. The Wentz Wagon was rolling in La-La Land and all the quarterback had to do was drive.

"LeGarrette out there on the field," said Wentz. "That man is angry."

* * *

There are all kinds of memorable quotes to describe the motivation behind the game of tackle football, which is a uniquely American pursuit.

"You can't play scared," said Jim Brown, perhaps the greatest running back to play the game. "If you got a little rabbit in you, this game's not for you."

"Football is a game of the heart," former long-time head coach Marty Schottenheimer said.

"As a coach," said Hall of Fame head coach Bill Parcells, who won two Super Bowl titles with the New York Giants, "you need two things: You need to give the players a good plan. And then you got to be able to motivate them to execute that plan."

It's one thing to have the tactics, the strategy, the plan, as Parcells said. Anybody can draw up superior X's and O's on a white board. Chip Kelly could do that all day, all night, all week long.

But you got to have the right psychology bag to lay on these players—something that will get them to put their hearts into it. It's an unnatural act to go out and hit somebody. Not everybody walking down the street has the desire, willingness, wherewithal, or skill to do that.

My father, Vito Mario Paolantonio, who coached me in baseball and football, used to say, "You gotta wanna."

Translation: Your heart's got to be in it.

And on this perfectly spectacular Southern California afternoon, the type of day the Mamas and the Papas used to sing about, LeGarrette Blount's heart was into it.

Blount just hammered away. Two yards. Three yards. Eight yards. Ten yards. The Chargers' "NASCAR" outside pass rush of Joey Bosa and Melvin Ingram could not fire off on Wentz. Blount was trying to take away the Chargers' willingness and desire to take him down—take away their desire to get hit in the mouth.

Pederson sprinkled in Wendell Smallwood and Corey Clement, attacking the edges. Both backs would finish the day with 10 carries.

The San Diego safeties had their heads on a swivel—come in and take on Blount's forearm or stay back for Alshon Jeffery and Torrey Smith. Or chase Clement and Smallwood down the sideline. Pick your poison.

Jeffery caught a touchdown pass to open up the game. Pederson's plan was working. The Eagles fans pumped up the volume and Wentz went to work into the body of the Chargers' defense with Pro Bowl tight end Zach Ertz. But Ertz only had two catches. The Chargers had decided he wasn't going to beat them.

Still, the threat of Ertz was enough. Wentz threw to him four times in the first half. The Eagles' offense was like a heavyweight boxer, working the head, then the body, wearing out the Chargers' willpower and legs.

In the halftime locker room, the Eagles were up 16–10. That's exactly where Pederson wanted his team to be—and not to be. He didn't want them to be complacent.

He reminded them that was Philip Rivers playing quarterback with the lightning bolt on his helmet. He had already shocked them with a 75-yard touchdown pass. Nothing was over. "Got to finish this," Pederson said. Wentz was watching Rivers operate. "You never knew what he was going to do, strike from anywhere," said Wentz. That's something he was trying to imitate on the fly.

Pederson was prescient, again. The Eagles' defense was weary. And Rivers had a fourth-quarter surge in his hip pocket. At the beginning of the fourth quarter, rookie running back Austin Ekeler found the edge of the Eagles' defense unmanned and sprinted 35 yards for a touchdown. And just like that, the Chargers had closed to within two points, at home, with momentum. It was just 19–17, Eagles.

Bosa and Ingram were coming hard at No. 11. So, Pederson sent Clement to the edge, give Bosa something to think about. Four-yard gain. That's not going to do it.

Second-and-six at the Eagles' 29-yard line. No first down here and the Eagles would be forced to punt and give the ball back to Rivers. Remember, Pederson had just come from the AFC West. He knew that Rivers was more than capable of sending you home wondering how you'd lost. So, Pederson didn't want to risk an interception at that juncture of the game. That would be worse. That would kill the drive. Give Rivers a short field. And the Eagles' defense was giving up big plays.

So, Pederson put Wentz under center and called for a simple trap play through what is called the A-gap—LeGarrette Blount right up the gut.

Sixty-eight yards later, the Eagles had first-and-goal at the Chargers' three-yard line.

"They opened up a pretty big hole. It wasn't that hard to see," Blount said. "Obviously, you get into the secondary and you become an open-field runner. It happened pretty fast. In order to be a good back you got to make guys miss."

Except Blount wasn't making guys miss. He broke four tackles. And then he didn't seem to be interested in making guys miss. He was looking for somebody, anybody, in a powder blue uniform, to hit.

And, as he rolled toward the Chargers' end zone, he began to feed off the reaction of the Eagles fans, who roared louder and louder as he rumbled through the second and third levels of the Chargers' defense, throwing off the yoke of frustration of being left out of the game plan for three weeks, of all the doubts and disrespect hurled his way, as if to say, "This is what I do. If you like it, keep feeding me the football."

Nobody tackled Blount. He was finally pushed out of bounds at the three-yard line. On the sideline, Malcolm Jenkins and the defense got up off the bench and whooped and hollered and running backs coach Duce Staley, a bowling ball of a human being who had made his reputation making similar runs in an Eagles uniform for Andy Reid, could not contain himself.

It was fists in the air, chest bumps and high-fives all around. "I had a pretty good view of it," said Wentz. "It was a simple inside zone run. The offensive line gave him a crease. It was one of the most incredible runs I've seen in my life."

Except one little problem. The Eagles' offense could not punch it in. On the next play, Pederson inexplicably gave Blount the ball again—even though he was on his way toward to the third-most rushing yards of his career and just basically pulled off the impossible by gashing the home team for 68 yards, breaking through tacklers and huffing and puffing his way out of bounds. Next run: One yard.

One more run: No yards. Next run: Minus four yards.

Wentz was sacked. Blount carried for minus one yard and Wentz threw incomplete. Six plays and the Eagles were stuck at the three. A field goal here would give them the lead, but would also feel like a surrender, giving Rivers new life.

Wentz lined up in the shotgun. Blount was out of the game. Instead, Wendell Smallwood carried for three yards and the touchdown—his only touchdown of the season. In fact, for the remainder of the championship season, Smallwood would not see much action after that play. Blount had proven he had the job, for now.

When the Chargers scored again, it was Blount who was called upon to close the game. He had runs for three, six, and 15 yards. Wentz took a knee and the stadium erupted in the Eagles' fight song, "Fly, Eagles Fly."

"No one will ever forget that feeling," said center Jason Kelce.

Least of all Blount. After the game, his body was battered, bruised, and sore. Of his 136 rushing yards, 109 had come after first contact with a Chargers defender, according to ESPN Stats & Information—the fifth-most in the last five seasons in the NFL. (Two of those top five were recorded by running back Jay Ajayi in a Miami Dolphins uniform against the Buffalo Bills in 2016. That's clearly one of the reasons why the Eagles acquired Ajayi four weeks later.)

"Big win for us, no doubt," said Wentz. "Winning three out of four on the road. Last year, we could never find a way to win tight ballgames. We are starting to learn that a little bit."

And he was starting to understand the power of the Eagles fans. "It's huge," he said of the support at StubHub. "It's honestly huge. You get to go on regular cadence, you don't have to worry about silent cadence. We just feed off that energy. But to go on the road, go across the country to L.A. like this and have that kind of atmosphere, it makes it really enjoyable to play."

* * *

The Eagles were now 3-1—propelled over .500 by two improbable plays by two players who were not even on the team six months earlier: A walkoff 61-yard field goal by a rookie kicker and a 68-yard gallop by a running back no one else wanted.

They were in first place in the division. In 2016, they got off to a good start, but they could not win on the road and they could not close out the close ones.

And it was happening with the franchise quarterback playing his part, not trying to do too much. Wentz finished 17-of-31 for 242 yards with a touchdown. But it was also his second straight game without an interception. And Pederson could feel a calmness developing in his young quarterback. He could see it in his eyes. Wentz was a film study rat—in the NovaCare building before everyone else.

"Every day I go in at 7:00 AM," said Pro Bowl defensive tackle Fletcher Cox. "Carson's vehicle is already there. He beats me every single day."

It was this type of quiet commitment that was beginning to build the kind of leadership capital that any young quarterback needs to lead. Mature, quiet, tough as they come.

"He's learning, they're learning," Pederson said after the game. "Even though we're four games in, this team is really beginning to believe in themselves, believe in each other. The offense is bailing out the defense, the defense is bailing out the offense. Special teams sometimes bailed out everyone... They're coming together. That's exciting. It's fun to watch."

* * *

The next day, Les Bowen, the long-time Eagles beat writer for the *Philadelphia Daily News*, got the first question to the head coach.

"What would you say your offensive identity is now after four games?" Bowen asked.

"Pound and ground," Pederson said. The hard-bitten group of reporters who had grilled Pederson on this very subject for more than a month burst out in laughter. "That's what you want, right? All right, that's my answer."

And that was Pederson, is Pederson. *Never show on your face how hard your ass is getting kicked.* Packers quarterback Brett Favre would always say to Pederson, "We're having too much fun to give a crap." Only he wouldn't say "crap."

After having a little fun with the press corps, Pederson tried to give a straight answer, giving offensive line coach Jeff Stoutland credit for designing the blocking schemes and putting together the run-first game plan.

Stoutland is all offensive line coach: Crusty, tough, silent. Walks with his head high, but looks right through you. If you offer a hello, he's friendly. If not, he's thinking about the next week's game plan. In 2016, Stoutland, who coached one of the best offensive lines in the nation at Alabama in 2011 and 2012, helped the Eagles battle injury after injury on the offensive line—fielding seven different combinations. Still, the two Jasons—left tackle Peters and center Kelce—would make the Pro Bowl. Prior to the game against the Chargers, both went to "Stout," as they call him, and said, "Let's run the rock. Get back to what we do."

Pederson listened to the advice. The Eagles rushed for 214 yards against the Chargers, the most the team had amassed in a game with Pederson as head coach.

"Listen, we want to go in and establish that run, play-action with Carson, being able to move him around a little bit," he said. "It's sort of the direction that I think our offense needs to go in."

It was about to go in that direction in a major, major way. And the rest of the NFL simply was not ready for what was about to happen next.

One important statistical note: After scoring in Super Bowl LII, LeGarrette Blount would have 11 rushing touchdowns in 11 postseason games, tying him with Marcus Allen for sixth-most in NFL history. Allen plus the top five (Emmitt Smith, Thurman Thomas, Franco Harris, Terrell Davis, and John Riggins) are all enshrined in the Pro Football Hall of Fame in Canton, Ohio.

Final score: Eagles 26, Chargers 24

Postscript: Remember, this would be the first of two trips to the West Coast for the Eagles in 2017. The second one was two months away, in December, when the team would play two beasts—the Seahawks and the Rams—on back-to-back Sundays. Pederson had already decided to practice out west between those two games.

And he knew now that the fans would play an important role, traveling strong, helping to sustain a high level of energy for 60 minutes in a tough environment with their special brand of Philly pride and motivation.

"To get on a plane for five hours and feel like it's a home game, that was unreal," said Pederson.

"I'm kind of starting to not be stunned by our fans," Wentz said. "It's unbelievable."

Chapter 5

Carson's Team

It was about three hours before game time on Sunday, October 8, 2017, a wet, sticky, humid morning in South Philly, and my instructions were simple: Meet Eagles head coach Doug Pederson outside the team breakfast room at the Marriott Hotel at Concourse C at Philadelphia International Airport.

Pederson had agreed to try something no other NFL head coach had ever done before. He had invited me into the team's inner sanctum on game day, then for a ride with him from the team hotel to Lincoln Financial Field. And we were going to do this ride-along with a camera—live on national television on *SportsCenter*.

To understand the magnitude of that and what it says about Pederson and his style of coaching, his personality, and why players, coaches, and the front office personnel gravitate toward him so effortlessly, you have to understand how secretive pro football coaches can be. Many of them think of themselves as military generals, guardians of the battle plans so much so that any slight intrusion into the routine, however small, will allow an opening for the enemy forces to steal the tactics, interrupt the chi, or distract from the smallest habit of preparation for Sunday's game.

Example: The New England Patriots hang black curtains to keep cameras from even recording the time-honored ritual of players arriving to the game. Nothing to see here, so keep moving. The home locker room at Gillette Stadium is hidden from prying eyes. Tom Brady arrives in a golf cart and if the cameraman follows him down the hall, a member of the public relations staff will soon appear out of nowhere with a reprimand.

When head coach Bill Belichick arrives at the stadium, he has total tunnel vision. He blocks out everything except the five feet of concrete in front of him.

Pederson is the opposite. Open, friendly, quick to say hello and joke around. In short, he's grown up his whole life around the game of football and the whole world is his locker room.

"He's always been happy in life," his mom, Teri "Mama Bird" Pederson, told me.

At the airport Marriott, my intrepid New York producer Brian Franey, my lieutenant adjutant all things NFL, who I'm loathed to be without on the road, met Eagles vice president of security Dom DiSandro—Big Dom—in the hotel lobby—just to make sure the coast was clear.

Pederson popped out of the breakfast room. Right behind him was quarterback Carson Wentz, who was all business, as usual. Wentz was on a mission. You could see that in his eyes. He was ready to get on one of the team buses. I think he would have played the game on one of the airport runways if that's what Pederson asked him to do.

We had a convoy going—Pederson in his car with us, followed by the buses, snaking north on I-95 with an escort of Philadelphia motorcycle cops. Only one difference: It was happening on live TV. If something went wrong, this whole experiment would be a big, fat embarrassment—maybe good TV, but it would have been the last time it was ever tried. The hair was literally standing up on my arms. Pederson was as calm as Jeff Gordon on race day.

"I'm ready," said Pederson. And we all jumped into his SUV—I sat behind Pederson, who was driving. The cameraman was riding shotgun. Franey folded himself up in the back.

"I was out at the stadium earlier, Coach, even though the weather is bad, I can tell you that the fans are already tailgating for this one," I said, in my broadcast tone and vernacular. "The passion in this city is unbelievable for this team right now."

"It is crazy," he said. "I've been a part of the city when the team has done well, and they've won, and we've just got to keep it going. It's a one-game-at-a-time mentality, and to see the fans this early at the stadium, it just shows the love of the team and the passion these fans have for the Eagles."

I asked, "When you're riding in, does your wife, Jeannie, ever call you on the phone and say, 'Good luck, honey,' or 'Hey, you left your wallet on the kitchen counter back at the house'?"

"No," Pederson said, "she knows how I am on game day. I get a little more focused in and lasered in. We had our conversation earlier this morning before breakfast and I will see her at the stadium here in a little bit."

I paused and imagined asking the next question to Belichick—on the morning of the game. "What did she say to you this morning?"

"She just wishes me luck, says, 'Get after them,' and 'Do what you do best.'"

"What's the checklist in a head coach's mind as you ride to the stadium?"

Pederson: "First thing is *not* to hit the police officer on the way. We don't want to do that."

"No, we don't," I said. Franey was trying not to laugh.

Pederson continued: "You know, really, I open up those curtains in the morning. I check out the weather, I want to see what the weather is going to do. We knew going in that this game might have a little rain early in the morning, but it should be out of here...And then I kind of mentally prepare. Go back through my openers, go back through some of the game situations that we've talked about during the week, and really begin to sort of dial down and get that focus toward kickoff."

"You ever allow yourself," I asked, "the joy of, as you're riding into the stadium, 'Hey, we're 3-1, we lead the division, so let's go play football'?"

Pederson: "I do, and I have to kind of stop and just sort of catch myself or pinch myself and say, 'Listen, we're in a great situation. We are 3-1.' And you have to enjoy these moments and if you don't, you're going to worry yourself to death... These are big opportunities for our team and for our city."

Pederson pulled into the coaches' lot under Lincoln Financial Field. Franey and the cameraman took off to feed the rest of the interview back to ESPN.

With the camera gone, I wanted to ask him about Wentz.

"Is Carson okay?" I said. "He didn't even look at me back at the hotel." I have interviewed and talked to Wentz dozens of times since he was drafted by the Eagles in the spring of 2016. We have had a good relationship. I thought he might be put off that I was intruding into his space—even though I was there with the permission of the team and the head coach. Covering a 53-man roster, a coaching staff of about two dozen, and the front office is a delicate operation, even after 25 years. You've always got to remind yourself that you're in their home, always their guest. You got to tread lightly, especially when it comes to the triggerman.

"Carson's great," Pederson said. "We had an unbelievable week of practice. He's about to take off."

Boy, was that an understatement.

* * *

"The great thing about Nick Foles is that he understands this is Carson's team."

Doug Pederson said that in a national radio interview about three weeks *after* winning Super Bowl LII. At that point, he was

In an NFL first, I ride with Doug Pederson in the team convoy to Lincoln Financial Field before the game against Arizona in Week 5. "First thing is not *to hit the police officer on the way," said Pederson. "We don't want to do that." (ESPN)*

trying to convince the football world that even though Foles was the Super Bowl MVP and that he might be feeling some ownership of that quarterback job, everybody needed to know how much Foles understood that Wentz was the foundation—in the past and in the future. And, that, of course, begs this question: When exactly did it become Carson Wentz's team?

I believe it happened against the Arizona Cardinals in Week 5 at Lincoln Financial Field. Wentz and the Eagles would beat the Cardinals so thoroughly on this day, so completely, that it would be the day that Arizona's front office had to realize that it was all over for the team's head coach, Bruce Arians, and its aging star quarterback, Carson Palmer, the former Heisman winner from USC. In 2017, the Cardinals had the oldest roster in the NFL. And they played like it—slogging through the afternoon while Wentz and the Eagles seemed to play on roller skates.

The Eagles won the game 34-7. But it wasn't even that close. Carson Wentz threw four touchdown passes, but he might've thrown two more.

LeGarrette Blount hammered out 74 yards on just 14 carries, but the Cardinals could not stop backup running backs Kenjon Barner and Corey Clement, either. The Eagles finished with 122 rushing yards. The Cardinals? Just 31.

Lincoln Financial Field that day with 69,596 fans filling every seat and every inch of standing room along the rafters on the second deck was a rollicking homecoming block party of joy and mayhem.

Before the game, as the Cardinals' buses arrived in South Philadelphia, they were pelted with eggs. It's a ritual that's part celebration, part intimidation. Like Halloween.

Visiting players expect it, but they always seem surprised that it still happens—because it rarely happens anywhere else. And definitely not every single Sunday afternoon. "You mean, this still goes on?" That's usually the reaction. It's 2017, but it still happens. Always will.

The Dallas Cowboys, the New York Giants, and the Washington Redskins—of course—get it the worst. But all the visiting players get warned. And they tell their friends and families: Don't come to Philly wearing our colors or our jerseys. If you do, you're in for a rough day. For years, it got so bad that the Philadelphia police department stationed undercover officers in the stands wearing the visiting jerseys to catch hooligans. Those caught were brought to a makeshift Common Pleas Court in the basement of old Veterans Stadium. And a little jail. Like the Wild, Wild West. While Randall Cunningham was carving up the Cowboys, a judge held arraignments. One-stop shopping. No get-out-of-jail-free card here. You acted out, it was straight to the slammer.

* * *

On this day, inside Lincoln Financial Field, it was party time. After beating the Chargers on the West Coast, it was a triumphant return for a team that had defied the odds and the critics. Now, they had put a big exclamation point on it. And No. 11 wrote his signature all over it.

Against the Cardinals, Wentz threw for a career-high four touchdown passes—the most by an Eagles quarterback in a single game since his backup Nick Foles threw seven touchdown passes in Oakland in 2013, a feat which landed his cleats in Canton.

Wentz came out firing, burying the Cardinals with three touchdown passes in the first quarter. Backup tight end Trey Burton: 15-yard strike. Zach Ertz collected an 11-yard touchdown pass. Then Pederson called on Wentz to go deep to Torrey Smith. It was effortless and precise: 59 yards and a touchdown and the stadium shook.

In the third quarter, Wentz went deep again. This time, he hit Nelson Agholor for 72 yards.

While Agholor did a happy half-moonwalk back to the sideline, six-time Pro Bowl cornerback Patrick Peterson went to the other side of the field and started shouting to no one in particular. These two teams were going in every possible opposite direction. (After the season, Arians and Palmer would go into retirement. This game had to have them thinking about it already.)

Wentz threw 13 passes to Smith, Agholor, and Alshon Jeffery, and the three wide receivers caught 10 of them. If that kind of accuracy and production persisted throughout the season, the Eagles were going to steamroll to the playoffs—and beyond.

It gets better. On third down, Wentz connected on 11-of-12, a completion rate of 91.7 percent for an average pass completion of 18.8 yards, including the 72-yard touchdown bomb to Agholor.

"To be that efficient," said Wentz. "That's huge."

Since the beginning of spring practices, offensive coordinator Frank Reich had made it a priority: Wentz and the offense would work on third-down situations every day.

"That's something we talked about since the day he walked in the building at the start of the off-season program—had to get better on third down if he wanted to become an elite quarterback," said Reich. There would be whole days of film study that crept into the evening, past dinner, and into the night where Wentz would study his third-down tendencies and make sure he wasn't tipping off the defense. And each week, he knew exactly what defensive look a team had shown in the past on third downs. The Cardinals were fairly predictable. Nothing surprised Wentz.

"What really sets you apart as a quarterback is how you perform in situational football," said Reich. "That's third down and red zone. Are you moving the chains? Getting first downs? Are you putting your football team in the end zone? We are here to score points. And that's the quarterback's job. That's what really separates those elite players."

Reich, a backup to Jim Kelly in Buffalo, and Pederson, a backup to Brett Favre in Green Bay, were witnesses to that kind of Hall of Fame greatness. Now, they were trying to take the raw talent of Wentz and shape it into something truly special.

* * *

They saw the potential back in North Dakota.

Ron Jaworski was on the phone. He was calling from Fargo.

"Sal," he said, "we just found the Eagles' next quarterback."

Jaworski, who took the Eagles to their first Super Bowl in 1980, was on assignment for ESPN, covering the Pro Day at North Dakota State, featuring Carson Wentz at quarterback.

North Dakota State University of Agricultural and Applied Sciences is one of the original land grant colleges established in 1890, one year after the Territory of Dakota was admitted to the Union as the states North and South Dakota. It's a massive campus on more than 260 acres in the town of Fargo, made famous by the Coen Brothers movie that depicts a godforsaken place where the forces of good and evil reside as surreal partners in daily life.

The movie could not be further from the truth. Fargo is a tough place to live—cold and harsh most of the year—but the citizenry is ready to do the right thing, in the name of family, country, and God. At least that's the impression Ronald Vincent Jaworski and the entire Philadelphia entourage got on March 24, 2016.

"I got the same question all day long," said North Dakota State football coach Chris Klieman "They always ask, 'Is there anything we're missing? Why is this kid so perfect?'"

And Eagles owner Jeffrey Lurie, who is the only owner in NFL history to give two quarterbacks $100 million contracts (Donovan McNabb and Michael Vick), was looking for perfect. Since trading McNabb on Easter Sunday in 2010, Lurie had cycled through quarterback after quarterback, trying to find the magic formula, replacing Andy Reid with Chip Kelly and turning to Reid's back-to-the-future protege Doug Pederson to save his franchise.

Lurie bought the Eagles in 1994, just four months before Robert Kraft bought the New England Patriots. In fact, Lurie wanted to buy the Patriots, but it didn't work out. Since then, Kraft—by hiring Bill Belichick and drafting Tom Brady—had collected five Lombardi Trophies. And Lurie had been shut out.

Amiable if sometimes misguided, those who know him say Lurie's heart is usually in the right place. He's the heir to the General Cinema Corporation fortune. His mother gave him the cash to buy the Eagles. So, he doesn't need money. He needs a quarterback who can take him to the Super Bowl.

So, Howie Roseman and Pederson persuaded him to take a road trip. If the Eagles were going to take Wentz in the first round, they would have to move up. It would take a whole lot of wheeling and dealing and the investment of draft picks and patience. Wentz played in Division 1-A football, one notch below the big leagues of college ball. Drafting him in the top of the first round would be unorthodox. Phil Simms played at that level in college. Roseman and Pederson had to convince Lurie that Wentz could be the next Simms.

It didn't take much convincing.

Wentz's workout was scripted, yes. And it was held in the Fargodome, where North Dakota State had just won two of the previous three Football Championship Series national titles. So, it was all familiar territory. Still, it wasn't the fact that Wentz completed 62 of the 65 passes he threw—it was the way he did it.

"He had pinpoint accuracy and he's got a rocket for an arm," said Jaworski. "He can make all the NFL throws."

John DeFilippo, the Eagles' quarterbacks coach, added, "We knew he could move. But we didn't know he could move like *that*."

"I knew that day was important," Wentz would tell me later. "We knew there were questions because of where I played. I really wanted to go out and show my athleticism. I knew I had to show the ability to throw on the run, throw in awkward platforms and still deliver the football."

That's what Pederson wanted to see—the accuracy on the run. It was downright Favre-like. "I saw Brett in him right away," Pederson told me.

As luck would have it, a snowstorm prevented a lot of NFL teams from getting to Fargo on time for the workout. Some of them wanted North Dakota State to postpone it. No dice, said Klieman. He and the Wentz team wanted to stick to the script.

Only 18 of the 32 NFL teams were represented. The Cowboys sent a scout. The only head coach other than Pederson to attend was Hue Jackson of the Cleveland Browns, who put Wentz through a smaller workout after the 95 throws.

Jaworski had seen enough. Now, he wanted to *hear* more about Wentz. The storm had delayed his flight. So, he stopped in town to get something to eat and just talk to people—a little boots-on-the-ground reporting.

"Every waitress, every cop, everybody had something nice to say about the kid," he said, calling me from his rental car, unable to hide his excitement. "We're going to draft this guy. You watch."

The question was how.

* * *

Wentz, with his parents, his two brothers, and his girlfriend, drove three hours back to his hometown of Bismarck. Lurie and his coaches got on the plane back to Philadelphia and began plotting how to draft the savior of football in Philly. It wasn't going to be easy. Roseman told Lurie it would be a long and winding road of trades and maneuvering and it would require a lot of faith in the process—and even then, it would take the cooperation of the Los Angeles Rams, who held the No. 1 pick.

Roseman told Lurie there was no way the Eagles could move all the way up in the first round to the first pick. The Rams were going to use the pick, take a quarterback. Which one? The Rams held all the cards. The choice was either Wentz or quarterback Jared Goff of the University of California, Berkeley—tall, blond, photogenic. In short, Goff was straight out of central casting for a team looking to sell tickets in Southern California.

Wentz was blue collar and no-nonsense. He looked like he'd be comfortable carrying his lunch—maybe a bologna sandwich and a Yoo-hoo—in a brown paper bag to work in a factory in Northeast Philly. Goff looked like he just walked off the set of *Beach Blanket Bingo*.

The Rams wanted Goff. At the annual league meeting in the spring of 2016, the team's general manager Les Snead told Roseman that Goff was the choice. Was he bluffing? Could

Roseman trust Snead? If the Rams changed their mind and took Wentz, would the Eagles be happy with Goff? Probably not.

This was Roseman's big gamble. He was not only risking players and draft picks. Roseman was rolling the dice on the very future of the franchise—with an increasingly impatient and surly fanbase that had just about enough of these two out-of-towners (Lurie from outside Boston, Roseman from New York) playing hit-and-miss with their beloved Eagles.

Time was running out on Roseman. Chip Kelly had sent him into exile—literally making him move his office to a wing of the NovaCare Complex that was separated from coaches and the scouting staff. Kelly wanted him out of the building altogether.

Roseman had been with the team for 16 years. He came from the New York Jets. He had been hired out of the Fordham University College of Law by former Jets general manager Mike Tannenbaum, who had been plucked from obscurity by then head coach Bill Parcells. Parcells called Tannenbaum "Mr. T." Everybody just called Roseman "Howie." But when Kelly said his name, he lathered the final syllable with sarcasm: "Howeee."

But Lurie vetoed Kelly's decision to jettison Roseman. They were kindred spirits. And Roseman had a near photographic memory for players and numbers. Lurie wanted to save that. So the owner saved Howie. Now Roseman had to save the owner.

But first he had to find a way to move up in the first round.

After the Rams, the Cleveland Browns picked second. Hue Jackson did not have a franchise quarterback, but he did not like Wentz—he didn't think Wentz's collegiate experience translated to the NFL. So, the Browns put a for-sale sign on the No. 2 overall pick. And Roseman went shopping.

Roseman waited patiently until he got a call from Browns director of football operations Sashi Brown. If Roseman called first, the price would go up—maybe too rich for the Eagles to pay.

Roseman's offer was solid gold from the beginning. It said to the Browns that the Eagles were not fooling around. There was no one else they needed to call.

Roseman offered the Browns the No. 8 overall pick, third- and fourth-round selections in the 2016 draft, a first-round pick in 2017, and a second-round pick in 2018. The Eagles also got a conditional fifth-round pick (a compensatory fourth-rounder, if available) from the Browns in 2017.

All for the No. 2 pick. Brown said to Haslam and Jackson that they were crazy to turn it down. Eagles fans thought Roseman was crazy to offer it.

"It's hard to be great if you don't take some risks," Roseman said. Eight days later, the Rams took Goff and the Eagles selected Carson Wentz.

* * *

On the day Wentz was drafted, I saw two things that I will never forget.

The first was the look on Carson Wentz's face when I told him this little fun fact of Eagles history: The last quarterback to pilot the Eagles to an NFL championship was Norm Van Brocklin in 1960. That year, the Eagles beat the Green Bay Packers in the championship game, the only postseason game Vince Lombardi ever lost.

Van Brocklin wore No. 11. Wentz was going to wear No. 11.

Wentz looked at me like we both needed a drink, or a prayer. Or both. "I didn't know that," he said. "Well," I replied, "now you do."

The second was the look on Doug Pederson's face after I interviewed him—live on ESPN's draft show—about selecting

Wentz. The cameras were off. We moved out of the make-shift studio we had at NovaCare for the draft.

I asked Pederson about veteran quarterback Sam Bradford, who had left the team in a huff when he found out Roseman moved up in the draft to select Wentz. Bradford was AWOL. Pederson had texted him, got nothing back. "He walked out on us," he said to me. I knew then that Pederson was already moving on from Bradford, that the public plan to play him in 2016 while Wentz sat and learned was just for show. Bradford was as good as gone right then and there.

It would take a summer of waiting, and another leap of faith. Wentz got hurt in the preseason. But then the Minnesota Vikings lost quarterback Teddy Bridgewater to a freak knee injury right before the season and Howie was on the phones again. The Vikings offered a first-round pick for Bradford and, just like that, Wentz was handed the keys to the Eagles kingdom eight days before the season opener.

* * *

After the blowout of the Arizona Cardinals, I walked with tight end Zach Ertz from the field back through the tunnel which was adorned with screaming, joyful Eagles fans, to the locker room.

"Carson is just playing instinctive right now, but that's because he studies, he understands the offense, understands the defense," said Ertz, who had replaced Jordan Matthews as Wentz's closest friend on the team. "You can't do what he just did on third down without putting in the work. Our skill players are playing at a high level. But we all know that it helps to have a guy like Carson pulling the trigger."

"Now," I said, "you gotta turn around and do it all over again in five days in Charlotte."

"Our confidence level is so high right now, we could play tomorrow, if we had to," he said.

Of course, that was a bit of boasting. An NFL game is described as like being in 1,000 car wrecks. Your body needs time to recover.

The players dread nothing more than having to truncate that recovery time and play on *Thursday Night Football*, especially on the road. But that's exactly what the Eagles would have to do—in Charlotte, against the 2015 NFC champs, the Panthers.

One important statistical note: Carson Wentz entered that game 28th in the NFL in completion percentage (33 percent) on passes traveling 15 or more yards downfield. On Sunday, however, he was 4-of-7 (57 percent) for 163 yards and three touchdowns on such passes.

Final score: Eagles 34, Cardinals 7

Postscript: With Eagles fan Mike Trout watching from an end-zone seat, Philadelphia's wide receivers decided to perform an homage in the end zone after one of Wentz's touchdowns: Agholor pitched to Smith, who used the football as a bat, with Jeffery catching and Wentz playing, of course, umpire. The windup, the pitch, and Smith hit it out of the park.

"We just did that on a whim," said Wentz. "Zero preparation. We're just out there trying to have fun." Trout, named by Sports Illustrated *as the No. 1 player in Major League Baseball, is from Millville, New Jersey, not far from where Wentz has a home. Wentz's golden retriever, Henley, gave birth to eight puppies in November 2016. He kept one. Named it Jersey.*

PART II

THE MAKING OF AN MVP

Chapter 6

Believing in Big V

The Eagles at the Panthers
Thursday, October 12, 2017 •
Charlotte, North Carolina

Fletcher Cox could not believe it. He rolled into the parking lot of the Eagles' practice facility on Monday, October 9, several hours before sun up. He thought for sure that Carson Wentz had taken his time this morning, taken time to reflect on what he had just accomplished, at least hit the snooze button and indulged the sweet dreams of the four touchdown passes he had thrown the day before—or perhaps enjoyed an extra cup of coffee appreciating the maddening effect he had on cornerback Patrick Peterson, who was left shaking his head on the sideline.

Nope, Wentz was already there.

"You got to be kidding me," Cox mumbled to himself, shaking his head. If there was any doubt that this was Wentz's team, arriving this early on this morning erased it all.

Wentz was watching film of the Panthers' defense, already trying to find any clues at all about the movements of Carolina's two insanely talented linebackers, Thomas Davis and Luke Kuechly, who played the game of football with the kind of anticipation and foresight which led most quarterbacks to believe they were extra-terrestrial—aliens from another planet who wanted to decapitate your friends and teammates. In the game of professional football, there was nobody smarter, nobody more violent than Davis and Kuechly. And the game was just four days away—and one of those days was a travel day.

That's why even though the game against the Cardinals and other postgame obligations had been completed just seven hours ago, Carson Wentz was already in the building, studying every nuance he could.

Also there was Halapoulivaati Vaitai, the 6-foot-6, 320-pound second-year offensive tackle—Big V—who was about to get his first start of the year. Starting Pro Bowl right tackle Lane Johnson suffered a concussion and would not play on Thursday night.

This was nothing new for Vaitai. In 2016, when Johnson was suspended for 10 games for using performance-enhancing drugs, Big V was a rookie and tried to step in. Johnson's suspension torched a promising start to the season—Vaitai was determined and tough, but Johnson was a former top-four pick in the NFL draft. He was being groomed to take Jason Peters' spot at left tackle. But Peters was not interested in letting his job go, and when Johnson got snagged for the second time by the NFL for using PEDs, the team had serious doubts about whether it could count on Johnson long-term. As long as Peters—who, at age 35, was one of the three oldest starting offensive linemen in the NFL—stayed healthy, he wasn't going anywhere.

Pederson would proclaim to the press later in the day that he wasn't sure about Johnson, that he was still in the concussion protocol. But he also said it would be a small miracle if Johnson was cleared in just four days. The coach knew that Big V needed to get himself ready. Davis and Kuechly would not be accepting any excuses. Johnson suffered the concussion about midway through the Cardinals game. Big V started the third quarter. And the Eagles' offense did not miss a beat. But that was the Cardinals at home. This was one of the best defenses in the league—on the road.

"For him not getting a ton of reps at tackle to come off the bench like he does is just a tribute to the way he prepares himself and the way he battles," said Pederson on that Monday afternoon. He was speaking to the assembled reporters in the NovaCare auditorium, but he was also talking through them directly to Vaitai. Head coaches often use their press conferences to send subtle messages to their players. This one was not subtle: Big V better be in the film room.

* * *

There are a lot of things that are sexy and glamorous about professional football. Film study is not one of them.

Imagine yourself in a darkened room for hours and hours and hours, looking at a projected image of a football play on a big screen, going over the footwork of a defensive end—a 300-pound Baryshnikov—and looking at the way he bends a knee or plants his foot to find just the right leverage point. You want to keep him from blowing up your afternoon. All it takes is one slip, one play where you get beat by that defensive end, and within a half-second, he's got his helmet in your quarterback's rib cage, he's violently separated the football, which is slithering out of your reach while some linebacker appears out of nowhere, and scoops it up like the fish in the bottom of a boat and scampers into the end zone, beginning a dance that ignites your opponents and their fans and turns momentum against you—for good.

While you're studying the footwork of this dancing bear on roller skates with 20-inch biceps, there is a man sitting next to you, your offensive line coach. His name is usually Mudd or Stoutland or Grimm or Munchak, and he's a football lifer and his breath smells like nine cups of coffee or five-day-old cigarette butts—and he's breathing down your neck, asking you questions, making sure you are seeing what he's seeing on film, because if you're not, "We're all in big fat trouble."

Those are all real last names of offensive line coaches. Howard Mudd was the offensive line coach for many teams. In 2012, after two years with the Eagles, Philadelphia was his last stop before retirement.

He started playing pro football in 1964, the year I was in the eighth grade, and started coaching offensive linemen in the NFL in 1974, the year I graduated high school. He worked for the Chargers, Niners, Seahawks, Browns, Chiefs, Seahawks again, Colts, and Eagles—Mudd coached coast to coast, a hired gun who knew the secret code of how to do one thing very, very well: Block the other guys so they don't kill your quarterback. If you don't have a good offensive line coach, you're simply not going to be able to play winning football on Sundays in America. Mudd was a great one.

I had a ton of respect for him. The feeling, apparently, was not mutual. I didn't find that out until I casually went to ask him a question.

Mudd turned to me with a grin made of granite and said, "Listen, Sal, I understand you're trying to do your job. But I don't think you know what you're talking about."

I respectfully didn't respond. I had been thrown out of the Eagles' locker room once by Rich Kotite, the former tough-talking head coach from Brooklyn. He poked his finger in my chest in front of Fred Barnett's locker. We were separated by the late trainer Otho Davis. Andy Reid once barred me from training camp in Lehigh. And Bill Parcells threw me out of Weeb Ewbank Hall at Hofstra University on draft day because—on live TV—I asked him too many questions about Keyshawn Johnson's new book.

And when I covered politics for the *Philadelphia Inquirer*, it was worse, much, much worse. You just have to know when to walk away. Let the other guy have the last word. Privately, I had three reactions to Coach Mudd:

I had no idea he even knew my name.

I had no idea he paid attention to anything I said.

He was probably right: I probably don't know what I'm talking about.

I've always tried to approach this job with that basic understanding. I'm not the one in that film room, hour after hour, day after day. Having been in the military, I have always respected the level of tactical preparation that goes into an NFL game, always tried to understand that these coaches and players were trying to keep secrets from their opponents.

It was my job to get a hold of those secrets and tell the world. One of my favorite producers at ESPN, Mark Gross, always says to me, "Sal, take people behind the scenes, take people where they can't buy a ticket to go."

That's exactly where coaches and players don't want you to be. So, you have to ask questions, find out what happens behind closed doors, in those meetings and film study sessions.

I did that job willingly, but I had to be ready to take the consequences.

To replace Mudd, Reid hired Jeff Stoutland, who had toiled at the high school and collegiate level for more than two decades. Philly was his first pro stop. His last college job was working for the incomparable Nick Saban at Alabama, where he helped the Crimson Tide win a national championship in 2012.

Stoutland just looks like he was born to coach football. He has a squat body with a cinderblock head—in the Marines, he'd been a gunny sergeant, the guy all the troops turned to in a firefight. To paraphrase Colonel Jessup, "You want him on that wall."

The Eagles' offensive linemen worshiped him, called him "Stout." Stout means portly, but it also means brave and determined. The nickname said it all. Pederson also relied on Stoutland and his assistant Eugene Chung to give him advice, now, on the running game—when and how to use it.

"Those guys are in the box, they are seeing things I don't see," he said, referring to the coaches' box at the press level. "Coach Stoutland and Coach Chung, the guys that are seeing the run game from a distance and making those necessary adjustments during the game and the course of the game."

But, right now, in Week 6 of this improbable run of the Philadelphia Eagles toward respectability, it was Stout's job to whip Big V into shape, get him ready to replace Lane Johnson, a Pro Bowl tackle and one of the team's highest-paid players— in just four days.

There was quite a bit of skepticism about Vaitai's ability to start for Johnson. Pederson and the team believed in him. Mostly everybody outside the NovaCare facility had their doubts.

What nobody knew at the time was that this would not only be a debut for Big V, but a dress rehearsal for a much bigger responsibility to come.

* * *

This was a big showdown on national television. The Eagles were 4–1 and led their division. The Panthers were 4–1 and led their division. But Vegas had installed the Panthers as just a 3.5-point favorite. Usually, the oddsmakers would give a team, especially a team that had just beaten the Patriots in Foxboro and the Lions in Detroit, three points alone for home-field advantage.

Making it feel worse was that the favorite was 4–0 against the spread and straight up in the last four meetings between these two teams.

But the fact that the line was so close indicated to South Philly bookies that the Eagles were gaining respectability. In short, take the points. "The line is telling me something," said one bookie. "They got a legit chance down there," he said. "Go Birds." I ran into him in the Philly airport. He was on his way to the game.

So was half of South Philly. It's an easy hop from Philadelphia to Charlotte, a central booking point for American Airlines. And the flights were filled with "Birds" fans flocking south.

But Pederson wasn't buying all the happy talk. The truth was he was worried about how in the world this team was going to sustain this level of success. Veterans on the team agreed with him. Malcolm Jenkins said in the locker room after beating the Arizona Cardinals that the veterans spoke up quickly about not getting complacent after such an easy win. LeGarrette Blount jumped in, too. "We ain't won nothin'," he said he told the team.

Jenkins won a Super Bowl in New Orleans. Blount had just gotten through the school of Bill Belichick's hard knocks: Shut your mouth, do your job, I'll tell you when it's time to celebrate.

Said Jenkins, "I told them to keep their feet on the ground and be here now."

"You really don't have time to dwell on your past success," Pederson said after hearing Jenkins and Blount. "But we've got guys on this roster who have played in the Super Bowl, who have played in playoff games, and coaches on this staff that have been in those games. They know what it takes to stay focused. They know what it takes to stay grounded. You're only as good as your last win or your last loss. It's tough because these players are probably more out in the community, they're doing more appearances and those are the things that we have to guard against, complacency."

Pederson also knew Panthers head coach Ron Rivera, who worked for Reid in Philadelphia. Rivera, who comes from a military family, was as single-minded in his approach as they come. Never wavered from the task. His team was rolling. But he wanted to get back to the Super Bowl—and this time win it. And his old friend Doug Pederson was standing in his way.

These were two football sons of Big Red—one who was just in the Super Bowl, one on his way—doing battle. They met at midfield before the game. Shook hands. Embraced. Both are friendly, down to earth, married men, close to their families. But, to win a football game, there was no quarter given. Especially this game. Doug Pederson, in his second year, was not going to come into Rivera's house with a second-year quarterback and beat his team on national TV. No way, Rivera said to himself. Not gonna happen.

Rivera had quarterback Cam Newton, who was coming off his best game of the season, steamrolling the Lions with 355 passing yards and three touchdowns.

Just to put on a show for the cameras and the Eagles fans peppered all over Bank of America Stadium, Newton hitched his stretch band to a post along the end-zone sideline and began pulling and pushing, trying to loosen his massive hamstrings, like a preening heavyweight ready to show these interlopers and a national television audience why his team was ready to return to the Super Bowl.

In the basement tunnel of the stadium, I ran into Kuechly, who has been plagued by concussions, but refuses to quit the game he loves and has mastered. "How you feeling?" I said to him. "Never better, bro," he said with an easy smile. "Never better."

After seeing and hearing that, I thought Vegas had it all wrong.

* * *

One of the most underrated traits of a head football coach is knowing when to shut up. And on the day of the game against the Panthers, Doug Pederson didn't have much to say. Didn't have to.

He knew his team had been grinding for three straight days, getting their minds right, getting their bodies ready to land in Charlotte and take on a conference beast. The team plane landed in Charlotte on Wednesday afternoon, just about 72 hours after the beatdown of the Cardinals.

Pederson kept his message to the team short and sweet. I texted him and asked him what he said.

He texted back: "I told them: Consistency in all three phases. Ball security and execution."

Lane Johnson was definitely not available. Big V would make his first start of the year. But Pro Bowl defensive tackle Fletcher Cox, the team's highest-paid player, was back after a two-week absence with a nagging calf injury. That was key. The Panthers under Rivera wanted to run the football and the Eagles needed Cox to plug up the middle. If Philly was going to have any chance to put any pressure on Newton and stop the Panthers' offense in its tracks, it would start with stopping the run.

* * *

A bit of historical perspective: According to the Eagles' stellar public relations staff, the last time the team played three of its first five games on the road and started the season 4–1 was 1954. This was a history-making squad about to make more.

Carson Wentz threw three touchdown passes and the Eagles intercepted Newton three times.

The first two interceptions came inside Carolina's 20. And Newton could not be blamed for either one. Cox slammed Newton as he got rid of one pass. Another pass was bobbled by the usually sure-handed running back Jonathan Stewart.

With just over three minutes to go in the game, with Newton bringing the Panthers to the doorstep of a go-ahead touchdown, Jalen Mills made it a hat trick for the Eagles' defense to seal the win.

"I told them tonight after the game I haven't been part of a team that has battled through so much injury and adversity in the first month of the season," Pederson said. "The resiliency of the football team started to show last year at the end of the year. They're learning from last year. They're learning how to finish games and just the overall consistency from the leaders leading this football team. They are sacrificing for each other—themselves for the football team. It's a fun thing to watch."

But Wentz took a lot of punishment—he was sacked three times and hit eight more. Big V had his moments, but for the most part the offensive line struggled. Perhaps they were all keeping one eye on the right side, wondering how Big V was holding up, or perhaps they were just tired and worn out from the short week. Wentz shrugged it off.

"That was a hard-fought win, on the road, on a short week, on prime-time TV," he said. "So, to come out of it 5-1, that's big for us."

But not for Vegas. On the flights back to Philly next day, everybody who took the Birds and the points was flush with cash and optimism.

One important statistical note: The Eagles had won four of their first five games heading into Thursday night. But three of those victories came against the New York Giants, Los Angeles Chargers, and Arizona Cardinals, who had a combined record of 3-12. Now, they had beaten a team that was in first place in its division.

The team had a few days off, followed by three straight games at Lincoln Financial Field. But the questions about whether this team was for real would be resurrected quickly: The next three games were against the Redskins, who would finish out of the playoffs, and the Niners and the Broncos, who would finish last in their respective divisions.

Final score: Eagles 28, Panthers 23

Postscript: Sadly, Luke Kuechly suffered another concussion in the game. He slumped to the turf after a collision with massive Eagles right guard Brandon Brooks, who was pulling on the play. All of the Eagles' touchdowns came after Kuechly left the game. The following week, the Panthers would lose to the lowly Bears in Chicago. They would finish 11–5, but the back-to-back losses meant the Saints would win the division and the Panthers would have to start their postseason run on the road in New Orleans, where they would lose, 31–26.

Chapter 7

Next Man Up

The Redskins at the Eagles
Monday, October 23, 2017 • South Philadelphia

Jason Peters has always looked bigger and stronger than everybody else his age.

Nine years old, growing up in the east Texas town of Queen City, Peters was removed from a Little League game. The umpire, after getting a complaint from the coach in the visitors' dugout, was convinced that Peters was too old. It was silly. Everybody knew everybody else in town. Queen City has a population of 1,476, fewer than most city blocks in South Philly. But the ump wanted proof.

"I struck out nine batters in the first three innings," Peters said. Nine up, nine down. "My mother had to go home and get my birth certificate. I was allowed back in the game. After I went back in, I hit a home run." He dreamed of going to

New York and pitching for the Yankees. But he had a body that said football.

Peters crossed the border and attended the University of Arkansas. He was a redshirt freshman and played defensive end, running with the scout team. He moved up on the depth chart, but was passed over again. Peters went undrafted in 2004.

The Buffalo Bills, always adept at picking up rookie talent after the drafting was done, took a chance. They signed Peters to a rookie free agent deal. They made him a tight end. His signing bonus: $5,000. A year later, the Bills moved him to offensive tackle, a brilliant move. Peter King of *Sports Illustrated* named Peters as one of his All-Pro offensive linemen.

But, in 2009, Peters was stuck in a contract stalemate with the Bills. That's when Andy Reid picked up the phone. He offered Buffalo a first-round pick. Reid called Peters and said he wanted to give him $60 million. And that was how the Eagles landed their franchise left tackle.

Peters has been to nine Pro Bowls. In the fall of 2017, he was the anchor of an offensive line that had the leading offense in the conference and was running the football at a remarkable clip of 132 yards per game, better than any team in the NFC except the Chicago Bears (which without a passing game had no choice but to run the football).

In short, Peters was leading the way for a team that—at 5-1—seemed to be headed for greatness. And Monday night, October 23, 2017, there was to be a little coming-out party at Lincoln Financial Field on national TV.

And that's when Jason Raynard Peters was lost for the season.

In the third quarter, in one of those freak accidents caused by 300-pound men doing the line-of-scrimmage tango at a high rate of speed and violence, Peters was inadvertently pinned under Redskins defensive tackle Ziggy Hood.

His right knee got twisted. Two ligaments were immediately shredded and, as Peters was stretched out on the field in agony, his teammates knew right away that it was serious. If not, Peters would have been up off the deck. Veteran tight end Brent Celek pulled off his helmet and just stared at Peters. He was concerned about his good friend—they had served side by side in the trenches for nearly 10 years—but also worried about his team surviving such a loss.

A cart was brought onto the field. There was a hush over the Monday night crowd. The party was on hold. An air cast was fitted onto Peters' right knee. Once that happens, every

All-world left tackle Jason Peters is carted off Lincoln Financial Field after blowing out his right knee, with Eagles fans chanting his name all the way to the locker room.

player knows that it's over. The Eagles' sideline emptied and everybody came over to tap Peters' shoulder. On the Washington sideline, the Redskins clapped out of respect. The game was losing a true pro, an indispensable talent who could not possibly be replaced.

As the cart left the field, with Peters holding his head high, the Eagles fans chanted his name. He did not cry. He did not have to. His tortured face gave away the range of emotions running through his blood.

* * *

You can preach the Next Man Up philosophy all you want as a head coach. But when you're talking about replacing your left tackle, who is responsible for protecting the blind side of your franchise quarterback, whose résumé has "Future Hall of Famer" emblazoned across the top, who has started 166 games and embodies the soul and attitude of your offensive line, that's where platitudes begin to sound hollow. That's when you just got to find a way to win a football game.

So, the next man up was obvious: Halapoulivaati Vaitai. Somebody suggested moving Lane Johnson from right tackle to left and giving Big V the right side. Offensive line coach Jeff Stoutland vetoed that immediately. Pederson agreed. No need to disrupt both sides of the O-line at the same time. Johnson was on a mission. He was run blocking with a vengeance and his pass blocking was giving opposing defensive coordinators fits. Week after week, the opponents were throwing everything at him—free rushers from the edge, a defensive tackle slamming into his ribs to get him off his spot, or two players off the edge to force him into a choice that provided the slightest hesitation. Johnson was a stone wall. The opposition couldn't move him—why would Stoutland try?

* * *

Vaitai was a wall of a man, too. He liked to stand tall with his arms folded like Shaquille O'Neal, although Yao Ming, the 7-footer from China, was his favorite NBA player. This, even though one of his two dogs is a chihuahua. The dog's name is Coffee, because, Vaitai said, "he's hyper." Big V is not hyper. Far from it. He's as calm as the warm, soft breezes off his native island of Tonga.

Indeed, since the day he was drafted, Vaitai walked around the Eagles' locker room with a serene, stoic look on his face. He rarely said a word to reporters. His best answer to any question came after Eagles website editor Dave Spadaro asked him what it was like to be Tongan.

"We like to eat," he said. Mostly burgers and fries. Big V's parents left the Kingdom of Tonga in the 1980s, when the Reagan Administration, with the help of the Mormon Church, opened up the floodgates to Polynesian immigration to the United States. It's an archipelago of 169 islands. Only about 40 of them are inhabited. Most of the kingdom is poor. But the people are rich in personality and extraordinarily giving. And they love American football. Former Eagles punt returner Vai Sikahema—who once famously used the goal post padding at old Giants Stadium as a punching bag after a punt return for a touchdown (his father taught him to box)—was the first Tongan to play in the NFL. He joined the Cardinals when they were playing in St. Louis in 1986 and many more followed in his footsteps. There are currently 21 Tongans wearing NFL uniforms. It's a tight-knit family within the pro football community.

Why do they love football?

"It's because of the way Polynesian culture is set up," Sikahema told me. "Chiefs rule villages. And they rule islands.

Questions were not asked to the chief or they were simply killed. So, the idea of a football coach, the one guy in charge, was perfectly acceptable to the Polynesian athlete." The Polynesians are the Italians and Irish of the late 20th century, Sikahema explained. "We've only been in this country for 30 or 40 years. So our culture is still very much with us. That father figure on the football field works in our culture because it *is* our culture. Fathers have ultimate authority in our homes—that's the nature of our people."

And, it's still very much a warrior tradition. In Texas, Tongan schoolboys who dominate some high school football teams still do a pregame performance of the Haka, the ancient Polynesian war chant and dance that calls for a fight to the death.

"You know, our community, we're the most friendly people outside of sports, and we're also competitive," Big V said. "All of us hate to lose. I really appreciate that because growing up a lot of my family members were competitive. You've got to take what's yours, you know? You've got to go in there with that mentality. A lot of Polynesians are like that. But we're just caring guys. We like to take care of each other."

Take care of each other. But take what's yours. Doug Pederson heard that, liked it a lot.

Vaitai—who tried to emulate Peters when he was in college at Texas Christian, who worked out personally for Stoutland down in Fort Worth, Texas, and was only 24 years old in his second professional season—was now going to take care of the left side of the most successful offensive line in the NFL for the remainder of the season.

All across Philadelphia, all across America, the question was all too obvious: The Eagles can't possibly win a Super Bowl with Halapoulivaati Vaitai at left tackle, can they?

* * *

Just 54 seconds were gone in the third quarter of *Monday Night Football* when Peters was carted off and the Eagles had the lead, 17–10.

"You got into make-a-play mode," said quarterback Carson Wentz. Peters' departure did not stop the Eagles' offense. They were in the middle of an 86-yard drive. Wentz finished the deal. While scrambling, Wentz was sandwiched by two Redskins. As he fell forward, he floated a nine-yard pass to rookie running back Corey Clement. In the booth, long-time *Monday Night Football* analyst Jon Gruden was nearly speechless.

"That was amazing," the gregarious Gruden would say later. He knew Pederson from their days in Green Bay together. "With that kind of quarterback play, the sky's the limit."

After the game, Pederson gushed. "One of the best plays I've seen in a long time and by two young guys," Pederson said. "To hang in there and take shot after shot, it's amazing to me."

In the locker room after the game, Lane Johnson heaped more praise on Wentz: "That's what makes him so special. He's just got great field vision. He's got what a lot of guys don't have."

But how long could Wentz take this kind of week-to-week punishment and survive?

The Redskins sacked Wentz three times—bringing the total times Wentz had gone down with the football in his hands behind the line of scrimmage to 19 for the season. And the Eagles' season was only seven games old. That was almost three sacks a game—that projected to 48 sacks for the season. His rookie year, Wentz was only sacked 33 times.

The sacks only told part of the story. Wentz was getting hit, pushed, shoved, and smacked around much more than the box score indicated.

"We knew he was getting whacked, but we tried everything," said one Eagles coach. "First of all, it was his style of play. We didn't want to inhibit him in any way. Remember, he was the MVP of the league."

Indeed, with the season almost half over, Wentz was the clear favorite to win the MVP. Why screw with a good thing?

Still, behind closed doors, the coaching staff, led by offensive coordinator Frank Reich and quarterbacks coach John DeFilippo, hammered home the same sermon: Wentz had to learn to protect his body more. He had to get rid of the football. Learn to slide when he got out of the pocket. Get down or get out of bounds. Don't expose his body to needless punishment. Don't take on the hits. Avoid them at all costs. Watch Tom Brady. There's a reason why he's still playing at a high level at age 40.

Publicly, when asked about it, Wentz had several stock answers: "I'm not going to change my style." Or, "I'm trying to make a play for my team."

When you're 6-foot-5 and 237 pounds and you're 24 years old and your No. 11 jersey is breaking sales records and the fans are chanting "M-V-P" every time you step onto the field, you feel invincible.

"I'm just playing football," he said.

* * *

Carson Wentz didn't like answering all these questions about himself. He was fast becoming the most popular professional football player in Philadelphia in a generation. But he was not interested in that aspect of the NFL. He talked to reporters only when approached or asked.

After he met with the media the week before the Super Bowl, when he was still rehabbing his knee injury and had said nothing for weeks, I asked Wentz why he chose three days before leaving for Minneapolis to go public. "I do what I'm told," he said to me.

To his teammates, Wentz was outgoing, giving, and friendly. To the press, he was polite, but definitely aloof. He clearly wanted to keep his heart hidden from the picklocks of the media. He was not cultivating any kind of image off the field. He did not want to be a quote unquote star. And he definitely did not want to be a celebrity.

In August, just at the end of training camp, in a private session with a number of Philadelphia football writers, one reporter said to Wentz, "A lot of quarterbacks are flamboyant, hang out with celebrities. You're different. Why so private?"

"I feel like what I am and who I am is kind of out there, that's pretty much all there is to it," Wentz said. "I'm pretty simple. I do like being low-key. I do like being private, for the most part. I think this business, this world that I've come into, is really cool, but it can be a lot sometimes and sometimes it's just nice to go home and be chill."

Wentz asked his older brother Zach (and Zach's wife, Andrea) to come to Philadelphia to sift through the demands of being the franchise quarterback in a football-mad city. Zach Wentz handles the family foundation and sets up the hunting trips—Carson Wentz's passion away from football.

"It gives me peace of mind away from the game," he said. "Brings North Dakota to New Jersey. I'm not going to let the culture I live in and where I live kind of change me. I'm just going to keep being me."

In that interview, Wentz was asked about the one quarterback he watched and learned from. Without knowing what the future held for him and the Eagles, Wentz quickly mentioned Brady.

"He's done it no matter who's there, every year," Wentz said. "He's been doing it for so long no matter who's around him." Before the season started, Brady lost his most productive wide receiver, Julian Edelman, whose spectacular catch against the Atlanta Falcons in Super Bowl LI helped fuel what is arguably the greatest comeback in NFL postseason history. Now, Wentz would have to go on without Jason Peters.

* * *

Up 24-10 on the Redskins after the Clement catch for a touchdown, Philadelphia's coaches and veteran players were once again warning on the sideline against complacency. Watching the scoreboard is only natural, especially at home. At Lincoln Financial Field, the crowd is right on top of the bench. The stadium was designed like that on purpose. Joe Banner, Jeffrey Lurie's long-time lieutenant who had a falling out with his boss as Andy Reid's tenure unraveled, was a huge proponent of putting the Philly fans right on top of the players. Banner, who had a hand in designing every inch of the elegant Eagles palace in the South Philly sports complex, wanted the players to feel—and hear—the passion. It worked both ways: The opposition got a profane earful for 60 minutes. The Eagles players fed off the emotions of their faithful. So, when the game was a laugher like this one, there was a natural tendency to channel what the fans were saying and doing. The party was back and all Carson Wentz's rowdy Philly friends were enjoying it.

Once again, it was Malcolm Jenkins' job to put the hammer down. In the defensive huddle, he reminded his teammates about the resilience of Redskins quarterback Kirk Cousins.

"This cat ain't going away," said Jenkins. "We got to put him away."

Easier said than done. "This cat" Cousins was playing for his team's season and also out to prove to team management that fiddling around with his long-term contract status was a mistake. For two straight years, Cousins had been shackled by what is called the franchise tag, deals that kept him out of free agency. The franchise tags were lucrative. Cousins cashed in—more than $50 million. But he thought he earned the right to be like all the other starting quarterbacks. And that meant one of two things: Freedom or long-term security. And that doubt went two ways. The front office and the locker room wondered about Cousins' commitment to the Redskins franchise. After the season, long-time Washington defensive back DeAngelo Hall said on *SportsCenter*, "We kind of felt like the commitment wasn't there from Kirk." Cousins could feel that. He wanted to make sure his teammates felt he was all in.

Late in the third quarter, Cousins hit his favorite target, tight end Jordan Reed, for a five-yard touchdown pass. The Redskins cut the lead to seven points. The Eagles were in a one-score game.

Pederson thought he could ice the game with Blount. He thought wrong. On their very next drive, the Eagles tried running up the middle and got a paltry two yards. Quickly, Philadelphia had third-and-eight on their own 27 and needed something to keep the drive alive. Wentz did not want to give the ball back to Cousins.

He dropped back to pass. Nobody was open. He decided to take it himself, coaches and critics be damned. Wentz scrambled right up the gut of the Redskins' defense—for 17 yards and a first down. On the Washington sideline, Jon Gruden's little brother Jay, the Redskins' head coach, just marveled that a guy that big with that kind of arm could also move like that.

"His ability to make plays with his legs—that's what separates him from a lot of guys playing quarterback in this league," he said.

The 17-yard scramble put fear into the Washington defense and opened up the Eagles' passing game. Football can appear complicated at times. But it's really a simple game: If you have to dedicate a defender to even thinking about the quarterback running, you're short-handed in pass defense. It's simple math.

Wentz went to work. He hit Ertz for six yards, Jeffery for 24, Ertz again for 12, and then Agholor for a 10-yard touchdown pass, opening up a comfortable two-touchdown lead.

Cousins hit Reed for one more touchdown. And Jake Elliott missed a field goal. That kept the national television audience engaged deep into the fourth quarter. But there was a feeling of inevitability, that on this night, the torch was being officially passed from the promise of Cousins in Washington to the fulfillment of Wentz in Philly.

"We got something special going on here," said Jenkins. "Just got to keep it going."

One important statistical note: After beating Washington, the Eagles had won seven straight games against NFC opponents. The last time they did that was 2004, the last time they went to the Super Bowl.

Final score: Eagles 34, Redskins 24

Postscript: In metered market results, the Eagles-Redskins Week 7 game on Monday night scored a 7.9 rating. That was up a whopping 30 percent in the early numbers for ESPN from the previous week's Monday night game between the Tennessee Titans and Indianapolis Colts.

Yes, the East Coast markets are bigger. But people were falling in love with Philly's gunslinger. The Eagles, with Carson Wentz at the helm, were starting to become America's Team.

Chapter 8

Catching the Jay Train

The 49ers at the Eagles
Sunday, October 29, 2017 • South Philadelphia

Carson Wentz was pulled in the fourth quarter. Not because he played poorly. No, Wentz played efficiently, let's say okay—good enough for the Eagles to pull away in the final minutes against the San Francisco 49ers, who stunk on wheels.

Up 33-7 late in the game, Pederson told Wentz to turn in his helmet for an Eagles baseball cap. Backup quarterback Nick Foles trotted onto the field. No one could even remember when the Eagles had pulled their starting quarterback in a fourth-quarter blowout. It would be the first of two straight home games when Pederson said, okay, enough is enough. A head coach doesn't make that decision lightly. It's the ultimate insult, like announcing to the national TV audience—and the fellas on the opposite sideline—hey, you're not good enough to hang with us. Drive home safely.

Indeed, after the game, first year Niners general manager John Lynch may have said to himself, that's it—if we're going to return to the glory years that brought five Lombardi Trophies to the Bay Area, we have to do what the Eagles did—get us a franchise quarterback. (Weeks later, Lynch would be gifted Tom Brady's young backup Jimmy Garropolo by Bill Belichick in a trade that shocked New England. Brady was not far from retirement and Patriots fans liked Jimmy G—thought he was heir apparent—and getting a second-round pick was not enough in return.) San Francisco didn't need another Joe Montana. Just somebody who could put it in the end zone once in a while.

The Niners had waltzed into what I like to call the City of Brotherly Shove and thought they had a shot to compete against the best team in the NFC in front of a rabid, sold-out crowd—with C.J. Beathard at quarterback. Even playing a subpar game, Wentz and the Eagles' offense steamrolled through the Niners' frustrated defense. (Frustrated was an understatement. The team bus got egged as it arrived at Lincoln Financial Field and the Niners' offense could not get out of its own way.) It was 17-0 at halftime and the Eagles coasted to victory.

In the fourth quarter, Foles was given one mop-up drive and took a knee to end the game. It was his first action of the 2017 NFL season. The Eagles and their 69,596 fans had no way of knowing that No. 9 replacing No. 11 on this day would foreshadow a moment in time that no one could possibly contemplate or, right now, possibly comprehend.

Least of all Doug Pederson. Pederson had his eyes on the immediate future. The Niners were a winless team when they arrived and winless when they left. But with Jason Peters gone, the offensive line struggled and the Eagles' running game was pedestrian. As a team, they broke the 100-yard barrier—112 yards in all. But they averaged just 3.6 yards per carry. Sluggish. What's worse, LeGarrette Blount was held to just three yards per carry. That simply was not championship football. The team needed help and vice president for football operations Howie Roseman had just the answer.

* * *

The word down in Miami was that veteran running back Jay Ajayi was not happy with the Dolphins. And head coach Adam Gase was not happy with him. Ajayi ran hard but didn't like the fact that once the team got inside the 20-yard line, Gase did not call his number. His friends on the team thought maybe the organization was trying to limit his opportunities to score and thus reduce his financial value to the team. As a result, his attitude, along with his knees, were grouchy. Roseman's old mentor Mike Tannenbaum—Mr. T.—was looking to move on. Roseman offered a low-round draft pick, assuming Ajayi passed a physical. The Eagles wanted to make sure the knees would go on long enough to give Blount a break—and a little competition.

"We'd seen him run on tape," said another NFC team scout that needed a running back. "And it looked like to us that Ajayi lacked breakaway speed. He could not separate. That's probably why the Dolphins didn't trust him in the tight spaces inside the 20. He couldn't open up."

For Roseman and Pederson, what Ajayi showed them was good enough. "He is a great piece to the puzzle at running back for us," Pederson told me.

There were immediate reports that with Ajayi in town, Blount was gone. I got nervous. Pederson had sold me that the Eagles were not looking to make another move at running back, that Blount was staying. I reported that. He's never lied to me, never misled me. Nevertheless, there is an old saying in journalism: "If your mother says she loves you, check it out." So I went back to him, and checked one more team source. "Blount's not going anywhere," the source said. "Doug loves him and the team loves him."

Here was the exchange between Pederson and a reporter on November 1:

> **Question:** Will Blount embrace playing less?
> **Pederson:** Who said that?
> **Question:** I'm asking: Will Blount embrace playing less?
> **Pederson:** Who said he was going to play less?...I can't speculate on that.

How this was going to work, then, was anybody's guess. Blount was filled with pride and his past suggested he could go off the rails at any time. Clement was at the front end of the learning curve. The last thing running backs coach Duce Staley wanted to introduce to the rookie was diva drama in the meeting rooms and practice field. And that was the reputation that Ajayi brought from Miami.

* * *

Ajayi brought two other things with him: Big talent and a big personality. He was born in London to Nigerian parents. He was raised in Texas, where he attended Liberty High School in the state's northern plains, just south of where Jason Peters grew up.

North Texas is a long way from Nigeria and London—in many ways big and small. But there is one universal language there that everybody understands: Ajayi could speak Friday

Night Lights—even if he had a British accent. And from the day Ajayi started carrying the rock, he lit it up. As a senior, he was named second-team all-state and was voted a *Parade* Magazine All-American, averaging 10 yards every time he touched the football. He ran with the 100-meter, 200-meter, and 400-meter district championship track squads. Translation: He could run fast. And he was a National Honor Society Scholar, which means—as anybody who's gone to high school in America knows—that your teachers like you. Ajayi was personable and popular, on and off the football field.

He got a full ride to Boise State and the Miami Dolphins took him in the fifth round of the 2015 NFL draft. A year later, Ajayi accumulated 1,272 rushing yards, third-most in team history just behind another guy from Texas named Ricky Williams. In just year two, Ajayi was in the Pro Bowl. In year three, the wheels came off.

In his second year as head coach, Adam Gase began to clash with his young running back. Gase was hired in January 2016, the same month the Eagles hired Pederson. At that time, Pederson, Gase, and Ben McAdoo were all competing for seven NFL head coaching vacancies. The top three destinations were considered the Giants, the Dolphins, and the Eagles, which interviewed all three. The Giants were in New York and had Eli Manning and Odell Beckham Jr. and a front office flush with cash ready to spend lavishly on a new defense. So, they were considered the most desirable option. The Dolphins had tradition and South Beach and no income tax in Florida—players loved to play there. And they had a young quarterback, Ryan Tannehill. Thus far, Tannehill had failed to live up to the billing, but he had enough promise to succeed—if he had a stud running back. The Eagles were in total rebuild, without a franchise quarterback.

Pederson, who was not interviewed anywhere else, took the Eagles job. McAdoo got the supposed plum: The Giants. Gase went to Miami, inheriting Tannehill and Ajayi.

But there is a strange phenomenon that sometimes happens in NFL locker rooms. When disagreements begin to bubble to the surface for any reason—playing time, tactical approach, persistent losing—coaches and players will often abandon each other for no other reason than this: "He's not my guy." A coach likes to have "his guys" with him. Bill Parcells was like that. He wanted the guys he knew and could trust. They carried the message in the locker room. And they were the capos, making sure those who stepped out of line, who questioned the padrone, the coach, were either brought into the fold or shipped out the door.

What happens behind the scenes in an NFL locker room is rarely reported accurately. But here is what was written in the *Miami Herald* by one of the best reporters ever to cover pro football, Armando Salguero:

> The reason Ajayi was traded has to do with team culture and chemistry and player buy-in.
>
> And the Dolphins weren't liking what Ajayi was doing on those fronts. Yes, he was missing holes and assignments on occasions, too.
>
> He was among the players coach Adam Gase was referencing when he said players don't take work home with them.
>
> "At the end of the day, guys have got to actually take this stuff home and study it," Gase said a few days ago. "They're not going to just learn it all in meetings. We've got to find guys that will actually put forth effort

to actually remember this stuff and really, it starts with our best players."

Yes, like Ajayi.

I know Salguero. He's a tough, careful reporter. He's not writing that in one of the nation's most prestigious newspapers if he doesn't have it solidly sourced. He talks regularly with Gase—on and off the record. So, there is no doubt he wrote that with the coach saying something like, "You're on solid ground." Here's what he wrote next:

[Ajayi] complained bitterly about not getting the football. He stormed out of the locker room—get this, after wins—because he hadn't gotten what he deemed to be enough carries. And, oh yes, he didn't exactly light it up on the field.

And here's the thing: All this was done undercover. Ajayi complained to his position coach. And he carried around an attitude around other teammates. But he never took his concerns to the only voice that matters and that's Gase.

This report was all over talk radio in Philadelphia and what reporters carried into the press conference with Pederson. And what Ajayi brought to the Eagles, who had achieved a perfect chemical balance on their way to the best record in the NFC. What was Roseman doing? Was he doing a favor for his old boss, Mike Tannenbaum, taking a malcontent off his hands? Was he playing fantasy football the way his old boss in Philly, Joe Banner, was often accused of doing? Yes, Blount's production was tailing off. But would Ajayi push Blount or create a current of discontent that dislodged the moorings of a great season?

Roseman was taking another big risk. But did he go too far this time?

Roseman quickly came out and said Blount remained the starter. That was to mollify the fan base and the press, but it was also one of those instances where a team official was using the podium to send a message to the locker room—in this case, a specific player who was well-liked and respected.

First things first: Pederson knew Gase. He knew about the whispers that Ajayi wasn't a film room rat, didn't like homework. But when he talked to reporters the day after the trade, Pederson did his best to play dumb. He was trying to give Ajayi a clean slate and proscribe the approach that his assistant coaches and players should take with this new player who arrived with a sports talk radio segment wrapped around his neck. One long-time listener, first-time caller after another ranted about Ajayi. And the only thing the talk show hosts could do was repeat the *Miami Herald* report and then play Pederson's response. It had become a sideshow and the last thing Pederson needed to do was pump up the volume.

"I can't speak to how they ran things down there," said Pederson. "What I do know is that he was about a 1,300-yard runner last year and had three 200-yard games. That's pretty impressive in the National Football League. And we're trying to bring the same skill set here."

Pederson didn't have time to do much homework on Ajayi. After the game against San Francisco on Sunday night, Roseman came to him with the trade plan. "We were playing a game on Sunday, we knew the trade deadline was coming. He was definitely [in the conversation] on Monday and yesterday for me," Pederson said.

When Pederson was asked if Ajayi would play in the upcoming home game against the Denver Broncos, he sent another message to his locker room.

"It all depends on how well he does pick up [the Eagles' offensive system,]" Pederson said. "Listen, you can't throw everything at him right away. He's got to sort of push Miami's offense out one side and embrace ours. It's harder to do than easier…It's hard. All he's known is Miami. We got to get that out of him."

Pederson gave Duce Staley the assignment of getting it out of him, spending extra time with Ajayi. They went over a few good running plays he liked. It was up to Ajayi to make sure he fit into the Eagles' culture. Pederson referred to Staley as "the great equalizer." Staley was tough and quick-witted. His demeanor and bowling ball size suggested he wasn't interested in anything but winning football games. If you had any other agenda, don't even try it here. There's the door.

"He has the right demeanor to deal with LeGarrette, to deal with Wendell [Smallwood], to deal with all the guys we have," said Pederson. "He's the perfect fit and the perfect coach for handling this situation."

And there it was: *This situation.* By uttering those two words, Pederson revealed that there was, in fact, a situation that the team would have to deal with. It took a while, but the assembled reporters had finally gotten it out of him. Pederson had been grilled for what seemed like forever. In all, Pederson would field 27 questions about the trade. No White House press briefing goes on that long about one single subject. And it was all carried live on the city's two sports talk radio stations, WIP and The Fanatic, as though Pederson was announcing the normalization of relations with North Korea. He was well within his rights to get a little testy.

"As hard as it is probably for you all to believe," he started one answer. Then he paused and caught himself. "First of all, I can't speculate on what happened in South Florida. But I trust the guys on this team to handle players. Everybody has a past. Everybody has a past and as hard as it is probably for you all to sit here and believe that, I was in a situation where we brought in a player, and there were reports of character issues and all kinds of things. You know what? Guys rallied around him. And there was not one issue whatsoever with this player and we went on to win a Super Bowl."

Question: So, you're depending on the culture of the team to take care of everything?
Pederson: Yes.

* * *

Carson Wentz called Ajayi. Blount texted him; the two running backs knew each other from playing in the AFC East together.

"Me and L.B. had a good relationship through playing games when he was on the Patriots, to even when we were out here for joint practices," Ajayi said. "So I've been able to build a little bit of a respect relationship with him, and we had conversations here and there. Now being a teammate, it's just a really cool dynamic now, and it's fresh, all of us in the running backs room are all trying to feel each other out, especially with me being the new guy. I'm just trying to join whatever they've got going and not try to be a distraction or anything, just try to be a help. I think it's a great dynamic in that RB room."

But now it was time to see if Ajayi fit in. That's what professional athletes do. They hear what you say. But they watch what you do. Do you show up for meetings on time? When it's your turn to speak to reporters in the locker room, are you hiding in the training room or players lounge, leaving your teammates to take the heat? Or are you doing your part to feed the hungry daily media churn?

New Eagles running back Jay Ajayi, always cracking jokes, gets a laugh out of defensive tackle Fletcher Cox during practice.

"I'm telling you we had no problem with the guy from day one," Chris Long said later. "He knew he was coming to a 7-1 team and that we had strong leadership and we weren't going to let anybody get away with anything." With Long and Fletcher Cox and Malcolm Jenkins, there was a quiet policing that went on by example. Cox was a burly, amiable sort, but he ruled with a quick look and big paycheck. And he made plays. Long had the pedigree. And he stood with his hand on Jenkins' shoulder during the safety's anthem protest. He had cred. And Jenkins was like a lion, roaming quietly—the king of the locker-room jungle. Blount learned to fit in. So had Alshon Jeffery. Ajayi had no choice.

* * *

SB Nation called the trade "a blockbuster." Sky Sports in Britain, where they followed Ajayi's career daily, called it "a shock." The 24-year-old running back, after dominating the league in year two of his career, was jettisoned in year three. Ajayi, taking the practice field at NovaCare just 48 hours after the trade, had been coached up on how to handle the Philly press.

He praised the Dolphins. He said he was excited to be in Philly. He said "God" has another plan for him.

So did Doug Pederson.

One important statistical note: After eight games, the Eagles led the NFL in scoring differential, plus 76 points. And Philadelphia led the NFL in time of possession at 33 minutes and 37 seconds. The team also led the league with 16 scoring drives of five minutes or more. The Eagles also led the NFL with 121 plays of 10 or more yards and a league-leading 35 running plays of 10 or more yards. Which begged the question: Why did they need to take a chance on Jay Ajayi?

Final score: Eagles 33, Forty-Niners 10

Postscript: When the Eagles published their unofficial depth chart for their Week 9 game against the Denver Broncos at Lincoln Financial Field on Sunday, November 5, LeGarrette Blount was listed as the starting running back. The backups to Blount were listed as Wendell Smallwood, Corey Clement, and Kenjon Barner. Ajayi was not listed.

Chapter 9

Lurie's Lament

Trap game.

That's what everybody was calling it.

The low-hanging fruit known as the 49ers had been picked. The dreaded division rivals, the Cowboys, were on the horizon, waiting in Dallas for a Sunday night showdown on national TV after the Eagles' bye week. Time to get away, think about the second half of the season.

And on their way to Philadelphia were the underachieving Denver Broncos, arriving with a head coach, Vance Joseph, who proved to be in way over his head, and a quarterback, Brock Osweiler, who had been bounced around the league like an unwanted orphan.

A little letdown was natural. Nobody could blame the Eagles if they were a little flat when they came to work on Monday morning, even a little distracted.

That's exactly what Doug Pederson was worried about. Inside and outside the NovaCare Complex, all the talk was about Dak Prescott, Dez Bryant, about going down to Big D in two weeks and finishing off the Cowboys just as the Eagles had buried the Redskins. Pederson listened to gospel music in the car on the way to work, but people told him about the talk on sports radio. And he heard the whispers in the hallways and cafeteria. Dallas, Dallas, Dallas. Not Denver. And he was not happy about it.

To anybody who would listen, he warned against complacency. And reminded everybody of one more little annoying statistical fact. Yes, the team was setting all kinds of records on offense and defense. But the mistakes were starting to pile up, beginning with penalties. After eight games, the Eagles had been penalized 543 yards—the most in the conference. One smart aleck replied to one of the coaches that the New England Patriots also had 543 yards in penalties. The coach said, "Yeah, well, a) they got Tom Brady. And b) they already got five Super Bowls."

Pederson told his position coaches, especially on offense, to remind his players that the Eagles had already coughed up the football nine times in eight games. "That's got to stop," said Pederson.

Pederson tried to get his team focused. Yes, the Broncos had already come east and lost to the Bills in Buffalo and lost to the Giants at home, scoring just 10 points with quarterback Trevor Siemian, who graduated from Northwestern and somehow landed in the good graces of Hall of Fame quarterback John Elway, who was now running the Broncos.

But, he reminded them, Denver was coming into town with what was statistically the No. 1 ranked defense in the league. The Broncos had Von Miller and one of the best pass rushes in the league. They would make you get off the field, leading the league in third-down defense, and punish your quarterback in the process. Take the Broncos too lightly and the Cowboys won't matter. Remember, the penalties and the turnovers. And, we have this little issue of getting Jay Ajayi ready for his first action—in a crowded backfield in front of a skeptical home town.

Denver, Denver, Denver. "That's all I wanted to hear about," Pederson said.

* * *

This is exactly what Jeffrey Lurie loved about Doug Pederson when he hired him in January 2016.

Lurie was looking for a head coach who would listen to his building, be in touch with his players, be part of the daily dialogue, who wasn't haunted by the ghosts of what people might be saying about him, who had some semblance of social skills, who was well adjusted to the little nuances of daily life.

Somebody to replace Chip Kelly.

Lurie called it "emotional intelligence."

Emotional intelligence is a simple management concept that has been popular for years. Enlightened corporations used it. It was all over college campuses. Even senior officers in the Pentagon threw it around. The definition of emotional intelligence is pretty straightforward: The capacity to be aware of, control, and express one's emotions, and to handle interpersonal relationships judiciously and empathetically.

In other words, be comfortable enough with who you are so that when somebody says something to you, you don't get all bent out of shape.

The day he introduced Pederson as Kelly's replacement, Lurie first mentioned that Pederson was smart and well-prepared. But he quickly gave a long-winded explanation of what set Pederson apart from the 24 other candidates the Eagles vetted.

"Communications skills, unparalleled," said Lurie. "A key ingredient for me, and I think when you go into this it kind of defines differences between candidates, and that is who is the most comfortable in their own skin. And when I say that, what I mean is an ability to be genuine at all times. I got to spend a lot of time with our players at the beginning of this coaching search, and the message was loud and clear—which I agree with in terms of leadership in today's world—no matter what, you've got to be comfortable in your own skin in order to be able to reach out, be genuine with those you want to get high performance from, be accountable to them and make them accountable to you."

Echoes of Bill Parcells there. You got to give the players a good plan, yes. But that's only half the equation. Today's pro football players are from all over America, from poverty, from the wealthy suburbs, from the Polynesian islands, from Nigeria to North Dakota. You got to get them moving in one direction to implement that plan. Tell them you care—first and foremost.

And you've got to listen, and adjust your plan. Situational game-planning and situational management styles. Pederson had both. This is what Lurie and his search team discovered and what everybody else missed.

Finally, Lurie said, he wanted a coach who had "the emotional intelligence to open up his heart to the players."

According to noted management experts, leaders who regularly practice emotional intelligence follow these precepts: Exercise empathy—put yourself in your team member's shoes, look through their lens. Create a culture of transparency—stay visible and grow trusted by your team. Invest time in the relationships you have with your team members and give freedom for relationships to grow between them. Never allow adversity to get you and your team down—change the narrative to see challenges as opportunities. Provide a purpose higher than self. Give your team the opportunity to align with something mission-driven, and it will elevate them.

Where Kelly failed was not on the chalkboard. His machine-gun-style offense, which he brought from Oregon, was wildly successful at first. The NFL was caught gaping at the sheer speed of it. Kelly fired off offensive plays every two seconds, dictating matchups to the defense with the speed of the snap, not necessarily formation or personnel variation—the time-honored way to deceive the opposition. Without the ability to substitute, defenses were at a disadvantage. But Kelly's plays were too predictable. And defensive coordinators caught up, quickly. Defensive personnel would be calling out the play and the blocking scheme in advance, dooming Kelly's system. And he refused to adjust.

Then he had the spat with Roseman, banishing him to the opposite side of the building. And, in the process, Kelly alienated long-standing employees, keeping his head down, moving around the halls without the small talk or pleasantries you need to survive in a big operation. Late in the season in 2015, on the way home from an emotional upset win in New England, Lurie sat next to running back DeMarco Murray and got an earful about what was wrong with the team. Murray struggled in Kelly's offense and complained to the owner that he was being underused. Lurie started to talk to more players and staff about Kelly and the direction of the team. He didn't like what he heard. In retrospect, it's shocking that it took Lurie this long to figure out what was happening right underneath him. Some in the organization thought the owner was clueless, that he was not paying attention to the damage that Kelly was doing to the culture of the team.

Then it all came apart over a Christmas party. Kelly complained that the team's annual off-site holiday gathering—Lurie's way of giving back a little love to his employees—was held on a Monday night, and would interfere with game prep. Lurie didn't want to cancel it. So, he moved the party to a Friday afternoon in the team's practice facility. Of course, it just didn't have the same feel. Lurie was embarrassed and apologetic to the staff. And not happy.

You can be a lot of things. But you can't be the office Scrooge. By forcing Lurie to move the party, Kelly had crossed the line.

On the day after Christmas, the Eagles lost to the Redskins at Lincoln Financial Field. Kirk Cousins was running around the field after the game. The burgundy and gold of Redskins fans decorated—some would later say desecrated—the stadium. The visiting team celebrating in South Philly, there's nothing worse. It's taken personally. Team president Don Smolenski came out of the tunnel from the Eagles' locker room to watch. I stood next to him. His face was gray and sullen. He didn't say a word. He didn't have to. Kelly had hijacked the team and now the Redskins had taken over the stadium. I knew right then and there that the Eagles were going to fire Chip Kelly.

He was gone 72 hours later.

* * *

Jeffrey Lurie bought the Eagles in 1994. The day I met him he was still in the process of negotiating with then owner Norman Braman, the car salesman from Miami who had grown tired of answering to the fans and the press about his skinflint stewardship of what they considered their civic enterprise. Lurie and his first wife, Christina, both children of wealth, were sitting in the 92nd Street Y in Manhattan. We were all guests of a Lurie family lawyer, the erudite and gentlemanly Dan Kaplan, who was old friends with late New York mayor Ed Koch. Kaplan ran the 92nd Street Y, one of the most prestigious positions in New York, and was major domo at Proskauer Rose, one of Manhattan's oldest law firms. We were all in the audience, listening to a talk about the Brooklyn Dodgers. The Luries were sitting behind me. Kaplan had arranged it. I turned around at exactly the right time to introduce myself. I found Lurie then, and still to this day, to be a thoughtful man who clearly was uncomfortable with notoriety. He grew up sheltered, went to Hollywood, tried to make some movies, but really wanted to own a professional sports franchise. Don't we all? But Lurie had money. His uncle, Dick Smith, had left his mother a fortune. She lent her son the money which Lurie and his partners parlayed into $185 million to buy the Eagles from Braman.

When Lurie bought the team, people in Philly initially didn't like what they heard. He was from Boston. He liked the Red Sox. Okay, Philadelphia could live with that. The Phillies played in the National League. But he openly talked about going to Celtics games and rooting for the Bruins. Major no-no. He was called a carpetbagger and worse. He was accused of being motivated by money, not winning championships.

He was deemed a dabbling rich guy in a town of working class heroes. He had a doctorate in social policy from Brandeis University. His thesis was about the depiction of women in American cinema. He was before his time, a free thinker, a liberal from Chestnut Hill, Massachusetts. His father died young. His brother has autism. He's a philanthropic, caring individual who became one of the most misunderstood and underappreciated people in the long, complicated history of Philadelphia sports—mostly because he made promises that were nearly impossible to keep. He promised Super Bowls, plural. And said that his stewardship of the team would be "the gold standard"—words that would be derisively used against him for years and years as the team wandered through the wilderness of one disappointment after another.

His teams were a big tease. While Robert Kraft delivered five Super Bowl titles to his native New England, Lurie could not quite get there. His teams captured seven NFC East titles and went to five NFC title games, but lost four. In their only trip to the Super Bowl under Lurie, the Eagles lost by three points to the Patriots when Donovan McNabb threw three interceptions. But coming into the 2017 season, Lurie's teams had played 23 playoff games with 11 postseason wins—both more than all the other owners of the franchise combined.

But no title. Across the state of Pennsylvania, the Pittsburgh Steelers had six. Down I-95, the Ravens had two in Baltimore, a city that franchise occupied the year after Lurie bought the Eagles. In North Jersey, the Giants had four. Down in Washington, the Redskins had three. All around Philadelphia, there were Lombardi Trophies—in another words, Super Bowls, plural.

Lurie's pursuit of a championship consumed him. And his quest would become costly for him personally. He would get divorced and re-married. His boyhood friend, Joe Banner, a young businessman who would run the Eagles for more than a decade, would leave, go to the Cleveland Browns, and get thrown out of the NFL for good. Lurie stayed with Andy Reid as head coach for 14 seasons, three years after nearly everybody around the team said it was time for him to go. Lurie could not go out much. He got ugly looks. There were groans and mumbles and occasional boos when he went onto the field. But, hey, who doesn't get booed in Philly? Still, it was getting uncomfortable. And personal.

His belief in Kelly almost resulted in Roseman bolting. It took him a while, but Lurie finally decided he had to take his team back—or his franchise might go down a road that would take a decade to return from. After owning the team for nearly a quarter century and no Super Bowl title to show for it, it was time to do what just felt right. That was hire Doug Pederson.

* * *

To Eagles fans, however, hiring Doug Pederson just felt wrong. It had the feel of Lurie trying to re-package what he had with Andy Reid, that he longed for nostalgia, not something new. A back-to-the-future thing. People in the city were not buying it: Pederson's only head coaching experience was at the high school level. He did not have the professional résumé to lead one of the top franchises in the NFL. And worse, he was just mini-Andy.

Pederson recoiled at the questions, which were so pointed and, he thought, unfair.

"Listen," he protested, "Andy Reid is a mentor. I'll be the first one to tell you that he is. But I'm also here to tell you that this is not an Andy Reid football team and it's not a Doug Pederson football team, this is a Philadelphia Eagle football team. So I'm going to bring my spin on it, I'm going to bring my personality to it, and we're going to make it our team going forward."

But there was more. What happened in Foxboro, when Pederson was given the play-calling duties in the fourth quarter of Kansas City's last playoff game and squandered all that time on the clock and the Patriots just laughed about it all the way into the locker room? It had shades of the Super Bowl when McNabb and Reid showed no sense of urgency in the fourth quarter and ate up the clock. This kind of storyline was not what Philly wanted to hear, or repeat. Pederson had some explaining to do during his first press conference in Philadelphia:

Question: How much responsibility did you have for the Chiefs' final drive in the playoff game against New England?

Pederson: I'll tell you—I'll even go back a little bit further. I was able to call plays [this season] really since the Pittsburgh game on, if you follow the Kansas City Chiefs. Coach Reid and I had a great understanding and a great feel for the game. He allowed me to call the second half of every football game from that Steeler game on. The second half of our playoff game the other night, I had the second half. I did have the second half and so I called the entire second half at that point.

Question: Why did that drive take so long?

Pederson: It took us time because No. 1, we did not want to give Tom Brady the ball back. We knew we were going to score. We knew we had timeouts and time. We were also limited with the number of receivers; we had Jeremy Maclin out of the game at the time. We were down numbers. We felt like at that point, not to give the ball back to Tom Brady. We still had timeouts and time, even with the onside kick, to put ourselves in a position to tie the football game.

Few people bought that explanation. The Chiefs needed two scores. An onside kick has little chance of working, especially in the postseason against a Bill Belichick team. But Lurie was satisfied. That's all that mattered. Pederson made him feel comfortable with his team again. Clearly, the new coach was going to learn on the job. But he was willing to learn. That was good enough for Lurie. And Pederson wanted to fit in, wanted to be part of the Eagles tradition that was already established, not remake it in his image. And Lurie liked the way he handled the questions from the media. There was a sense of calm, not entitlement—a sense of "this is part of the job, I get it, and we'll get through it just fine."

Several days after Pederson was hired, I had a short conversation with him. I asked him what was the best piece of advice he ever got about being a head coach.

"Just be yourself," he said. That was his father, Gordon, talking.

* * *

The Eagles demolished the Broncos on November 5. They had 419 yards of offense, including 197 yards rushing.

In his first series in a Philadelphia Eagles uniform, new running back Jay Ajayi found a seam off the left shoulder of left tackle Halapoulivaati Vaitai and just took off in front of the Eagles' sideline. He sprinted past running backs coach Duce Staley, who pumped his fist in the air, and Doug Pederson, who smiled like he was watching one of his sons sink a three-point shot and LeGarrette Blount, who watched his new teammate stretch the football across the goal line for his first touchdown in South Philadelphia, which erupted like it was everybody's birthday: 46 yards, touchdown. Eagles up 31–7.

After the game, I talked to Ajayi as he was walking off the field. "Great football town," he said. "This is special here. I think we can do a lot of special things here."

Wentz had thrown four more touchdown passes. He now led the NFL with 23, 17 in his last five games, astounding for a second-year quarterback with two new wide receivers and three new running backs and a novice left tackle.

"Don't care about the stats," he said. "I just care about being 8–1."

"What I'm seeing from Carson is what I saw in Brett," Pederson told me, invoking old No. 4 in Green Bay. When he did that, I always kind of tried to hide my skepticism, my reporter's eye roll. "No, I'm telling you," Pederson continued. "Guys want to be around Carson just like that. Carson elevates your game because you want to be on the field with him, in the huddle with him. He's just fun to play with. In the end, these guys want to have fun and win. That's really all it's about. Not much more than that."

Once again, Pederson had pushed all the right buttons. He felt the team had earned the right, now, to make the trip to Texas to play the Cowboys. They were in the right frame of mind to take on Dallas Week.

One important statistical note: Wentz dismantled the so-called best defense in the league. Especially when it counted most. He was 9-of-15 (60.0 percent) for 109 yards and two touchdowns against the Broncos' blitz. He now had a league-high 10 touchdowns against the blitz this season with no interceptions. That's the most such touchdowns without a pick in a team's first nine games of a season since Tom Brady's 11 in 2007, according to my friends at ESPN Stats & Information. Wentz was not only supremely athletic, he was also utterly prepared. He was becoming blitz proof. "He knows what's coming," said Blount.

Final score: Eagles 51, Broncos 23

Postscript: On the day he was hired, January 19, 2016, Pederson was asked if this team could go back to the playoffs fairly quickly. With his owner sitting next to him, Pederson gave this answer: "I do. There's some talent here and I do believe that you can put yourself in a position to not only win the [NFC] East, but have a chance to get yourself into the postseason and then go deep into the postseason."

PART III

THE FATE OF THE SEASON

Chapter 10

Desperate in Dallas

The Eagles at the Cowboys
Sunday, November 19, 2017 • Arlington, Texas

The Eagles' team plane arrived at Dallas/Fort Worth International Airport late Saturday afternoon, November 18, 2017, for a nationally televised Sunday night game with the same NBC crew that would call Super Bowl LII. This game had a little snap, crackle, and pop to it. There is nothing like playing the Cowboys in the massive football palace Jerry Jones built, with all its excessive show biz accoutrements: The cheerleaders, the 90-foot TV screen hung from the rafters, the players walking through a Snapchat-hungry gauntlet of football fans. But Doug Pederson was having none of that. "This is the ultimate business trip," he told his team. The Eagles, after having a string of successes in Dallas, lost down in Big D in Pederson's debut season, in overtime, after a series of decisions made by the rookie head coach that landed him in sports talk radio purgatory. But Pederson was not looking for redemption or revenge. He just wanted this team to "keep rolling," as he liked to say, rolling all the way to the division title. And the Cowboys were in their way, plain and simple.

The Eagles, many of them wearing those noise-cancelling headphones, silently loaded up on the team buses, which cruised through Saturday night traffic in the Dallas Metroplex straight to the team hotel. Pederson had called for an early team meeting, not unusual for the night before the game, especially a big game like this.

The Eagles were coming off a mini-vacation, a midyear gift from the NFL schedule maker, something called the Bye Week. It came at exactly the right time, but also at exactly the wrong time.

The players needed to recharge. They were on a seven-game winning streak and had been to Kansas City and Los Angeles and Charlotte and they were at the lofty perch of 8-1. The Eagles were the only NFL team to score 20 or more points in every game in 2017 and they had scored at least four touchdowns in five straight games—the only team in the league to do that, too. So, the whole sports world was watching—what the Eagles were doing and what they planned to do next.

And that included the Dallas Cowboys, an absolutely desperate football team playing without its best player, running back Ezekiel Elliott, who had been suspended by the NFL following accusations of domestic violence. After a series of fruitless court battles that erupted into a nasty public feud between NFL commissioner Roger Goodell and Jerry Jones, Elliott finally began serving the six-game suspension in Atlanta the previous Sunday. And the Falcons, the defending NFC champs, promptly dismantled the Cowboys' offense, battering quarterback Dak Prescott, who—it was finally proven—could not fully function without Elliott's rather important contribution on the ground. Against Atlanta, Prescott was also without his left tackle, Tyron Smith, who would also miss the game against the Eagles. "The quarterback position is a dependent position," former Eagles quarterback Ron Jaworski would remind his radio audience that week. "A complementary position." But this was no time to worry about the care and feeding of Dak Prescott and the Dallas Cowboys—Pederson wanted to make sure of that.

The Eagles players filed into the hotel ballroom. Big Dom made sure all the doors were closed. Pederson got up in front of the room. He sensed his squad was a little grumpy, a little anxious. They had waded through the bye week like a pack of lost wolves that had become accustomed to constantly looking for easy prey. It felt odd to some of them that the rhythm of the hunt had been interrupted, and that it was now suddenly back to the business. "We were a hungry group all year long," said center Jason Kelce. Pederson laid out the new menu for the season, which included no future and no past. The team, as Malcolm Jenkins was fond of saying in the locker room before the media walked in, needed to put its feet on the ground and think about being in the here and the now.

"Our goal is to be 1-0 on Sunday night," Pederson said, relaying his speech in a text to me the following morning. Desperate or not, the Cowboys are not what we care about, he said. "We can't worry about them," he said. "We got to worry about us."

No time to feel sorry for the other guys, especially *these* other guys.

"A football team is like an army," former head coach Tom Coughlin, who won two Super Bowl titles with the New York

Giants, once said. "At some point, it has to decide whether it wants to survive, or it wants to kill."

* * *

The Eagles wanted to go for the kill. But the first half of the game against the Cowboys sure didn't feel like it.

They couldn't convert on third down—came up short on six straight tries. Carson Wentz was misfiring all over the stadium. He completed just seven of 18 pass attempts. When No. 11 is way below 50 percent, something has to be radically wrong. And with Jay Ajayi, LeGarrette Blount, & Co. stuck in neutral, Wentz was the leading rusher in the first half with a paltry 10 yards on two carries. Not good, especially since he landed on the trainers' table in the first quarter after a nasty hit. He was asked if the team put him in the concussion protocol. "Yes," he confirmed. "I was fine. It was just a back of the neck situation. I was just trying to speed it up and get out there as fast as I could." Wentz never missed a down, but the offense was missing its mark.

The Eagles had a tenuous 7–6 lead and had a chance to put the Cowboys down. Prescott, under pressure from Philly's rookie defensive end Derek Barnett, threw his first interception. Safety Rodney McLeod picked it off and ran it back to the Cowboys' 15-yard line. First-and-10 for the Eagles inside the 20. But three plays later, they were lining up for a field goal and kicker Jake Elliott left too much air under his foot and the ball sailed wide right. It was too easy of a field goal to miss. Something was wrong with the rookie kicker. Midway through the next quarter, it was finally announced to the national television audience that he was being evaluated "for a head injury." At halftime, Pederson was told he would have to play the rest of the game without a placekicker.

They would not need him the rest of the second quarter—the offense could not put it together. The Cowboys' defensive line was playing with a lot of energy and the Eagles didn't match it. Philly went three-and-out on three straight series, squandering another gift interception by Prescott at midfield. The Cowboys added a field goal and took the lead, 9-7.

"We didn't have our mojo," Wentz said. And the Eagles went into the halftime locker room an angry bunch.

* * *

In the long, nasty history between the Philadelphia Eagles and the Dallas Cowboys, there has been a lot of anger.

The greatest sportswriter in Philadelphia history, Ray Didinger, once wrote, "Walk up to any Eagles fan and say the following two words: Dallas Cowboys. Better step back to watch what happens next. The eyes will narrow, the nostrils will flare, the fists will clench. There will be growling and, most likely, profanity."

It is said that, in Philadelphia dictionaries, the word "Dallas" is followed by the word "sucks."

The Eagles once knocked Roger Staubach out of a game. Carried off on a stretcher at old Veterans Stadium with a horrible neck injury, wide receiver Michael Irvin was cheered—not because the Philly fans were applauding his bravery. No, they were celebrating the fact that he might be paralyzed.

In 1987, many of the Cowboys players crossed the picket line during the NFL players strike. Dallas humiliated the replacement Eagles, 41-22. Buddy Ryan accused Tom Landry of running up the score.

There was The Bounty Bowl. Jimmy Johnson accused the Eagles of putting a bounty on the heads of his kicker and star quarterback, Troy Aikman. The Cowboys had the stars and the hardware. The Eagles had Buddy Ryan, who never won a playoff game. The Cowboys had Landry, with his holier-than-thou approach. The Eagles had the "dese, dems, and dos" Rich Kotite, the Brooklyn native who liked to call Steven Seagal his friend. Veterans Stadium was a concrete monument to misguided municipal policy that had a turf field once described as asphalt with a green bed sheet pulled over it. The Cowboys played in a stadium with a hole in the roof so the team "could be closer to God." The Cowboys—with the cheerleaders in designer outfits and the Big Star on their helmets—were America's Team. The Eagles were America's punchline.

There was one brief shining moment delivered by Dick Vermeil and Ron Jaworski in 1980. To earn their first Super Bowl berth, the Eagles beat the Cowboys at Veterans Stadium. Up to 2017, it was considered the highest point in the franchise's history. Wilbert Montgomery's touchdown run in front of the Cowboys' sideline on that frigid Sunday afternoon was the one highlight played over and over as a reminder that there was once a beautiful day when the Eagles truly put the Cowboys in their place.

This 116-game rivalry went back and forth. After Jerry Jones purchased the team and he and his boyhood friend, Jimmy Johnson, turned the franchise into a dominant force in the 1990s, collecting three Lombardi Trophies, there had been a long drought in Big D. Under Andy Reid, there was a resurgence in Philadelphia that helped keep the Cowboys from going back to the Super Bowl. Even with Reid gone, the Eagles did not feel intimidated by Dallas, especially *in* Dallas. In 2013 and 2014 and 2015, the Eagles rolled through AT&T stadium, known as "Jerry's World," and ran up big wins, the last one in overtime.

"We always felt like it was just a big place to play football—it was a show," said former Eagles quarterback Michael Vick. "You never felt like the fans were against you, I mean really against you, like in Philly."

Playing in Philly felt like the Saturday night fights. Playing in Dallas was like going to church on Sunday.

"On the scoreboard here," said one Eagles player, talking about AT&T Stadium, "they tell the fans what do, how to act. In Philly, they don't have to." He was speaking anonymously for a reason: "Don't need to provide the 'Boys with no bulletin board material."

The Eagles may have had the beat on the 'Boys, but it was Jerry Jones who was enshrined into the Pro Football Hall of Fame in the summer of 2017. Lurie has never been considered for Canton, might never be. Even while Jones' teams lost and Lurie's franchise dominated in recent years, it was Jones who went to the Hall. Why? Because he had taught the other 31 NFL owners and the league itself how to turn millions into billions. He was the league's rainmaker, even if his team signed the troubled players and could not win a playoff game. Irked Philly to no end.

And now, the Eagles were coming off a bitter overtime loss in Dallas in 2016. Prescott threw two touchdown passes, one late in the fourth quarter and one in overtime, in a come-from-behind win. Pederson took a beating in the media. Here's one example from the well-respected Matt Lombardo, who writes for a number of New Jersey newspapers: "Pederson turned down a long field-goal attempt, stowed timeouts, and shackled his quarterback with predictable play-calling as the Eagles blew a 10-point fourth-quarter lead to lose on a five-yard TD pass from Dak Prescott to tight end Jason Witten." It appeared under the headline, PEDERSON TO BLAME FOR LOSS TO COWBOYS.

"This is the second time in two weeks when Pederson faced game-altering situations and his decisions when it comes to play-calling and clock management have been called into question," Lombardo continued, referring to the previous week in New York. "After Sunday's late-game collapse, it appears evident that just climbing into the playoff race will be a daunting task for this Eagles team that is now 0–2 against the NFC East, with losses to potential wild card teams—the Detroit Lions, Washington Redskins, and Cowboys."

That loss to Dallas was considered a watershed rookie moment for Pederson and Wentz. And that kind of criticism was widespread. It stung, even if the coach and the players would not admit it publicly. Wentz was asked whether the way the game ended in Dallas in 2016 was a motivating factor going into 2017. "We have enough motivation playing a division rival like the Cowboys," he said. "We have enough motivation from this season alone."

And now a bad first half of football—against a team that was a historical rival and had mortally wounded the promise of last season.

* * *

"The big boys up front kind of came out angry."

After the Eagles turned it around, reeling off 30 straight points, demoralizing the Cowboys and embarrassing their owner, that's what Carson Wentz said to Michelle Tafoya in the postgame on-field interview on NBC. The "big boys up front" were, of course, the Eagles' offensive line. And, in the halftime locker room, nobody was happy with the state of the team. When a star player admits after the game that there was "frustration" in the halftime locker room, that usually means somebody threw something, and said something that was loud and profane. Who knows what exactly was said, but one thing has been established: One of the angriest of the bunch was center Jason Kelce.

This is what you need to know about Jason Kelce that tells you he was born with the kind of controlled rage perfectly suited to play football in the trenches on Sunday afternoons: Jason Kelce's first job was at a hockey youth camp. He was 14 years old, teaching kids bigger and smaller than him how to play with passion. His dream job: To be a center on the Philadelphia Flyers, "The Broad Street Bullies."

He played linebacker and fullback for the Roxboro Rockets in the seventh grade in Cleveland, Ohio.

Before an NFL game, he listens to Christmas music. And he combs his beard. In Minneapolis for Super Bowl LII, Kelce showed up looking like a cross between Robert Redford in the movie *Jeremiah Johnson* and The Unabomber.

His favorite movies are *The Last Gladiators* and *The Big Lebowski.* He certainly abides by very little.

His brother, Travis, tight end for the Kansas City Chiefs, is considered the wacky one. Yet, Jason, the older brother by two years, said all he would need on a desert island would be duct tape, a lighter, and a fishing pole. He's a survivor. On the football field, he hunts—for people to knock to the ground. His favorite NFL player of all time is Chuck "Concrete Charlie" Bednarik, who played center, linebacker, and special teams for the Eagles' last championship team in 1960 and was captured in a photograph—frozen for eternity—standing over New York Giants halfback Frank Gifford, celebrating that he had just knocked Gifford out.

Kelce's grandfather, Don Blalock, played football at Ohio University and took his grandsons fishing. He liked to quote this passage from Calvin Coolidge, the nation's 30th president: "Nothing in this world can take the place of persistence. Talent will not. Nothing is more common than unsuccessful men with talent. Genius will not. Unrewarded genius is almost a proverb. Education will not: The world is full of educated derelicts. Persistence and determination alone are omnipotent. The slogan 'Press On' has solved and will always solve the problems of the human race."

After winning the Super Bowl, talking to reporters, Kelce tried to recite the poem repeated to him many times by his grandpa. But he could not finish. He just kept breaking down in tears.

On this Sunday night, still 10 weeks from that moment, Kelce came out of the halftime locker room in Dallas determined to make the Cowboys feel some of that midwestern persistence, some of that controlled rage.

With Kelce, the problem for the opposition was two things: That persistence, that rage was often just not under control. And he liked to take it on the road. By the road, I mean outside the confines of what is called "the trenches" in football, the space between the offensive tackles and within three to five yards of the line of scrimmage. It's called "the perimeter." And if you have an offensive lineman who can and will take that rage on the perimeter and inflict bodily harm on defenders in his way, you're going to be very successful running the football on the edges, outside "the box," where running backs can create in their own space with shiftiness and speed, compile chunks of yards, and then cash in at the box office and their bank accounts.

Greg Cosell is the nephew of Howard Cosell. If you don't know who Howard Cosell is, you probably aren't reading this book. Howard Cosell basically invented modern sports television commentary by "telling it like it is." His nephew pretty much has the same attitude. But he also happened to invent the best X's & O's show ever put on television, *NFL*

Matchup, the longest-running pro football studio program in the history of TV. (I'm proud to host the show, but Cosell is the brains behind the entire operation.)

The show, which has been appointment viewing by NFL players and coaches since 1984, emanates from NFL Films, where Cosell has a cozy little office on the second floor. There, he will stare into a TV screen, watching every play of every NFL game for 16 weeks and into the playoffs.

After the Super Bowl, Cosell and I were sitting at a dinner in Atlantic City to honor the recipients of the annual Maxwell Awards, the oldest in college and professional football dating back to before facemasks and television were introduced to the game.

It was four weeks after the Eagles had won Super Bowl LII and I asked Cosell a simple question. I knew he had studied the team and the game all year long and had intimate knowledge of the schematics of what the Eagles tried to do each and every Sunday. Who, I asked him, was the most important player on the team in this championship season? He hesitated for only a beat.

"Jason Kelce," he said.

People sometimes forget that the 2017 NFL champion Philadelphia Eagles finished third in the league in rushing. And they did it with Jay Ajayi, a fifth-round pick, 149th overall in 2015, LeGarrette Blount, who went undrafted in 2010, and Corey Clement, who was not drafted in 2017. How'd they do it? Design and execution. And a special trait that can only be pulled off if a team has an athletic offensive line.

"They have a perimeter-based run game," Cosell added. "The key to that perimeter run game is Jason Kelce. It's his athleticism that allows him to get outside the tackles, find unblocked defenders, get in their way, or lock them down long enough for Clement, Blount, or Ajayi to run free."

* * *

In the second half, emerging from the locker room ready to inflict pain on the Cowboys, the Eagles did just that. Hey, if you want to be America's Team, you had to beat America's Team.

First drive: Ajayi had two carries, Clement had three. That opened it up for Brent Celek, who had a 28-yard catch, and Alshon Jeffery, who made another grab good for 18 more yards. In just four minutes and four seconds, the Eagles scored a touchdown and, without Elliott available to kick the extra point, cashed in a two-point conversion.

That kickstarted the 30-point bolt of lightning that paralyzed the Cowboys. On the next drive, Kelce, right tackle Lane Johnson, and Ajayi just cut the Cowboys heart out.

"Tackle-trap play," said Pederson. Credit the design to offensive line coach Jeff Stoutland and his assistant Eugene Chung, with an assist from offensive coordinator Frank Reich. "We ran it several times in the game. Lane came around from the right to the left, came around the horn right there and it was just well blocked. It's a north-and-south between-the-tackles play and they just hit it and he took off." Ajayi ripped off a 71-yard run. The Eagles owned the line of scrimmage. The Cowboys overcompensated outside the hashmarks and Wentz slid an 11-yard touchdown pass up the middle to Torrey Smith.

That killed any chance of a Cowboys comeback. It forced head coach Jason Garrett to abandon any hope of playing it conservative. That unleashed the Eagles' pass rush, which played havoc with Prescott's competence and confidence. A total rout was on and over, just like that—a victory unleashed from one angry moment in an angry lifetime of football between two teams caught in the maelstrom of pro football history.

When the game was over, the Eagles had 215 yards rushing, after having just 35 in the first half. To run up and down the football field like that in the state of Texas against the home team with the whole nation watching was a civic embarrassment. Jerry Jones looked liked he had just seen somebody key his Cadillac in broad daylight. Either that or he

I interview Carson Wentz at the Eagles' practice facility in South Philadelphia. (Tony Florkowski)

was getting ready to leave Goodell an ill-advised voice mail: "Hey, Roger. This is Jerry, you killed our season. Thank you and the horse you rode in on."

In the Eagles' locker room, there was no containing the glee.

"We're having a blast," said Carson Wentz. "I love winning in this league."

One important statistical note: That was the first time the Dallas Cowboys were outscored by 30 points in the second half of a football game since 1962.

Final score: Eagles 37, Cowboys 9

Postscript: Running backs love seeing a guy like Jason Kelce on the edge, causing pain, opening up big holes.

One running back said to me, "Your eyes get wide open and then your heart pumps and you just take that energy and start moving your legs and your natural God-given talent just kicks in. You look for color. The color of the other guys. When there is none and just daylight, you start to tingle." That running back was Emmitt Smith, who had a Hall of Fame career with the Dallas Cowboys.

Another running back once told me, "It's better than sex. Well, almost."

Chapter 11

Survive and Advance

"My message to the team was this," said Doug Pederson, when his team returned from Dallas. "If you can't have fun doing what you're doing, you should probably find something else to do."

Coming home to play the Chicago Bears after steamrolling the Cowboys was almost like a second bye week for the Philadelphia Eagles.

In the last two meetings with the Bears, the Eagles won both, scoring a combined 83 points, holding Chicago to just 12.5 points per game. Total domination. With back-to-back games coming up on the West Coast—first the talent-rich Seahawks in Seattle, then the upstart Rams in Los Angeles—Pederson needed to take a breath and take stock. He liked what

141

he saw. "Even at this point in the season, you still find ways to keep it fresh and creative and have fun doing it," he said, "and the guys are having fun playing together. It's a family. Sounds corny. But that's what you're seeing now."

At this point in the season, the final game in November before a brutal five-game stretch when December kicks in, with three of them on the road, the 9-1 Eagles had the best record in the NFL. But the Minnesota Vikings and New Orleans Saints were both on their heels. Both were 8-2, only one game behind. Pederson's players liked one another. He liked the atmosphere. He knew the team had a real chance of winning the division, coasting into the postseason. But he was looking for more. He knew what Mike Holmgren preached in Green Bay, what Andy Reid talked about in Philly and Kansas City: Getting that No. 1 seed in the conference makes all the difference in the world. Get the No. 1 seed, get a first-week bye in the playoffs, and host the NFC Championship Game. That was the best road to the Super Bowl. He had a confident bunch, but playing the Saints or the Vikings in their domes for the conference title was problematic—even if Wentz had played and won a lot of games in the Fargodome at North Dakota State. What's more, the Saints—with Drew Brees and head coach Sean Payton, the master designer and play-caller—basically ran a pinball offense in the Superdome. You go down to New Orleans, you had to be ready for a track meet and a quarterback who has seen it all and won it all. That playoff math was all the talk outside the NovaCare building, not inside. Pederson knew it was out there. But he tried to guard against it permeating his thinking, that of his staff and certainly his players. "I try not to get caught up in a lot of that stuff right now," he said, two days before the Bears arrived in town. "Just win this game this Sunday." And then it leaked out that he clearly was having difficulty screening out all the outside noise. "You're still playing for a lot—one, playing for the division. Two: You're trying to get that home-field [advantage], if possible. So, it's tight. You saw what Minnesota did yesterday and what New Orleans is doing." The Saints were on a tear, scoring 30 or more points in three straight games. The Vikings had just finished off the Lions in Detroit and were in the middle of a seven-game win streak. Pederson knew that the Eagles had to take care of business, now. Beat the Bears at home, survive and advance.

* * *

That's just what an NFL season is after 10 games: A matter of survival. The body is breaking down, the mind is grinding through another week of detailed preparation. An NFL player has to be part Lou Ferrigno, part Bobby Fischer. Pro football is a test of endurance and strength, but it's also a chess match. You have to know the opponent's move in every situation before you can map out your own. And those moves are getting updated each week, with new schematics, new formations, and new personnel. "If you study," Ray Lewis once told me, "you have a chance. If you don't, you got no shot. It's like taking the SATs every week. And then your test is to see if you can survive on Sunday."

In many ways, even at 9–1, the Eagles were searching for ways to do just that: Survive. Injuries were beginning to pile up, if not take a toll. September 24: The ageless punt returner and utility back Darren Sproles was lost for the season with a knee injury. Three weeks later, special teams captain and backup safety Chris Maragos was gone for the year after a knee injury. The following week: Jason Peters was out for good, also a knee injury.

Starting middle linebacker Jordan Hicks was out, not coming back: Achilles injury. Hicks wore the green circle sticker on the back of his helmet, signifying that he had a radio in his helmet so he could get the defensive signals from Jim Schwartz on the sideline. Now, backup Nigel Bradham would wear the sticker and have to listen to Schwartz's instructions, which had all the unforgiving detail of biochemistry.

Another linebacker, Dannell Ellerbe, was sick. Fletcher Cox was still dealing with calf soreness. Running back Jay Ajayi had his ankle wrapped. Later in the season, he would have one hand in bandages, fighting off constant swelling after somebody had stepped on it. Backup tight end Trey Burton had back spasms.

"We just got to take care of business, and, at the end of the day, that's all that really matters," Pederson said.

Every team was dealing with it. The New England Patriots were hit hard in training camp, losing wide receiver Julian Edelman for the season. Young wideout Malcolm Mitchell was gone for the year. All-world tight end Rob Gronkowski missed some time with a number of problems. On defense, their best linebacker, Dont'a Hightower, was lost in October with a pectoral tear. Gone for the year.

But, as Bill Belichick would preach over and over again, it's not how the team looks in September or how it performs at the beginning of the season. It's how it finishes. He knew his teams would look different in the fourth quarter of the year. You plug in replacements, you advance.

And sometimes you don't. The Giants lost the mercurial, the pyrotechnic Odell Beckham Jr., who suffered a broken ankle in the first week of October. Eli Manning was never the same. The Green Bay Packers were considered the top team in the NFC all year, until Minnesota Vikings pass rusher Anthony Barr chased Aaron Rodgers down and viciously landed on him. Upon impact with the turf at U.S. Bank Stadium, the right shoulder of the Packers' star quarterback folded in half—right in front of the home crowd. Going off on a golf cart, Rodgers gave the Vikings' defensive huddle a snarky stare and had a few choice words—almost like he thought he'd been deliberately hunted down and knocked out: It was the second week in October and Rodgers was gone. The Packers? Sunk. His replacement, Brett Hundley, simply was not ready. Rodgers returned to start Week 15 against the Panthers, but the Packers lost and shut Rodgers down for the season as Green Bay missed the playoffs.

The 2017 NFL season would be plagued with bad injuries, especially knee injuries. The league saw 51 torn ACLs, according to ACL Recovery Club—the most since 2013, when the NFL had 63 players tear an ACL. Two AFC teams that were considered playoff contenders lost their quarterbacks to knee injuries: Deshaun Watson in Houston and Ryan Tannehill in Miami. You don't want to lose your starting quarterback. It's the true death knell in professional sports. It's like losing LeBron James or Sidney Crosby. It destroys your season and gives the league a new postseason calculus. One of the smartest things a front office executive can do is find a competent backup quarterback. That backup has to know the offense, run it pretty much like the starter with very little adjustment and seamlessly carry on. Second-string quarterbacks rarely see any action with the first team in practice during the week. It's impossible to develop any kind of chemistry with receivers, any kind of timing with the running backs and offensive line. So, that backup has to possess the kind of almost ego-less psychological makeup that says, "I know I'm not the man, but we're all going to survive. And advance. I promise." Rarely happens.

That's why Howie Roseman invested so much money in Nick Foles way back on March 13. It was a two-year contract that included $7 million in guarantees. Roseman was laughed at. You're doing *what?* Bringing Foles back? He's not Carson Wentz. He can't move like Carson. He proved he doesn't have

Wentz's arm strength. Seven million? What a waste. That was the talk of the town. And that's the way Roseman treated it. All talk.

* * *

When the Bears arrived in Philadelphia, it looked like the Eagles would never need Nick Foles, not this year or anytime in the future. Carson Wentz was the consensus Most Valuable Player in the NFL.

Wentz was leading the NFL with 25 touchdown passes. But it gets way better than that. He was just the fourth NFL quarterback dating back to 1950 to throw 25 touchdown passes and no more than five interceptions, joining Tom Brady, Aaron Rodgers, and Y.A. Tittle in that elite category. And none of them did it in just their second year in the league—a historic level of productivity for a young quarterback just scratching the surface of what he could do.

Wentz was downright unbeatable in the red zone, that area of the football field inside the 20-yard line, where a quarterback makes his reputation and his money. Thus far in the season, Wentz had completed 64 percent of his passes for 17 touchdowns, without throwing a single interception. On third downs, the so-called money down, Wentz had turned it into a disaster down for the opposition. He had completed 65 percent of his passes on third down with 11 touchdowns and just two interceptions, leading the league in third-down passing yards, yards per attempt, and passer rating.

The Eagles as a team were third overall on third-down conversions, trailing slightly behind the Carolina Panthers and the Los Angeles Rams. But, as a team, Philadelphia was first in red-zone productivity. Once they got inside the 20, you could not stop them.

Wentz was developing deadly accuracy and remarkable chemistry with his receivers, particularly tight end Zach Ertz and wideout Alshon Jeffery. But his strong, accurate arm was only part of the equation. Wentz could move—the kind of subtle movements in the pocket to avoid the rush, stay alive, and deliver the football. Wentz could really run, get away from defenders, make them miss or run over and through them. He was a big, strong wild horse. If the defense didn't dedicate a spy to watch his every move, it risked total embarrassment— or worse: Wentz scoring at will from anywhere on the field.

Thus, after 10 football games, the Eagles were leading the league in scoring: An astounding 32 points a game. If you go into a game knowing you had to break 30 points just to compete, you were in big trouble, especially considering that the Eagles' defense was keeping up its end of the bargain, giving up just 19 points a game—seventh-best in the league.

* * *

This one-two punch is what awaited Chicago, a 3–7 team lodged in the basement of its division, the NFC North. The Bears' head coach, John Fox, also a LaMonte client, had one foot out the door. (He would be fired at the end of the season.) Their quarterback was rookie Mitchell Trubisky. So, the Bears were outgunned before they got off the bus.

Wentz went right to work on the Eagles' second possession. He hit Ertz for nine yards, and Jeffery grabbed a 14-yarder. And then Wentz found Ertz down the middle for a 17-yard touchdown pass. With about six minutes left in the first quarter, the one-two combination of Ertz and Jeffery had given the Eagles a 7–0 lead and the rout was on.

Ertz and Jeffery represented what you have to do in the NFL: Draft well and find free agents to fill holes you can't with college players.

Ertz was the second player taken by former Eagles head coach Chip Kelly in 2013. And he turned into NFL royalty—in terms of production and star power.

He had three games of at least 13 catches and at least 100 yards receiving. Since 1960, that was second overall in that category among tight ends, trailing only Jason Witten of the Cowboys, who had four, and tied with Kellen Winslow Sr., the San Diego Chargers tight end who is in the Pro Football Hall of Fame, and future Hall of Famer Tony Gonzalez.

Ertz was born and raised in the Bay Area town of Danville, where he attended Monte Vista High School. As a senior, he caught 56 balls for 14 touchdowns and was named first-team all-state—in California. In 2008, the year Ertz graduated high school, there were 101,304 high school football players in the state of California, according to the California Interscholastic Federation—the highest number of any state not named Texas. So, Ertz was one of the top 11 offensive players among more than 100,000 football players. It doesn't get better than that. Stanford University never let him leave the Bay Area. He earned a degree in management science and engineering in Palo Alto.

"The thing we liked about Zach is that he could run every route, caught everything you threw to him, and never made the same mistake twice," said Kelly. "He's a really smart guy."

Smart but sneaky athletic. It's in his blood. His father played football at Lehigh University and his uncle played college baseball. In 2016, Ertz won the Eagles' annual home run hitting contest at Citizens Bank Ballpark, where the Phillies play across the street from Lincoln Financial Field. In March 2017, he got married to Julie Johnson, the World Cup champion soccer player. They got married in Santa Barbara where NFL players mingled with some of the top women soccer players in the world in a California celebrity wedding that was star-studded but understated. Ertz, soft-spoken and kind, is not flashy. But he is brutally competitive. He talks like he could be chairman of your local charity, but he plays like he wants to rip your heart out.

"Totally tough player," said fellow tight end Brent Celek. "But the best thing about him as a player is that he's always in the right place at the right time. He sees stuff on the field that helps Carson. Carson trusts him."

Going into the game against the Bears, Ertz was Wentz's top connection, leading the Eagles with 45 catches for 536 yards and six touchdown receptions.

Jeffery was not far behind. He was second on the team with 38 catches, 567 yards, and six touchdowns. But that's where the comparison ends.

Jeffery grew up on the other side of the country, and a world away, in rural St. Matthews, South Carolina, in Calhoun County, population 15,175 in the latest census—one-third the number of people than Danville City alone.

In high school, like Ertz, Jeffery was all-state, but at defensive back. A 6-foot-3 power forward and center, Jeffery led Calhoun County High to four state titles in basketball. He got a full ride to the University of South Carolina, where he played wide receiver, and was drafted in the second round by the Chicago Bears in 2012. (Jeffery was the 45th overall pick. Ertz was the 35th overall pick.)

In Chicago, Jeffery had a solid career, but he had the reputation as a player who just could not get out of the trainers' room—a bad rap to have. He missed seven games in 2015 and was suspended four more games in 2016 for violating the league's ban on performance-enhancing drugs.

So, when he hit free agency in the spring of 2017, few teams went after him. But the Eagles were desperate for wide receiver help. Howie Roseman took a chance on him, signing Jeffery to a one-year, bargain basement deal. The promise was simple: The Eagles were an up-and-coming team with a promising young quarterback. Sign for a year, stay on the field, and we will take care of you at the end of the season.

Game by game, his connection with Wentz improved. "People think it happens overnight, but it doesn't," Jeffery told me. "You've got to work at it, stay with it." What's more, he was keeping a secret that would not be revealed until after the season. In training camp, Jeffery injured his shoulder. But he wasn't coming off the field. He would play all season with soreness and pain. He had made a promise. And he knew if he did come off the field, he could kiss a new contract good-bye.

Jeffery's production was solid, but not Pro Bowl quality. Going into the game against his old team, he had yet to have a single game with more than 100 receiving yards, the benchmark for a top wide receiver in the NFL. Indeed, the Eagles had yet to have a 100-yard receiving game all year. Wentz liked to spread the ball around to the plethora of options he possessed. Jeffery had 92 receiving yards against the Chiefs in Week 2. That's as close as he got. But he was proving his worth, and his durability. He was keeping up his end of the bargain. Roseman started talking to his agent about an extension, giving Jeffery further incentive. The new deal—and a possible Super Bowl berth—was pretty good incentive.

* * *

In the second quarter against his former team, Jeffery caught a neat little eight-yard touchdown pass. It put the Eagles up 24–0 over Chicago. Blount finished the game with 97 yards rushing at a clip of 6.5 yards per carry, which means the Eagles' offensive line was just brutalizing the Bears' front seven. Corey Clement added 6.8 yards per attempt. Wentz ran five times for 29 more yards. In total, the Eagles had 176 yards rushing and Wentz tossed three touchdown passes.

Ertz caught 10 of the 12 passes Wentz threw to him—which is something you would expect if there was nobody else on the field. To do that against an 11-man defense in the NFL is absolute domination. It's like the Bears didn't even bother to show up. And Ertz amassed 103 receiving yards—the first time an Eagles receiver had broken the 100-yard barrier all year, remarkable considering they were leading the league in offensive production.

"It just shows you how unselfish this team is," Pederson said. "The fact that it's not all about one guy. It's everybody. Everybody's making plays on offense. It's everybody contributing. The fact that we're spreading the ball around and everybody's involved and we're still being efficient on offense is a tribute to the way these guys work and practice each week."

Jeffery liked to bring his mother and his wife and family to the home games. They would walk across the field in the evening light to just soak it all in—living in Philly, getting a new lease on life. It was all working for him. I would be on the field, doing postgame live shots for ESPN. We would talk about the season and family and you could see it in his eyes. He was happy, really happy, he said, for the first time in his career. Once in a while, Jeffery went across the street in South Philly with LeGarrette Blount to watch Joel Embiid and the Philadelphia 76ers. He liked to go out in Philly, be recognized, be appreciated.

Walking across the field with his family after beating the Bears, he told me, "I really love it here. People here are

151

great. They are starving for a championship. I'm going to do everything in my power to bring it home."

Six days later, the Eagles signed Jeffery to a four-year extension for $52 million, with $27 million guaranteed.

One important statistical note: The Eagles had 11 penalties in the game, costing them 70 yards. And they had four fumbles, losing three of them. And Pederson was not happy about it, especially with two road games against NFC opponents coming up. "It's unacceptable," Pederson said. "Can't do it. Can't do it. You can't put the ball on the ground like that."

Final score: Eagles 31, Bears 3

Postscript: The Eagles were now 10-1. It was their fourth consecutive win by at least 23 points and third in a row by exactly 28. The win reduced their magic number to clinch the NFC East to one—and it wasn't even December yet.

Chapter 12

Sloppy in Seattle

The Eagles at the Seahawks
Sunday, December 3, 2017 • Seattle, Washington

"We're going on the road for the next three games, so we've got to be able to take care of the football."

That was Doug Pederson's message to his football team. He was thinking about the next three weeks, playing in Seattle, Los Angeles, and finally North Jersey, against the division rival Giants, who were out of the race but out for blood. But he was more concerned about what was happening to his own team, what happened on Sunday against the Chicago Bears. His team was committing silly penalties and costly turnovers. You give the other team yardage and the football and it can kill the game, destroy your season. The Eagles had overcome these mistakes on Sunday because they were playing the lowly Bears at home, he reminded his coaches on Monday morning after the game against Chicago. Against the Seahawks and Rams and in the final month of the season when the Eagles were trying to close out the division and secure a favorable postseason position, those kinds of mistakes would doom their chances of going deep into the playoffs, he told anybody who would listen. Not that anybody needed to be told. Still, getting ready for Seattle, Pederson made eliminating the penalties and turnovers what coaches like to call "points of emphasis"—in the meetings and on the field, the coaches were to make it a priority to teach, correct, and coach it out.

"I'm not going to beat them up over it," Pederson told me that morning in a text. "But it's going to be a big part of our messaging, believe me." As difficult as it might be to imagine, a team that was 10–1 and had scored 30 points or more in five straight games (tied for the second-longest streak in franchise history dating back to 1933) needed to be coached up real good and real hard. But this is how you build a champion. Mike Holmgren taught that to Doug Pederson, who watched Bill Belichick in New England never give an inch to his players until they hoisted the trophy—no matter how many games they won on the way to that championship moment.

In the final question of his Monday morning press conference, Pederson was asked about the turnovers and penalties against the Bears. His answer sent a clear message to all those assembled and to his locker room on the other side of the building: "It's my job to make sure the guys stay humble and stay grounded. If we've got a certain goal in mind, we can't play this type of ball against the Seattles and the Rams and the playoff-type teams down the stretch and expect to win. So those things have to be tightened up."

What in particular had to be tightened up? It started during the Eagles' first possession against the Bears. Wentz had the offense on the move near midfield and right tackle

Lane Johnson was called for a false start—moving before the ball was snapped, a major no-no, especially for a veteran who was one of the highest-paid players on the team. That penalty killed the drive and the Eagles punted. Penalties and turnovers were what coaches like to call "field flippers," referring to field position, which almost always determined the outcome of a drive. Going 20 yards to score was much easier than going 80—simple math.

After the Eagles scored on the Zach Ertz touchdown catch and Malcolm Jenkins picked rookie quarterback Mitchell Trubisky, the Eagles gave the football right back in their third possession. Running back LeGarrette Blount took a handoff up the middle and rumbled 35 yards, but the football was stripped from his grasp. The Bears recovered. On the Eagles' next possession, an offensive holding call was charged to the other offensive tackle, Halapoulivaati Vatai. In the first quarter, the Eagles had two penalties and a fumble, a bad sign even in a game that was lopsided.

Pederson hammered that point home to his assistant coaches and to his players in the team meeting on Wednesday, three days before they left for the West Coast. He was as agitated as any of them had seen. Pederson was thoughtful, had the emotional intelligence (as his owner was looking for), listened to his players council and took suggestions. But he was not a so-called players coach. Phil Simms, who won a Super Bowl playing for Bill Parcells in New York and is seen in countless NFL Films features jawing with his head coach on the sideline, said to me, "That's the worse label you could ever have as a coach." Simms and I were discussing this subject one Sunday afternoon while walking across the field together at Gillette Stadium. He was about to call a Patriots game and we were discussing Belichick and his methods. Belichick would never be described as a players coach. "It means he's soft, that he will give in to the players too easily," Simms said. "It means he's afraid to work the team too hard, afraid to give it to them straight."

On this day, Pederson was standing in front of the players on his 10–1 team and giving it to them straight. And they were listening. "We're better than that," Jason Kelce said to me in the locker room after hearing Pederson. "Everybody in this locker room knows that. No one has to go around pointing fingers. But we all need to do our job better." Downright Belichickian.

Against the Bears, it got worse before it got better. On a 16-play drive to end the first half, the Eagles struggled through two more offensive holding calls before scoring a touchdown. In the third quarter, two more offensive penalties—a false start on running back Jay Ajayi and another one on wide receiver Torrey Smith—killed another drive. Philadelphia did not score in the third quarter. Were they sleepwalking through the lousy competition?

At the beginning of the fourth quarter, Ajayi scampered 30 yards into the end zone, but he didn't get credit for the touchdown. He fumbled the ball. Luckily, Nelson Agholor scooped it up and the Eagles tacked on another seven points, the only touchdown of the second half by either team. Both running backs had fumbled. And Vaitai had been called twice for holding. Even backup quarterback Nick Foles fumbled in mop-up duty in fourth quarter, giving the football back to the Bears, who promptly did nothing with it.

Malcolm Jenkins lectured his teammates about it. So did one of the culprits, Blount—a refugee from New England. Two days before the team boarded the plane for Seattle, Pederson endorsed what the veterans said. "That's exactly right," he said. "I wanted to make sure that they understood not only the positive that came out of this past game and these past few weeks, but at the same time as we go down the stretch, and we get into these playoff-type-atmosphere football games, particularly this week on the road, that we have to take care of the football."

The only one who seemed to be taking care of the football was the kid quarterback. Wentz had not thrown an interception in his last three games and only two in his last six. And, entering the game against Seattle, he had lost two fumbles all year.

* * *

That's why the quarterback position was invented. The forefathers wanted someone on the field who would take care of the football and control the game. American football evolved from the games of soccer and rugby, which were bequeathed by European settlers.

The first "football game" in this country is considered to have happened in New Jersey in 1869 between Princeton and Rutgers. But the game played that day was more of a blend between soccer and rugby. Not a single forward pass was thrown. And for the next decade, that's what was played on American soil. But both games proved to be unsatisfying to the American audience. Not enough scoring. Too much mass movement. It was a long, laborious game. American audiences were on the go after the Civil War. Manifest Destiny had convinced the country to expand west. With the industrial revolution gripping the nation, change was happening in every area of American life, including sports and leisure. American audiences were not attracted to soccer and rugby and the blended game being played here. There were too many other things going on.

Think about what was happening at that time, a bold multi-layered panorama of cultural experiences. President

James Garfield was shot dead in 1881. The same year, on the other side of the country, there was the showdown at the O.K. Corral in Tombstone, Arizona. Jesse James was shot by a member of his own gang in 1882, the same year that John D. Rockefeller—defying his critics and convention—formed Standard Oil Trust. In 1883, Mark Twain published *Life on the Mississippi*. America needed a game that reflected this dynamic landscape.

Said football founding father Walter Camp, "The rugby code was all right for the Englishman who had been brought up upon traditions as old and binding as the laws themselves." The non-descript running and kicking was not working in America, said Camp, who would become known as the father of American football.

An analysis in *The Princetonian* in 1879 went one step further: "Keeping the ball and working it by passing, running, and rushing is superior to the kicking game now in vogue."

In 1880, Camp, who was a professor and a coach at Yale University, called a conference of collegiate athletic officials from Yale, Harvard, Princeton, and Rutgers. The first rule change created at that conference was simple enough: The ball will be snapped to a man "a quarter of the way" behind the line of scrimmage. "That position will be called the quarter-back," who shall take possession of the ball and advance it as he sees fit. But that was not enough.

Two years later, in 1882, another convention was held and many more changes were put in place. The most important was the creation of the first down. "If on three consecutive downs a team has not advanced the ball five yards, they shall give it up on the fourth down," the new rule said. A little convoluted, yes. But translated into the affirmative, if a team advanced the ball five yards, it could keep it. It was later changed to 10 yards once it was quickly realized that the new quarterback position had opened up the game and the movement of the ball.

So, at its core, the game of American football is about two things: Possessing territory and possessing the football. Grab territory, hold it, defend it, and advance down the field. Keep possession of the football by making first downs and preventing the other team from taking it away from you. That's the way football in this country was designed by the game's founding fathers. The forward pass was put in place three decades later. Then the game really took off. With those rule changes, the position of quarterback evolved into the most important, glamorous, and well-paid in all of sports. But all the glory came with a high price: All the blame.

No one touches or controls the ball more than the quarterback. He can dazzle. But he can also disappoint. And the camera never blinks. Hero or goat, or dreaded "game manager." Doesn't matter. The focus is always on the quarterback.

* * *

Carson Wentz fumbled the football.

There is no good time to fumble in a football game, no good place to give it away to the other team. But Wentz managed to fumble it at the worst time of the game, at the worst place on the field.

The Eagles were down 10-3. It was a *Sunday Night Football* showdown on national television. Al Michaels and Chris Collinsworth in the booth. Michele Tafoya patrolling the sidelines for news. America was getting a firsthand look at the team with the best record in the league in a game with the best player in the league, on the road against a team that gave no quarter to any visitor. CenturyLink Field, home to the 12th man, was obnoxiously loud and unforgiving. It's a place where young quarterbacks could not hear themselves think, where winning streaks went to die.

Down by seven at halftime, were the Eagles getting exposed? They came out of the halftime locker room bursting through their shoulder pads with a combustible mixture of energy, anger, and anticipation. The Seahawks seemed ripe for the taking. But the Eagles, used to scoring 30 points a week, had been stoned by an injury-plagued Seattle defense. In 2016, the Eagles lost in Wentz's first trip to the Pacific Northwest. But this year's Seattle defense was without key players— Richard Sherman, Kam Chancellor, and Cliff Avril—and this Philadelphia offense was much better, more experienced than the one that visited in Wentz's rookie year. Yet, it had failed to cross the goal line. The Eagles trailed at halftime for the first time in as long as any of them could remember. So, they opened up the third quarter with an offensive drive filled with determination and grit.

First-and-10 from his own 25-yard-line, Wentz went right to work. He hit tight end Zach Ertz for 14 yards. Then he connected with Ertz again two plays later for 10 more. Wentz then threw to the left side for Alshon Jeffery for 11 yards and again to the left for Torrey Smith for 11 more yards, but it was one yard short of the first down. Fourth-and-one, on the road, down seven, Pederson needed a spark, needed to trust his team, his quarterback. Wentz went right up the middle, a keeper for two yards and a first down.

Then, he hit Jeffery again for a 23-yard gain. Now, the Eagles' offense was on the doorstep of redemption. Uncle Big Al was actually getting excited in the booth: A Philly TD here and the national audience would hang in there.

Wentz had first-and-goal at the four-yard line, the best chance the Eagles had to score all night. Blount was stoned for a two-yard loss. So, that's when Wentz, who had just made the fourth-down conversion, decided to go for it himself, again, a quarterback draw. As he lunged to the goal line, however, Wentz was stripped of the football by Seattle's newly acquired defensive tackle Sheldon Richardson. Instead of scoring a game-tying touchdown, Wentz lost the ball on the one-inch line. It rolled haphazardly out of the back of the Seahawks' end zone. Touchback.

"I saw the goal line so I thought it was going to be close," Wentz said. "Made that extra lunge and it cost me."

The cost was much, much higher than just *me*. Seattle took possession of the football and control of the game. Thirteen plays and 80 yards later, Russell Wilson had the Seahawks dancing in the Eagles' end zone. It was 17–3.

At the outset of the fourth quarter, Wentz did try valiantly to come back. And he made the kind of highlight-reel throw that forgives all sins and paints a glorious picture of a bright future and big paydays. It was third-and-13. The Seahawks' defense had the Eagles pinned on their own 16-yard line. Wentz rolled to his right and as he was careening toward the turf, he let the ball fly to Nelson Agholor, who snagged it and was pushed out of bounds after a 51-yard gain. Four plays later, another third down, Wentz hit Agholor again and the Eagles were in a one-score game with about 12 minutes left to play.

But Wilson took over, engineering a 10-play drive that showcased his ability to be creative on the run, elude the rush, and deliver the football accurately—all the same traits that Wentz possesses. Wilson, who piloted the Seahawks to a Super Bowl title in a blowout of the Broncos at MetLife Stadium after the 2013 season, hit a trademark 15-yarder for a touchdown and a 14-point lead.

"We thought we had a good game plan going against [Wilson]," Eagles strong safety Corey Graham said. "But as you see, you know how it is, better in person than it is on film."

Down by two touchdowns with just over seven minutes left, Pederson had to abandon any pretense of running the football—not enough time on the clock to score twice. So, the Seahawks started to race the Eagles' offensive line to No. 11, who dropped back to pass seven straight times, including an incomplete throw on a fourth-and-six play from the Seattle 40.

The Eagles got the ball back but Wentz was intercepted near midfield. It sealed the win for the Seattle. You could see that pick coming, considering how much pressure was on Wentz down the stretch. It was inevitable.

The fumble to open the second half, that was a different story, the case of the young quarterback getting too caught up in the moment, making a critical mistake he didn't have to make. Bottom line is if Wentz had not coughed up the football to Richardson and squandered a chance to score and flipped field position to the Seahawks in the beginning of the third quarter, the Eagles would not have been playing from behind the entire second half—and the game takes on a completely different dynamic.

After the game, Wentz's reaction to the fumble was puzzling. He either didn't like the tone of the question, the line of inquiry, or didn't understand the magnitude of what happened, which seems hard to believe.

"Yeah, I fumbled," he said. "It happens." If his answer sounds a little too casual considering the gravity of what took place, it was. He went on, stating the obvious: "It's tough to do that on the road in close situations like that, especially when you are down at the one-yard line. Tough to do that and expect to win. Especially coming back in the first drive of the second half the way we did. We were rolling there. Yeah, just can't put it on the ground."

Pederson's West Coast plan since the start of the season was for the team to hop on a plane right after the game in Seattle and travel down to Costa Mesa, California, where they would check into a Westin Hotel and relax for a while before getting ready to play the Rams. They would not start practicing at Anaheim Stadium, where the Angels play their home games, until Wednesday. So, the players had a lot of time to purge the loss to Seattle—but also agonize over what might have been. It was difficult to digest. There was a feeling that the Eagles let the Seahawks off the hook, that with all the missing starters on defense, Seattle was vulnerable. "Gave that one away," one player said to me after arriving in Costa Mesa. "We had them on the ropes."

Making matters worse, Wentz's favorite target, tight end Zach Ertz, took a vicious shot in the third quarter and left the game. He arrived at the hotel in California in the league's concussion protocol and was in jeopardy of missing the game against the Rams.

The Eagles needed time to recover—physically and mentally.

"We will be fine," said Wentz. "We are all frustrated about this one, but we're not too worried. I think we will be just fine."

Little did anyone know that soon enough the team *would* be fine—but without Carson Wentz.

One important statistical note: With the loss, the Eagles dropped to the No. 2 seed in the NFC. The Vikings held the tiebreaker over Philadelphia. It was the first time since whipping the Cardinals in Week 5 at Lincoln Financial Field that the Eagles did not own the best record in the conference. The pressure to beat the Rams was very real.

Final score: Seahawks 24, Eagles 10

Postscript: After beating the Eagles, the Seahawks were thought to be very much alive in the playoff picture. And no team wanted to go to Seattle in the postseason, especially the Eagles. "Everybody was ready to count us out," said Wilson.

But it turned out to be a mirage. The Seahawks lost three of the next four games and finished 9-7, out of the money. Wentz was right. Seattle had been ripe for the taking. But the Eagles gave it away.

Chapter 13

"We All We Got,
We All We Need"

The Eagles at the Rams
Sunday, December 10, 2017 •
Los Angeles, California

Sometimes when you're telling a story, you have to start with the end, because—in many cases—that's the most important part. And sometimes, as in this case, everybody pretty much knows what's coming. You have to get right to it. So, in this chapter, we start with what happens at the end of the game between the Eagles and the Rams, because what happened at the end turned out to be the beginning of a brand-new chapter for this Eagles team, and this Eagles season.

We will start there: When Carson Wentz got hurt. Wentz—the player who had become an urban legend, who captured our attention like a comet that arrives once in a generation, who created magic on the field with an effortless, Technicolor brilliance that seemed to be a gift from the football gods to a championship-starved fanbase—got hurt while diving into the end zone. He took off from about the three-yard line, his body horizontal like a wild animal lunging for prey. But by the time he reached the goal line, Wentz was twisted between two players weighing a combined 500 pounds, defensive tackle Morgan Fox and linebacker Mark Barron, who buried his helmet and his bad intentions in the quarterback's legs and destroyed his left knee.

It happened in the most unlikely of places. At the worst possible time. I was there, saw it happen. It felt like one of those slow-motion nightmares that take place on the edge of your mind. You want to grab it, stop it, reverse time. But you can't quite reach it. And you have that kind of awful feeling in the pit of your stomach that you can't shake.

So, here's what happened and how I reported the story. I will break it down into four parts: The scene, the game, the injury, and the speech that saved the season.

Part 1: The Scene

The Los Angeles Memorial Coliseum, modeled after the original in Rome, was dedicated to those who died in World War I, the so-called War to End All Wars. It was completed in 1923. The initial construction cost was $954,873. In 2018, the NFL's highest-paid player, quarterback Kirk Cousins, was due to make $1,647,581 per *game.*

The Coliseum seats about 100,000 for football, but never sells out for the home games of the Los Angeles Rams, who are using it temporarily until their new palace in nearby Inglewood is completed in 2019. It has none of the luxuries of modern stadiums, none of the suites or plush seating. There are only a handful of elevators, which do not go down to field level. You have to walk down after descending through the porticos that lead to the stands, which are more like high school bleachers than the seats you would see at any college or pro football stadium. It looks old and feels old.

But on this Sunday, as the Eagles and the Rams were warming up, the Coliseum felt re-energized. The field was lined with stars and celebrities, football and otherwise. They were there to see what all the fuss was about, to witness the showdown between the two young NFL gunslingers, Jared Goff and Carson Wentz, who went No. 1 and No. 2 in the 2016 NFL draft and had the Rams and the Eagles the talk of pro football, coast to coast. Indeed, it seemed like fate had brought us all together on this perfect day in the City of Angels.

Former Rams Eric Dickerson, Torry Holt, Marshall Faulk, and Vince Ferragamo were there. Movie and TV stars mingled behind the Rams' bench. The Hollywood feel to the game really started during the week. Pederson asked NBA champion Kobe Bryant, who is from Philly and grew up an Eagles fan but never wanted to play for the 76ers, to speak to the team at the hotel. It was a private meeting. But afterward, John Clark of NBC10 Sports in Philadelphia tracked Bryant down as he left the hotel—the only reporter who did.

"I think the character of this team is special," Bryant told Clark. "That's what wins championships—the character of the team, the spirit of the team. You have moments where you go up and down, but when the spirit of the team is a strong one, a collective one, then you have something that's truly special. Fingers crossed, they look to have that."

On the field, before the game, I ran into actor Ty Burrell, who plays the often silly but well-meaning dad on *Modern Family*. Burrell is a big sports fan. We recognized each other right away. He asked me who I thought would win. I looked around, gave him that "you talking to me?" look and said, "You kidding me, boss? We're standing behind the Rams' bench and there are about 40,000 Eagles fans here. That's a no-win question for me." I paused, looked him in the eye. "But," I said, "I got to go with the Birds." He gave me the same big belly laugh he has on TV. Blue California sky was bathing everybody and everything in a good vibe, even if the juxtaposition was odd: A modern slice of Americana in a stadium that looked like it was transported from an old movie.

And, yes, there were tens of thousands of Eagles fans there. It was an intimidating sight. They were loud and had the run of the place like somebody was giving away free pizza along Broad Street. At the peristyle arch entrance to the Coliseum, the Olympic torch was lit. The whole stadium, the whole day, was just *lit*—with excitement and anticipation.

"You gotta love this," said former Eagles wide receiver Mike Quick, part of the Eagles' radio broadcast team with Merrill Reese, the longest-serving voice of any NFL team. Quick looked around, soaked it all in. "I love it."

Part 2: The Game

The people who wrote about and talked about pro football for a living liked Doug Pederson. But they *loved* Sean McVay. When the Rams hired him as their head coach at the beginning of the year, McVay was just 30 years old, the youngest head coach ever in the modern history of the professional game. He quickly became a media darling. He's photogenic, smart, and a great young coach, the future of the league in a city where the NFL has been AWOL for a generation and desperate to plant the flag and grow.

In his first year, McVay marked his territory. The Rams vaulted to the lead in the NFC West and he had resurrected Goff, who languished under former head coach Jeff Fisher, who was finally fired after one of the longest and most overrated coaching careers in the history of the league. The Rams were scoring 30.1 points per game—identical to the Eagles to the decimal point.

The winner of this game had a chance to make a real statement, especially the Eagles. They wanted nothing more than to come here with their fans and just crush the hopes and dreams of La-La Land football and its pretty boy head coach—especially after giving away the game in Seattle. The players were in a mood to wreck a party—by any means necessary. And that started with Carson Wentz.

The one thing the Eagles were clearly concerned about going into this game was the Los Angeles Rams' defense, particularly the defensive line, anchored by a marauding beast of a football player named Aaron Donald, considered by many the best defensive player in the game. This was his fourth full year in the NFL. Donald had reached that prime level of maturity and mayhem. At just 6-foot-1 and 280 pounds, he was a menacing force of solid muscle with the right blend of quickness and ferocity. He dispatched with running backs who dared to come into his territory and terrorized quarterbacks. His specialty was arriving just as the quarterback got rid of the football, inflicting pain at the precise moment of delivery, when the quarterback's ribs were exposed—just a little shot in the breast bone to remember him by.

"Carson knows what he's up against," said offensive coordinator Frank Reich. "This is not Carson vs. Jared. This is Carson against the Rams' D. Physical, fast, disruptive."

Reich knew that the Rams would come after Wentz with everything they had. Rams defensive coordinator Wade Phillips is one of the smartest, toughest defensive coordinators in the game. He'd been around, seen it all. McVay at age 30 and Phillips at age 70 were the Odd Couple of the NFL. There was no greater age disparity in the league between a head coach and one of his coordinators. But Phillips had just led the Broncos' defense to a Super Bowl title—in a win over the Panthers two years earlier—by unleashing Von Miller on Cam Newton, watching the Carolina quarterback squirm and run for his life, then pout about it after the game. So, Phillips knew what he was doing. His calling card was to get pressure on the quarterback—early and often.

The Rams indeed came after Wentz and the hits were beginning to accumulate. Pederson, Reich, and quarterbacks coach John DeFilippo were well aware of what was going on. Wentz got punished by the Seattle defense, which never passed up a chance to deliver a little extra shot, a little extra push out of bounds, making sure blows were delivered right up to the whistle, right up to the moment where it might be a flag—or just a half beat beyond. Few penalties were being called for hits on Wentz. He was considered a running quarterback, and a young running quarterback at that. The bald truth is that guys like Brady and Brees and Rodgers get a little extra care and comfort from the referees. If it's close, it's a flag. These guys are proven rainmakers. They put fannies in the seats, make people at home put the remote down. Handle with care.

Rookies who are out on the edge making the same play do not. Just ask Cam Newton. Wentz was getting hit and rarely getting protected.

Several times in Seattle, Wentz returned to the sideline, wincing in pain. One time, Reich asked if he was okay.

"You good?" Reich asked him.

"Yeah, I'm good," said Wentz.

"I always have my eye on Carson and the hits he's taking," Reich said later. "He's a tough guy and this game is for tough players. I watch that. I'm aware of the amount of hits that he is taking."

Here is the breakdown of the number of hits taken by NFL quarterbacks in 2016 and 2017, provided by Evan Kaplan of ESPN Stats & Information: Cam Newton of the Panthers took the most hits, 303 in 31 games. Then it breaks down like this:

Tyrod Taylor: 249 hits in 30 games
Russell Wilson: 235 hits in 32 games
Dak Prescott: 174 hits in 32 games
Carson Wentz: 171 hits in 29 games

Kaplan did an analysis of Carson Wentz and Andrew Luck, two similar quarterbacks: Expected to be leaders of their franchises for the next 10 years, tough, strong arms, not afraid to run, put their bodies on the line. Both knocked out with injuries that required surgery to return—Luck with his shoulder and Wentz with his knee. Both trying to figure out how to get back on the field. If you compare the first 29 games (what Wentz has played) between Wentz and Luck, the Eagles' quarterback has been contacted 29 fewer times. Here is Kaplan's analysis:

	Luck	Wentz
Pass attempts	1,091	1,047
Rush attempts	112	110
Combined	1,203	1,157
Times contacted	200	171

But Luck learned to take fewer hits in his second season, something Carson Wentz didn't adjust to. Wentz was hit 14 more times through his 13 games in his second season than Luck was.

	Luck	Wentz
Pass attempts	464	440
Rush attempts	50	64
Combined	514	504
Times contacted	76	90

Wentz was getting hit more than Luck in year two of their respective seasons. Maybe the reason was as simple as a revolving door on the Eagles' offensive line. But it certainly was also the fact that Wentz was on a mission, not afraid to put his body on the line to get the job done. In the coaches' booth during games, DeFilippo was keeping track of every movement, every hit. During the week, he and Wentz would dissect the hits, make sure the young quarterback knew exactly what he was doing, and they would try to figure out how he could do a better job of protecting himself. But, in the course of preparing for that week's game, it was a miniscule part of the coach-player interaction. So much more time was being consumed on the game plan, the opposition, weight training, practice, breaking down practice on film, studying. Wentz had a style of play and, in the end, there was very little that could be done to change it. He would always come back to the same thing: "It's just football. I'm out there playing football." It made him one of the most attractive stars in all of American sports.

"Everybody is watching every move he makes," said Reich. "Everybody is. But sometimes as a player, and I think Carson falls into this realm, you thrive in that. It doesn't feel good, but you're in the game. This is what football is. It's a physical sport. And just because he plays quarterback, that doesn't mean he's not part of that. We all know that he's a little bit wired like that. But I still think he's done an excellent job of taking care of himself. I don't think he's taken a bunch of unnecessary hits. Except for the illegal ones."

There are hits. And there is something that veteran quarterbacks and coaches counsel against: Taking unnecessary risks. Bill Parcells first told me about the oldest, truest guiding principle of football, a sport that deals with injuries like no other: The number one ability is availability.

You got to be on the field. You can't lead from the bench. It is especially true for the most important player on the team: The starting quarterback.

Carson Wentz was intercepted in the first quarter. It happened on the Eagles' first possession, deep in their own territory. Three plays later, the Rams' brilliant young running back, Todd Gurley, shuffled into the end zone for a touchdown. And just like that, Los Angeles had a 7–0 lead. It felt like Seattle 2.0.

Wentz came back to the sideline. His teammates had never seen him that angry. And when the Eagles got the ball back, Wentz decided enough was enough. He wasn't going to let this opportunity slip away. The notion of coming out west and losing back-to-back football games because he continued to give the football away—he simply could not live with that. He had to re-focus. "Just go out and play football," he thought to himself.

He fired 28 yards to Corey Clement. Jay Ajayi put together two nice runs. Then Wentz hit Alshon Jeffery for 15 more yards. Blount found a small seam for two yards. Then Wentz looked for tight end Brent Celek. A pass interference call put the football on the one-yard line.

First-and-goal. Wentz decided to keep it himself, right up the middle. Wentz wanted to finish the play that he left on the field against the Seahawks. It was the exact same run up the middle that resulted in the fumble in Seattle. This time, Wentz scored. But right tackle Lane Johnson was called for a false start. Next play: Wentz threw a little five-yarder to Brent Celek.

Celek, the longest-tenured athlete in Philadelphia, started for the Pro Bowl tight end Zach Ertz, who was still dealing with a concussion. Celek would turn 33 in January and just wanted one thing after playing 11 years with only one team, the Philadelphia Eagles: To win a championship. He stayed around so long because he blocked so well, he played special teams, he did whatever the coaches asked him to do, and he did so to perfection. He did not score a touchdown in 2016. "I love players that sacrifice their personal stats for the team, and Celek leads the Eagles in that category," said Jon Gruden.

Wentz's pass to Celek was perfect. He scored easily. It was his first touchdown of the season.

But the lesson here was not the touchdown pass to Celek. It was that Wentz had playmakers around him. He was proving that all season long, and at the start of this game. He didn't need to do it all by himself—not in Seattle, not here. His lunge into the end zone on this drive was on first down, not fourth down. First-and-goal from the one calls for a running back plunge up the middle, not exposing your franchise quarterback to the business end of the Rams' defense—as we were all about to find out.

Pederson remained aggressive in his play-calling. It was now pretty clear that the Rams' defense had not faced anything like this kind of offense. Wentz kept firing. He hit another backup tight end, Trey Burton, for two more touchdown passes. The Eagles had a two-touchdown lead. But the Rams were far from done. Goff answered with two brilliant touchdown passes. And then the Rams blocked a Donnie Jones punt and returned it for another touchdown. The Eagles were in for a fight—they were down four points in the third quarter. That's when Wentz put together perhaps the best drive of his young career, a drive that would knock him out of the game and alter the course of the Eagles' season.

Part 3: The Injury

This is what the NFL schedule-maker, Fox Television, and all the thousands of Eagles fans who traveled across the country had hoped to see: Two young guns slinging the football around the oldest venue in the NFL, on a day bathed in the Golden State's afternoon sunshine. It was like Ali–Frazier, Yankees–Red Sox, McEnroe–Connors—Goff and Wentz would not be denied the chance for glory. They were like two gladiators in the bowl of the Coliseum with the thunderous crowd clamoring for more.

Wentz had the ball in his hands and the desire in his heart. He hit Jeffery for 13 yards and Torrey Smith for 24 more. He scrambled for five yards and hit Smith for six yards and Nelson Agholor for five yards. Ajayi had a supporting role, but this was all Wentz, running, throwing the football—a maestro, manipulating the Rams' defense with short throws and runs. On a third-and-three at the Rams' 11-yard line, he hit Agholor for six yards. The Rams were called for unnecessary roughness. The L.A. defense had seen enough. "We didn't want them to get in for another score, but we couldn't stop Wentz," Donald said after the game. "The guy's for real."

The Eagles had first-and-goal at the Rams' two-yard line. They had three chances to punch it in. Blount had just carried off left tackle for two yards. It would have been the perfect play to call. Instead, Pederson had Wentz in the shotgun. He wanted to throw the ball. Maybe he had Gordon Pederson in his head—stay aggressive.

The football is snapped. Wentz had two reads of the field: First a pass in the left flat to Agholor. He was double-teamed. Then Wentz quickly looked to his right for a quick crossing route to Celek. He determined that was not available. He had two choices: Throw the football away and live another down, try another play. Or keep it. Wentz decided to keep it, take it himself into the end zone. Remember, he's thinking touchdown. He had just scored on a one-yard run up the middle. He had a clear path to his right on this play. He took it. But that road to glory closed quickly.

No. 97, Morgan Fox, a backup defensive end for the Rams, came out of nowhere and met Wentz in midair. Mark Barron, a former first-round pick out of Alabama who played safety but was now listed as a linebacker, saw Wentz out of the corner of his eye and just leapt, driving the crown of his helmet into the young quarterback's legs. Close your eyes for a moment and think of one of those *National Geographic* films where the cheetah is captured in slow motion, leaping and grabbing the hind legs of a gazelle running for its life on a wide open African savanna. That's what Barron's takedown of Wentz looked like.

I was watching from afar through my binoculars, high atop the Coliseum in the press box, about 15 stories up on the east end of the old stadium. Behind me, the setting sun bathed the field in late afternoon light. I jumped out of my seat and stood on a concrete veranda on the right side of the press box so I could be closer to the end zone on the far left of the Rams' bench where Wentz got hurt.

Wentz had scored. But the touchdown was nullified by another penalty on Johnson, this time offensive holding. I could see Wentz knew he was hurt right away. He began rubbing his left leg. He said nothing. Later he would say it felt like he had been stabbed. He returned to the huddle. He was limping. But he had a football game to play, a drive to finish. He wanted to get the game back from Jared Goff and the Rams.

Pederson tried to run Clement twice. But the Rams could see that Wentz was hurt, too, and they loaded up, waiting for the Eagles to run the ball. Clement got nine yards and then one. No touchdown. Wentz's third-down pass was incomplete. Fourth down—stay aggressive—Pederson decided to go for it. A field goal would not be enough. He knew his quarterback was hurt. He wanted a touchdown. He put Wentz in the shotgun. This time Jeffery was open on the left where Agholor was not four plays earlier—touchdown. The Eagles had the lead again, finally—after 17 plays and 75 yards. It was 31-28, but Wentz limped to the sideline.

I left the press box veranda and started jogging down the cement Coliseum steps between the wooden bleachers, and disappeared through the portico directly behind the Rams' bench. If they were going to take Wentz to the locker room, I wanted to see the look on his face. I wanted to see who was with him, what happened in every critical moment of this young man's career and life, every second of time that was now suspended in this insanely unusual season of the Philadelphia Eagles. But getting to the locker room proved much more difficult than I anticipated. There was a stoppage in play on the field and a lot of the crowd filed out of their seats—to use the rest rooms or get something to eat. The lines on the second deck of the stadium were blocking any movement. I tried making a phone call to the news editors back at ESPN headquarters in Bristol. No service. Everybody in the stadium was on their phone, checking to see what had happened to No. 11. The only way I was going to get any real information was to get to the scene—to the entrance of the locker room. I looked at a young security guard in a yellow windbreaker and told him that I was reporter and that Carson Wentz got hurt and that I needed to get down the long winding causeway beneath the stadium to the visitors' locker room. He looked right at me and said, "I gotcha, Salpal." Gotta love ESPN, I thought. He knew who I was right away. He commandeered a nearby golf cart and hit the pedal and within minutes I was standing outside the Eagles' locker room as Big Dom and Wentz walked inside. Zach Ertz followed. The two best friends prayed together. It did not look good. I texted my producer, Shari Greenberg, who has lived in L.A. all her life and knew the Coliseum like her own neighborhood. I asked her to grab my backpack and meet me in front of the Eagles' locker room. The action was no longer happening on the field, I texted. It was all about Wentz.

Walking off the field at the L.A. Coliseum, head hung low, wondering what the future will hold, Carson Wentz goes to the locker room to get the bad news: Left knee injury, out for the season.

Dr. Peter DeLuca, in his 20th year with the Eagles, 15th as team head physician, examined Wentz and suspected right away it was going to be ligament damage, at least the anterior cruciate ligament, the ACL. DeLuca told Howie Roseman that Wentz would have an MRI on Monday back in Philadelphia and then he would know for sure. (Tests would later reveal that Wentz's left knee had not suffered just an isolated tear. There was other left leg damage in the knee meniscus and other muscles that would require a very long, difficult rehabilitation.)

While Wentz was in the locker room, Nick Foles was sent onto the field to save the game, and, little did anyone know at the time, the season. I walked out onto the field. When Eagles fans along the lower railings at the Coliseum, many of whom had seen me going into the tunnel to check on Wentz, saw that I came out and there was no sign of their quarterback, there was panic. I could see it in their eyes. They were looking for answers. Many of them knew that Wentz was hurt. Erin Andrews, the famous Fox sideline reporter, had already broadcast that Wentz was not coming back. Twitter was all over it. But the fans thought I might know more. I didn't. I just looked up at them and tried to console them. But my puzzled look did nothing to comfort them. I felt pretty bad. On the Eagles' sideline, there was a mixture of eerie silence and game chatter. John Gonoude, the team's young public relations assistant who handled the daily requests from the press for Wentz, just stared at the field, motionless. I didn't dare ask him a question. He wasn't going to tell me anything anyway. He's too much of a pro. But I had spent a lot of time with this young man in the last two years—that happens when you are that close to a team and a player like Wentz. I knew Gonoude was hurting. This was personal—for everybody.

Miraculously, the Eagles pulled themselves together— maybe it was a prayer from Wentz and Ertz. Foles finished the job. He led two scoring drives, both ending in Jake Elliott field goals. The rookie kicker was clutch, from 41 and 33 yards, with the game on the line. Foles hit Agholor with a beauty of a sidearm throw for nine yards on the penultimate drive.

The Rams got the ball back but Eagles defensive coordinator Jim Schwartz sent linebacker Nigel Bradham on a rare blitz at Goff. Bradham stripped the ball away from the young quarterback and Brandon Graham snatched it and ran 16 yards to ice the game. There was that bad man, again. Graham seemed to always in the right place at the right time—with the game on the line in the fourth quarter. He did in Washington in Week 1, he did it again on this Sunday afternoon to seal the win.

After the game, I was only interested in talking to one person on the field, the head coach. I caught Pederson's eye as he walked off the field with Big Dom. "Doug, what do you know?" I asked. "I don't know anything, yet. I'll see you after I get in there and talk to the doctors," he said.

Part 4: The Speech that Saved the Season

In the Eagles' locker room after the game, Doug Pederson tried to address the team. It was a good speech, hitting all the right notes about Next Man Up, about beating the Rams in their house, about recovering from the loss in Seattle, about being resilient and being a family. "We're playing for something bigger now, boys," he said.

Brandon Graham was riveted. Brent Celek was feeling satisfied but a little unsure. Torrey Smith, who won a Super Bowl with Joe Flacco in Baltimore, thought about how few of them had ever experienced anything like this. It was a wild array of emotions—joy for the team and sadness for Wentz.

LeGarrette Blount thought about how it might feel if, when he was in New England, the Patriots had lost Tom Brady.

Malcolm Jenkins looked around the room. He told me later that could sense the ambivalence. He knew the team had to speak with one voice. He asked Pederson if he could address the team. He got in front of his teammates and immediately began raising his voice. Here is his speech. I included the profanity, because without it, you don't get the real feel of him keeping it real:

> Carson being out of this shit, bro, that fucking sucks. But dig this, we set this up for whoever the fuck in this room—that's who we ride with, man. We said, we all we got, we all we need. Believe that shit. Feels great, man, celebrate that shit, man, know where we at. But at the end of the day, man, we got bigger goals. So we get back to work, man, you know what's in our minds, bro—championship and that's it. Nothing short of that, no excuses, don't fucking blink. This shit right here, this kind of win, on the road? That's big. This shit not going your way the whole time and it don't matter. It don't gotta be pretty, we just need a W. That's the mentality from here on out, man. Let's go. I'm proud of y'all boys. Family on three, 1-2-3, family!

The room exploded.

"'We all we got, we all we need'—we needed to hear that," Fletcher Cox told me.

In retrospect, was there a feeling that Jenkins was saying the team could live without No. 11, and that Wentz might've been hurt by that? "No, never went there," Graham told me. "Only Malcolm. Nobody else could give us that. He's our leader."

"It's what we had to have right in that spot," Lane Johnson said.

Jenkins later told me why he did it—and that it had nothing to do with Wentz.

"I know the media was about to come through that locker-room door," Jenkins said. "We needed to speak with one voice. Give us a message to tell the outside world. Or it could've have had the wrong feel to it. We all knew what was going on social media. We were getting texts from friends and family. 'How's Carson? What's going on with Carson?' Well, it wasn't about Carson. It was about us. We all we got, now. We all we need to finish the job."

Wentz was in the locker room, celebrating in his own personal way: He handed out NFC East championship hats. He left the locker room by himself, however, with a heavy air cast on his left knee and got his own food in the team chow line, walking along the tin pans while TV cameras recorded his every move. Big Dom backed a golf cart down the long causeway of the Coliseum and Wentz jumped in, cameras following.

After Jenkins' speech, the hats, and the realization that the Eagles were in the playoffs, the cross-country flight home was a lot more palatable. Foles had performed gallantly. He was a veteran. He had playoff experience. There was hope—not the kind that Wentz brought, but the kind that was explained with this preamble: "If the defense can hold up and Foles doesn't make too many mistakes, maybe, just maybe..."

One important statistical note: Carson Wentz finished his season with 33 touchdown passes, the most by any quarterback in Eagles franchise history. He did it in just under 13 games. Sonny Jurgenson had 32 in 1961 in 14 games. Donovan McNabb threw 31 touchdown passes in 16 games in 2004, the last time the Eagles had gone to the Super Bowl. Jared Goff and Wentz had a combined 55 touchdown passes as of that point in the season, the most by two quarterbacks taken first and second in the same draft in NFL history, according to ESPN Stats & Information.

Final score: Eagles 43, Rams 35

Postscript: As fate would have it, on the day I wrote this chapter, March 13, 2018, the Eagles announced the release of Brent Celek, one of my favorite Eagles players of all time.

An 11-year veteran, Celek was drafted by the Eagles in 2007 out of the University of Cincinnati and leaves Philadelphia with the fourth-most receptions in Eagles history (398). Celek, who missed just one regular season game in his 11-year career with Philadelphia, ranks fourth in team history with 175 games played behind David Akers (188), Brian Dawkins (183), and Harold Carmichael (180).

During his Eagles career, Celek totaled 398 catches for 4,998 yards and 31 touchdowns, marking the eighth-most receiving yards and 11th-most receiving touchdowns (tied) in Eagles history. He also played in nine postseason contests and added 27 catches for 257 yards and three touchdowns. In 2009, Celek recorded career highs in receptions (76), receiving yards (971), and receiving touchdowns (eight). His 971 receiving yards that season are the second-most by a tight end in Eagles history, trailing only Pete Retzlaff's 1,190 receiving yards in 1965.

A leader on and off the field, Celek helped the Eagles reach two NFC Championship Games (2008 and 2017) and capture the first Super Bowl title in team history in Super Bowl LII. Prior to his release, he was the longest-tenured active professional athlete in Philadelphia.

The Eagles' statement read: "Brent Celek defines what it means to be a Philadelphia Eagle. His dedication to his profession and this organization is unmatched and he will go down as one of the best tight ends in franchise history. Brent embodied the City of Philadelphia's temperament and character with his toughness and grit. He has been a huge part of everything we have been building over the last decade and it is only fitting that he was able to help us win our first Super Bowl last season. Unfortunately, in this business we are forced to make difficult decisions, especially this time of the year. This one is as tough as they come, but in our eyes, Brent will always be an Eagle."

The five-yard touchdown pass he caught against the Rams was the last time he crossed the goal line in an Eagles uniform. Such is the business of the NFL.

PART IV

THE SOUL OF THE CITY

Chapter 14

From Wentz We Came, In Foles We Trust

The Eagles at the Giants
Sunday, December 17, 2017 •
East Rutherford, New Jersey

Anthony Gargano could not sleep. He was not unlike most of the people in Philadelphia who follow the Eagles with a single-minded passion. On the long, lonely night the team traveled across the country at 39,000 feet, the city was sleepless. Instead of a full-blown celebration after the team conquered the high-flying Rams at the Los Angeles Coliseum, clinching its first division title under Doug Pederson, the city tossed and turned in the dark, waiting for dawn, hoping that it was all a bad dream, or just a bad case of indigestion that kept them up all night. Nope: The city awoke to a debate that would harden and calcify and remain lodged in the pit of the civic stomach—for weeks. The central question of that debate was simple enough: How far could the team go without Carson Wentz? The answer was unknowable, of course, launching full-scale examinations and evaluations in newspapers, on social media, television, and the city's two competing full-time sports talk radio stations.

Wentz was gone—the ghost of an unfulfilled promise, just like the rest of those agonizing disappointments that had haunted this franchise and the city's other sports teams over the generations. Gargano, who grew up in South Philadelphia, knew what it felt like. He had lived it. Now, he was re-living it, but he had to do so *live* on sports talk radio, four hours a day, beginning at 6:00 each morning—on the ESPN-affiliated station in Philadelphia, 97.5 FM The Fanatic. Luckily, Gargano spoke the language. He was one of them. He could feel their pain, because it was *his* pain. They felt like they could talk to him. In his big Italian family, Anthony—the son of Anthony and Florence Gargano—was shortened to "Antny." But in most cases, if you were really close, you called him just "Ant." On the air in Philly, Gargano was referred to as "Ant" or "The Cuz"—because, well, everybody was cousins in this great big *familia* that lived and died with the fate of the Philadelphia Eagles. On this morning, The Cuz knew what awaited him. And he was on no sleep. The city's sports fans would be looking for answers. And Gargano was supposed to provide them, first thing in the morning, as they drove back to work, back to reality. At the very least, he was to provide some kind of explanation or context or plan or—dare he say it?—hope. But, in truth, he had none.

"It was the most fatalistic I ever was in my life," said Gargano. "Everybody in the city felt the same way."

The city needed divine intervention. Gargano brought onto his radio show somebody he thought could talk directly to God, or at least the football gods. It was former Eagles punt returner Vai Sikahema, a bishop in the Mormon Church, to say a prayer for Wentz's mangled knee. "We just weren't sure. Doug had yet to make the official announcement," said Gargano. "We could see the foot and ankle dangling in the replay, so we *thought* it was a torn knee. But we just didn't *know*. When you don't know, you pray. So we prayed. And we prayed and we prayed."

Live on the air, The Cuz and Sikahema prayed for The Savior, Carson Wentz—may he come back to them, please God please. As they prayed, some fans commuting to work were moved to pull off the road, pull over on I-95 and the Vine Street Expressway and the streets of Cherry Hill and South Philly—Jew and gentile, didn't matter. They prayed together with The Cuz and Sikahema. But, truth be told, it did little to stanch the steady stream of despair and denial—Frank from South Philly: "Nicky could beat the Giants, I'll give you that. And the Raiders? He can take care of the Raiders on Monday night. But then what? What about the playoffs?"

They referred to Nick Foles as "Nicky." In the mezziginoro of Italy—the southern part of the country closest to Sicily, where farming and hill country means you were close to the land and each other—Nicky was short for Nicholas or Nicola, which, of course, rhymed with pistola, or pistol. Nicky, a perfect name for the quarterback, the triggerman. If you were called Nicky in an Italian neighborhood, it's a sign of respect. And Nicky Foles was respected. He had brought brief glory to Philly before. But, as a replacement for Carson Wentz, that was stretching the faith.

Harry from Bensalem: "What happens in the playoffs? What if it's the Falcons and Matt Ryan? We can't beat the

Saints—even with Wentz, the Eagles would have trouble with New Orleans. If it's Drew Brees and Sean Payton, fuhgettaboutit. No shot."

Vince from Collingswood: "If we get home-field advantage, Foles can get us to the Super Bowl. We got the defense. But, he ain't gonna beat Brady. No way, right Ant? No way."

That was the roiling debate that greeted the NFC East champions when they arrived in Philadelphia. There was no escaping it. As Phillies Hall of Fame third baseman Mike Schmidt once said, "In Philadelphia, you have the thrill of victory and the agony of reading about it the next day." But in this case, Schmitty might've felt the agony, too. That was the power and reach of Carson Wentz, a once in a generation athlete—just like Michael Jack Schmidt, who helped bring a World Series title to Philadelphia after decades of disappointment. Losing Carson Wentz at this time of anticipated greatness was just too much for even the most sober observers of the game to overcome. The headline on the SB Nation website: THE EAGLES DON'T HAVE A PRAYER.

* * *

According to Vincent J. Masi, the peerless guru of all things NFL at ESPN Stats & Information, only once in pro football history had a team started the season with 11 wins with one starting quarterback, lost that quarterback to injury, and then gone on to win a championship with another quarterback. That team was the New York Giants in 1990–91.

The quarterback who started with 11 wins for the Giants that season was Phil Simms. He was replaced by Jeff Hostetler. Those Giants won Super Bowl XXV in Tampa, beating the Buffalo Bills.

I called Simms and asked him to compare that Giants team to the 2017 Eagles team. "No comparison," he said. "Our team was so well constructed and had so many great pieces in place."

So, I asked him, would you say that Nick Foles' job was much more difficult than Hostetler's?

"Yes," he said without hesitating, "absolutely." And then Simms explained why.

The head coach of the New York Giants in 1990 was Bill Parcells. He had already coached the Giants to a Super Bowl title in 1986. So, there was experience and proven excellence at the top. And that was true for Parcells' coaching staff, including defensive coordinator Bill Belichick, who was with Parcells in 1986, and, of course, would go on to coach the New England Patriots to seven Super Bowl appearances (not including 2017), winning five. Parcells is in the Pro Football Hall of Fame. Belichick is a first-ballot lock. So, both coaches could draw on their coaching DNA and pedigree to adjust to the loss of Simms.

Belichick also had perhaps the best defensive talent in a generation, led by a once in a generation player at linebacker, Lawrence Taylor, who also went to the Hall of Fame. That defense was so stingy that it surrendered points during the opposing team's opening drive only three times all season. In 13 regular season games, the Giants' defense gave up zero, zilch, nada to the opponents on their opening possession of the football. "That always gave us a clear advantage on offense, so we never had to change what we did or how we did it," Simms said. The Giants' D gave up a field goal in Week 6 and a field goal in Week 7. It wasn't until Week 15 in 1990 that the Giants' opponent scored a touchdown on the opening drive—it was the Bills, the team the Giants would eventually beat in the Super Bowl about a month later. (The Bills did not score on their opening drive in that Super Bowl.)

This was the situation inherited by Hostetler, who was in his seventh season backing up Simms. In 2017, Foles had nothing close to that institutional knowledge or infrastructure in place to work with. "Jeff had a ready-made offense—a control-the-ball, control-the-clock offense," said Simms. As a result, the Giants that year only turned the football over 14 times, setting a record in 1990 for the fewest turnovers in a 16-game season in league history.

"With the offense Doug runs in Philly, Foles has to push the ball down the field," Simms said. "Jeff was the pretty much the same quarterback I was. Losing me was not like losing Carson Wentz."

So, in many ways big and small, what Pederson and the Eagles' coaching staff faced was unprecedented, presenting a set of challenges that none of them had faced, because no coach in league history had faced such uncharted waters. The first thing Pederson had to do was grab the helm and look for calm seas.

It was rough. On the morning of December 11, on the back page of the city's tabloid, the *Philadelphia Daily News*, the headline blared THE COST: AN ARM AND A LEG. One *Philadelphia Inquirer* columnist calmly stated, "The Eagles get a big win, but without Carson Wentz, Super Bowl hope is gone." That morning, facing reporters in Philadelphia for the first time since Wentz's injury, Pederson was asked seven straight questions about No. 11 and the status of the city's most important knee. Pederson confirmed the worst fears: A torn ACL (although he would not reveal the other injuries to the leg) and Wentz was having surgery and officially gone for the remainder of the season and the playoffs. The eighth question finally mentioned Foles, but it was a direct reflection of what was being said in the streets and on the airwaves of Philadelphia: "What do you say to fans who are as disappointed as they could possibly get with news like this? Everyone was just so thrilled the way Wentz was playing. Obviously, quarterback Nick Foles has done this before. But people suddenly think your Super Bowl chances are gone. What do you say to fans that are reacting like this?"

And just like that, live on two sports talk radio stations, the head coach of the Philadelphia Eagles was catapulted right into the middle of a public discourse that seemed to have no beginning, middle, or end, gripping his life, his team, and the future of the franchise. It's not like he was some anonymous caller or social media troll. His answer could help calm the fears and perhaps help his own team face the challenge—or backfire and make it worse. Remember, coaches use the bully pulpit of a press conference not just to answer the reporters, but to address the fans and send a message to their own locker room. What Pederson was about to say was supposed to accomplish all three of those objectives at once. He had to choose his words carefully, not give in to the obvious intent of the question—which was really one question, three statements, and another question. In other words, it was a reporter's soliloquy designed to illicit the right kind of soundbite or moment that would either mollify or inflame all the long-time listeners and first-time callers hanging onto every syllable from the head coach.

"That's a great question," said Pederson. He knew it was coming. His public relations assistant, Brett Strohsacker, in his first year leading the team's PR operation, had given Pederson a heads-up and talked through the possible responses. And why not? This was as important a public moment as any head coach would face. And he is the face of the Eagles, a $1.7 billion business with its future in doubt. Doesn't matter if you're fronting an automobile company or a major municipality, when there are *billions* of dollars at stake, you pay attention to the details and you get yourself prepared before you open your mouth. Pederson was prepared.

"You know what, people thought our chances were gone by the wayside when Jason Peters went down, too, when Darren Sproles goes down," he said. "To the fans out there, you can't lose faith. This has been a resilient football team all year long. If there's ever an opportunity for me as a head football coach to rally the troops, now might be the time. We just came off a tremendous victory to win the NFC East. Guys are riding extremely high. It might be a little bittersweet. But we got the Giants this week. We got an opportunity—you win Sunday, you got a first-round bye."

Pederson had told the team the same thing, leaving out the "bittersweet" part. But he also knew that comparing the loss of Wentz to the loss of Peters and Sproles wasn't entirely fair. Plenty of teams have lost a starting left tackle and survived to win a championship. As history clearly showed, what was happening to the Eagles had only been overcome once in pro football history. Pederson also knew that Wentz had achieved mythical status. "There was an aura about Carson," said Simms. "Foles doesn't have that about him. But he did have experience. He wasn't a young guy."

In 2012, Andy Reid drafted Nick Foles in the third round.

"I was here when we drafted him and we drafted him for a reason," said Pederson, who was Reid's quarterbacks coach at the time. "And then we went out and got him again this off-season for a reason. You never want to be in these circumstances, but my confidence is extremely high in Nick." Pederson acknowledged that he was privy to the outside noise. A good example of that, he said, was being second-guessed on a play-call late in the game against the Rams. It was third-and-eight. Pederson could have run the ball, taken his chances, and run time off the clock. Instead, he called a pass play and

Foles completed the throw to Nelson Agholor for a first down. "People ask me, 'Why did you throw the ball?' Because I've got confidence in Nick. I've got confidence in the guys. That's what I'm going to continue to do," Pederson said. "I'm going to continue to stay aggressive. I'm going to lead this football team. It falls more on my shoulders than it does on these players."

Then, addressing the question about why the fans needed to stay the course, Pederson spoke directly to Frank and Vince and the rest of the fellas listening in their cars or delivery trucks. "That's why they need to stay encouraged," he said. "That's why they need to stay excited about this opportunity we have in front of us."

And Pederson had another reason to stay encouraged: He had Jim Schwartz running his defense. Going into the game against the Giants, the Eagles' defense was ranked fourth-best in the league, leading the NFL in rushing defense and allowing teams to convert on third down just 30 percent of the time—third-best in the league. Most important, they were giving up just 19 points a game—fifth-best in the NFL. But when they rode up the New Jersey Turnpike to the Meadowlands swamp to play the Giants at MetLife Stadium, there was one little problem: The defense played like it should have stayed on the team bus.

* * *

Nicky Foles would throw four touchdown passes against the Giants and it would barely be enough to win the game. The Eagles' defense could not stop Eli Manning. All year, Manning had been blamed for everything from ruining the Giants' season to global warming. After Odell Beckham Jr. busted his ankle, Manning and the Giants' offense were pretty useless, convincing second-year head coach Ben McAdoo to bench

Manning. McAdoo's suggested replacement was Geno Smith, a reject from the New York Jets, who promptly lost to the Raiders in Oakland in his Big Blue debut. Giants fans threatened a boycott. McAdoo was fired. And Manning was resurrected. But he only managed one touchdown at home and lost to the Cowboys, 30–10. So, when the Eagles arrived, there was the distinct feeling that the Giants and their aging quarterback were playing out the string on a brutally disappointing season. Instead, the Giants ran up and down the field. And, on the Eagles' sideline, Jim Schwartz looked perplexed. He had no answer.

On their opening possession, the Giants reeled off a 16-play drive that covered 75 yards and ended with a neat one-yard plunge into the end zone. Manning was in the shotgun the whole drive. And the Giants did not huddle up, putting the Eagles' defense in a perpetual backpeddle. Manning never took a breath—completing passes of six yards, seven yards, five yards, six more twice in a row, then eight yards, a 25-yarder, another for 13 yards—most of the completions coming off a dizzying array of quick crossing routes that had the Eagles secondary talking to itself. Manning owned the middle of the field against Schwartz's defense.

This was nothing new. Against Schwartz in six previous matchups, Manning had completed more than 60 percent of his passes. Schwartz's use of the so-called wide-nine defensive front—putting the defensive ends outside the offensive tackle in what is called the "9 hole"—can open up the middle of the field. Schwartz wants his front four to get to the quarterback with a minimum of blitzing. If a quarterback can make quick work over the middle, Schwartz's defenses would be vulnerable. Manning had only been sacked four times by a Schwartz defense previous to this game and thrown nine touchdown passes. So, he had success in the past. And it was continuing this day—although it was shocking because the Giants had not been able to move the ball much the previous week in the embarrassing loss to Dallas.

Foles answered Manning. But then Manning quickly tossed two more touchdown passes, one for 13 yards and a killer 67-yard catch and run by shifty slot receiver Sterling Shepard. And just like that, the Eagles were down 20–7. Eagles defensive end Derek Barnett blocked the first extra point or it would have been 21–7 Giants.

Cornerback Ronald Darby finally intercepted Manning—why the Giants didn't just start pounding the running game was beyond comprehension. That set up a short field and a Foles touchdown pass to Zach Ertz. The Eagles blocked a punt, setting up another Foles touchdown pass, giving Philly the lead, 21–20. But, there was still no long-term answer for Manning, who put together an 11-play drive to end the half with a field goal and reclaim the lead. "We got the ball out quickly with some tempo stuff and that confused them a bit," Manning said.

In the halftime locker room, Eagles safety Malcom Jenkins was beside himself. The lack of communication in the secondary had to be fixed—or the Eagles were going to squander the coming-out party for Nicky Foles and re-ignite the citywide debate (which, marinating for the weekend, had concluded that Howie Roseman should pursue Colin Kaepernick as the only championship-ready replacement for Wentz).

To start the second half, Foles put together back-to-back scoring drives and the Eagles were up 31–23, providing a little cushion. Manning had a quick answer, tossing a 57-yard touchdown pass. But he was sacked on the two-point conversion attempt. An Eagles field goal gave them a five-point lead, meaning the Giants would have to score a touchdown late in the game to win. In an agonizing 15-snap drive going nearly 70 yards, including four penalties—two on the Giants and two on the Eagles—New York was stopped 11 yards short of the go-ahead touchdown. Manning's final pass went to rookie tight end Evan Engram at the back of the Eagles' end zone. It sailed high—incomplete. The Giants were irate. Manning thought after the play that Eagles safety Corey Graham held Engram's left arm.

"I definitely thought it was defensive pass interference," Engram said. "It was really obvious, but no call."

Game over. The Eagles earned a first-round bye in the playoffs. Foles had thrown touchdown passes to four different receivers. But had the defense been exposed? Manning had a total of 434 passing yards for the game, the fourth-most of his long career. The secondary and the pass rush had proven vulnerable to a veteran quarterback with superior field vision and a quick tempo who could strike in the middle of the field with an array of slippery wide receivers. A very bad sign.

What if that had been Tom Brady back there?

That night, Anthony Gargano could not sleep. In the morning, all across the airwaves, a new debate had been spawned. The Eagles were the No. 1 seed in the NFC, the perfect perch from which to launch a Super Bowl run. Nicky Foles proved to be a deadly triggerman. But what about the defense?

One important statistical note: According to ESPN Stats & Information, Foles completed 60 percent of his passes and threw two touchdowns without an interception against the Giants' blitz. Carson Wentz had 13 pass touchdowns and no interceptions against the blitz in 2017. The Eagles' offense had not missed a beat.

Final score: Eagles 34, Giants 29

Postscript I: A note about the title of this chapter. "From Wentz We Came, In Foles We Trust" first appeared on a billboard on the city's highways, courtesy of the city's tourism board, Visit Philadelphia. It soon appeared on T-shirts all over the region.

Postscript II: Gargano's ancestors came from the Italian province of Calabria, the heart of the mezziogiorno.

Chapter 15

Hoping St. Nick Would Soon Be There

The Raiders at the Eagles
Christmas Night, 2017 • South Philadelphia

Against the New York Giants, Nicky Foles turned into St. Nick. Only one problem—eight days later, on Christmas Night against the Oakland Raiders with the whole country watching *Monday Night Football*, St. Nick was a no-show.

The Raiders were the epitome of mediocre. They had been forced to travel across the country on Christmas Day, miss the festivities with their families, and stay in a Philadelphia hotel on the most cherished of all family holidays and wait to play football. They were about to fire their head coach and re-hire the guy in the booth calling the game, Jon Gruden.

Even with all that going for them, the Eagles' offense was a listless mess. Philadelphia had 14 offensive possessions. Here's the ugly list of results: Punt, touchdown, punt, punt, missed field goal, punt, punt, fumble, field goal, punt, interception, punt, punt, and field goal. Translation: After scoring a first-quarter touchdown, the offense hardly got a sniff again of the goal line. And Nick Foles took all the blame.

That's just the way it is in the NFL. Against the Giants, Foles got all the credit and praise for bailing out the defense, and perhaps the season. Just eight days later, Foles was the target of withering criticism. And, more important, he put the team and its legion of near-heartbroken followers back on the down slope of an emotional rollercoaster ride.

Never mind that the Eagles won the game, 19–10. This wasn't about beating the no-account Raiders—this was about whether Nick Foles could, in fact, be The Man. And now, after completing just 50 percent of his passes with an average gain per attempt of 3.5 yards (which would be mediocre if you were *running* the football), that was in serious doubt.

"I don't know what it was," said John DeFilippo, the quarterbacks coach. "We were just blah on offense. Just blah. Maybe it was the weather, I don't know. We could not find a rhythm."

On Christmas Night in South Philly, the conditions were brutal. Wind chill in the teens. Strong gusts whistled straight down the industrial plateau off I-95, careening off the long, flat, food storage warehouses that line the parking lots of Lincoln Financial Field. Felt like a bad day on the Eastern Front. "The field felt like cement," said one Eagles defensive player. He didn't want his name used, didn't want to insult the team's grounds crew.

The whipping wind did not help the passing game. But there was something going on with Foles. "He didn't have command of the team," said DeFillipo. "He just never took command."

Here was the most popular choice for newspaper headline writers the next morning: NICK FOLES DOES NOT LOOK READY FOR THE PLAYOFFS. The collective reaction to that headline was simple: No kidding. Only it was Philly, so there was a well-known profanity between the "no" and the "kidding."

Doug Pederson tried his best to spin it. "We found a way to win," he said. "That's the bottom line. We found a way to win." But as the late, great U.S. senator from New York, Daniel P. Moynihan, once said, "Everybody is entitled to their own opinion, but not their own set of facts."

And those facts were difficult to ignore. Foles could not get the football to his wide receivers. He threw seven passes to Nelson Agholor, who caught just four for a lowly 35 yards. Yet, on this pedestrian night, that yardage total led all wide receivers. Torrey Smith was thrown five passes, caught one for five yards. Alshon Jeffery had two balls thrown his way. No catches. He dropped one of them. Jeffery seemed the most effected by Wentz's absence. In the two games with Foles, he had just 49 yards receiving. He averaged more than 50 per game with Wentz. I asked him about it. He had no real answer. "It will come," he promised. "Give it time." Time they didn't have.

Against the Raiders, the five total catches by the wide receivers were their fewest of the season. They also set season lows in receptions, yards per attempt, first downs, and receptions that traveled 10 yards or more. Foles relied heavily on the running backs and tight ends. He tried to dink and dunk his way down the field. That takes patience. That takes accuracy. But to develop a sense of understanding of the offense (so-called chemistry) with the wide receivers, that would take time—on the practice field. Developing that in real game action is problematic in the NFL, especially in today's NFL. The collective bargaining agreement between the league and the players severely limits practice times and the number of practices where players can wear full pads and hit one another. It was designed that way to reduce injuries, especially head trauma. The first victim of that system? The backup quarterback, especially one who is behind a superstar stud in the second year of his development. As the backup, Foles saw virtually no time with the first-team offense. Wentz commanded the full attention of his teammates and coaches. Remember, at the beginning of the year, Wentz was just learning, too, to understand the subtle movements of Smith and Jeffery. He had never played with them before. No way was the offensive coaching staff going to give Foles even a taste of that experience with the new wideouts. It was Wentz's team. He was on an MVP path. Foles had to watch. Now, he had to get up to speed, quickly. And game action is at a totally different pace than practice. They try to simulate it. Coaches will always say things like, "Yeah, we had a good week of practice." Or, "Guys were flying around out there on the practice field." But the smart, experienced coaches save those quotes for the press. Those kinds of shopworn platitudes were never uttered inside the practice facility. Everybody in pro football knows that you just don't know how a new player or a new concept will do until, as they like to say, "the bullets start flying," meaning the action gets real. And by "real," it means until somebody hits somebody in the mouth, and then it's on.

And on Christmas Night in South Philly, with the wind blowing through their helmets' ear holes and 69,596 Eagles fans grumpy and grumbling in the stands, the Raiders slowly got in the mood to play spoiler. The Eagles had a chance to clinch home-field advantage throughout the NFC playoffs—and the Raiders decided they wanted no part of it. Head coach Jack Del Rio, already rumored to be replaced by Gruden, told his team this game was about pride. "We wear the silver and black," he said to his team before the game. "Let's go out and play like it."

So, the Raiders' defense came after Foles right from the beginning of the game—gave him no room to breathe. And Del Rio ordered his secondary and linebackers to hug the line of scrimmage to choke off the Eagles' ability to run the football. Jay Ajayi was the leading rusher—with a seriously embarrassing 52 yards, 3.7 per rush. LeGarrette Blount was worse: 2.4 yards a rush—just 12 total yards on the ground. With not even a crease to run the ball, Pederson was forced to call on Foles to pass. This is what a defense playing with house money (like the Raiders) will try to do against a team with an inexperienced quarterback: Make him play, make him beat you. This was a test for Foles and for Pederson. But when you telegraph that you have to throw the football, it becomes open season on the quarterback. Foles was chased and harassed, battered and smacked around. He was sacked twice and intercepted once.

The Eagles had just 12 first downs against the Raiders—a season low.

They generated just 216 yards of offense—a season low.

They ended the game with only 138 passing yards—a season low.

And the offense converted just once on third down—on 14 tries. That's a conversion rate of seven percent—another season low.

St. Nick's sleigh had to be pulled into the garage for a check under the hood. Even after he tried to put his best positive spin on the result, Pederson knew that.

"I'd love to win 40-3 or 34-28, but sometimes you're going to be in these games," he said, perhaps realizing his first attempt at an explanation was just not Philly Real enough,

On Christmas night, even the most loyal members of the Philly flock had their faith tested.

even on Christmas. The press was just not in a giving mood. "We got to be hard on ourselves as coaches and players looking at this film, moving forward, and get things fixed offensively."

As for Foles, Pederson was not going to try to dance around the issue for the press or the fans, or kid himself. They all saw it.

"He'll be hard on himself," he said. "He'll be critical. We'll just evaluate the film and make corrections."

The Eagles had two fumbles and an interception. More important, the penalties were back: Eight flags were thrown on Philadelphia for 60 yards. "We had holding calls," said Pederson, "and some missed assignments in the running game. We just couldn't find a rhythm."

Even the center snap to the quarterback, the most fundamental of all moves on offense, was an issue. Jason Kelce's snaps were low. Foles had trouble handling the football, bobbling the exchange. "Some of those are just the quarterback, just concentration," Pederson said. It's pretty rare for a head coach to say something like that about his quarterback in a postgame press conference for all the world to hear. Pederson was not about to blame Kelce, the fulcrum of everything the team does on offense and an indispensable leader of the team. Foles was a much safer target. Still, it was unusual. And everybody in the locker room paid attention. The players don't lie to each other. That's not how you get better, how you win championships. They could all see that Foles was jumpy in the pocket and that he could not get out of his own way. They were accustomed to seeing Carson Wentz glide and frustrate defenders with his quick explosion out of danger. Foles was awkward as he tried to move around the Raiders coming at him with bad intentions.

But there was also a single sliver of hope coming out of his ugly performance against the Raiders. There was one play where Foles seemed comfortable: The run-pass option, RPO.

* * *

Foles liked being in the shotgun, facing the defense from a distance, like the low-post basketball player he was in high school. At 6-foot-6, Foles can easily see the second and third level of the defense—the linebackers and the secondary. He could easily read their movements in real time after the ball was snapped.

DeFilippo could see Foles' comfort level on the Eagles' fourth play from the line of scrimmage against the Raiders. The Eagles lined up in "trips right" formation, with three wide receivers to the right side of the football. Foles was in the shotgun, about four yards behind Kelce. Ajayi was the running back. The play was called a rifle. It was a run-pass option. After the snap, Foles' job is to read the movement of the linebackers. If he sees the movement he likes away from Ajayi, Foles hands the running back the football. And that's what happened. Ajayi gained 11 yards. After that run and a three-yard pass from Foles to Blount, the Eagles rattled off nine more running plays in a row, giving Philadelphia the football on the Raiders' 17-yard line. On a second-and-eight, Foles decided to throw it to Ajayi—a 17-yard touchdown pass.

Run-pass option: That might work.

According to DeFilippo, the Eagles had used a smattering of run-pass option plays with Wentz at quarterback against the Chargers on October 1, against the Panthers on October 12, and against the Rams on December 10—all road games. They had mixed results. All three of those teams had active linebackers who could really run and tackle. Running the ball wasn't much of an option. Plus, a run-pass option play can be slower to develop after the snap. The quarterback has to read the movements of a key linebacker. That kind of play was not made for Wentz, who liked to strike quickly. The coaches were not crazy, either, about Wentz holding onto the football too long. They wanted him to get the ball out. He was deadly accurate and he had a cannon. With Wentz at quarterback, there was no need to worry about what the defense was doing. The opposition had to worry about what *Wentz* was doing. Not so with Foles. With Foles in the shotgun, creating doubt and deception for the opposing defense would add a needed dimension: What were the Eagles going to do here? It was another layer to the post-snap chess match that could be the difference between gaining three yards or 13.

DeFilippo saw that. As the quarterbacks coach, he was biding his time. He had already called the plays at the NFL level. It was DeFilippo, who has stone-cold total recall, a compass in his head for the football field beyond the rational mind, who tested Carson Wentz on play after play on film when the Eagles coaches wanted to know if Wentz had the goods to play—and play right away. "What do you do here with this route with quarters coverage? What do you call this play? What about this safety? How did you read him?" Each question was detailed and rapid fire. And each answer from Wentz was delivered correctly without the slightest hesitation. It was that Q&A session between DeFilippo and Wentz that so impressed Pederson and Howie Roseman and owner Jeffrey Lurie that they convinced themselves that they would pay any price—in draft picks and players—to get into position to draft Wentz.

It also was a clear indication that DeFilippo, who served as the Cleveland Browns' offensive coordinator in 2015 and was considered a rising star, would be near impossible to keep after the 2017 season. DeFilippo's contract was expiring and he wanted to go back to calling plays so that he could one day be in a position to be a head coach. Pederson was going to call the plays as long as Pederson was in charge. But, right now, Pederson—and his right-hand man, offensive coordinator Frank Reich—were all on the same page with what DeFilippo saw: Nick Foles was not going to turn into Carson Wentz anytime soon. Pederson was a former backup quarterback in the NFL. So was Reich. DeFilippo played quarterback at James Madison University. They all knew the difference between The Man and a guy trying to be The Man, between a guy who could move and avoid the rush and a guy who could not. Foles had been a starter before. But the difference between Wentz and Foles was too great. Foles needed help.

The team needed it, too. There were many tell-tale signs. Missed blocking assignments. Running backs sluggish. Jeffery out of sorts. Kelce simply not getting the ball snapped right. The team could not ride this rollercoaster much longer. It needed a defining element on offense, something that would calm everybody down, put them in a comfort zone. Paul McCartney said about his career after the Beatles, "When you cut into the present, sometimes the future leaks out." It looked like the Eagles might have a future in run-pass options.

After the game, in the locker room, with the door closed and just the team listening, Pederson had a very specific message to his players and coaches: "I just told them, 'Congratulations, man. Every team in the postseason, if we get a chance to continue on, is coming right through here.' That's what we wanted. That's what our goal was this week. We wanted to finish the game that way. And we did. And we're excited about that."

But then there was a warning. He also told the team this: "Now, we've got to get ready to play. You can't make the assignment errors and mistakes that we did tonight and expect to win a postseason game."

One important statistical note: Despite the ugly performance, the Eagles would get to stay home throughout the NFC playoffs. They were the NFL's only remaining unbeaten team at home (7–0). According to ESPN Stats & Information, home-field advantage throughout the playoffs has become more important in recent NFL seasons. From 2013 to 2016, seven of the eight No. 1 seeds—that's 88 percent—reached the Super Bowl. Now, let's look at the years 1990 to 2012, a much larger sample, but still instructive. In those years, only 21 out of 46 top seeds—46 percent—made it to the Super Bowl. Why this trend took place was anybody's guess. League-wide, there was better quarterback play, better passing, which favors the home team because they don't have crowd interference with the snap count. Get the ball off quickly and cleanly and fire away.

Final score: Eagles 19, Raiders 10

Postscript: Buried in all the bad news about the Eagles' ugly performance on offense, which dominated the airwaves and the headlines and spoiled the holiday week between Christmas and New Year's Eve, was the news that the Eagles' best pass rusher, Brandon Graham, who led the team with 9.5 sacks going into the Oakland game, had suffered a nasty ankle sprain. Graham, in a contract year, had not missed a game all season. Pederson would shut him down for the final game of the year: The Dallas Cowboys at Lincoln Financial Field on New Year's Eve. He knew that without Graham, the Eagles had no chance of going very far in the postseason.

Chapter 16

"Just Go Be Nick"

The Cowboys at the Eagles
New Year's Eve, 2017 • South Philadelphia

Nick Foles almost quit football. But fate called his bluff.

Fate came in the guise of Andy Reid. C'mon back to football, Big Red said. I got a spot for you in Kansas City.

Foles had been in exile from the game he had played since he was a kid, trying to find the emotional center of his life and profession. He left the NFL unceremoniously, perhaps pushed to the brink of retirement by the rather unfortunate way former Los Angeles Rams head coach Jeff Fisher cut him. The moment was televised on the HBO series *Hard Knocks*—with a camera rolling, Fisher called Foles on his white smartphone from the comfort of his training camp office and released him. "I hope you land on your feet," Fisher said, ending the small talk with about as much sincerity as a bad parody of a bad boss. You can't hear Foles on the other end of the phone. It was the first time that award-winning series had ever shown a head coach cutting a player over the phone. Fisher and the Rams had total editorial control over what would air, and what would not. The team chose to show it and immediately there was near-unanimous criticism of the team and Fisher for the way Foles had been treated. He didn't deserve that. No player did, but especially not Foles—who is about as selfless a team player as you'll ever encounter.

The nationally televised phone call was the culmination of a lot of mixed feelings for Nick Foles. So, instead of trying to find another team, Foles decided to take a step back, telling his father and best friend, Larry, that he needed time—away from the game—to think about the future. He was thinking of retiring, he said, and becoming a pastor. Foles has given many explanations for why he wanted to retire. But the most thoughtful one came when he was interviewed on a little-known Christian website called YouVersion: "After my time with a certain NFL team, I wanted to retire," Foles said. Notice how he doesn't mention the Rams by name—he's too classy for that. But his tone suggests that he was hurt by the way things went down. "I wanted to retire from the NFL, and I really struggled. I couldn't pick up a football for about eight months. I had no love for the game, and it was tough."

Foles had been on a fishing trip with friends. His phone was off for days. On his way home, he switched the phone on. There were dozens of texts and missed calls from family and friends. One text was from Reid, inviting him to come to the Chiefs. In 2012, Reid had drafted Foles in the third round, No. 88 overall, out of the University of Arizona.

"I went on a fly fishing trip with my brother Ryan, and just coming back talking to my wife, Tori, about it, I still didn't have a clear decision of what I wanted to do," Foles said. "But that's when I prayed and really asked God for guidance. There wasn't a sure path. I really just took a step in faith and I knew I would have more growth as a person going back to the game with knowing how I felt. And there were several teams that called, but the only one I was gonna play for was Kansas City—because of Coach Reid being there. And I knew he was a man who has always believed in me, no matter what has gone on in my career. He drafted me, and I knew if I went and played for him, he could find the joy and bring it out of me."

But Foles sat behind Alex Smith in Kansas City. He played in just three games and threw only 55 passes. And when Reid fell in love with a young quarterback in the 2017 draft—Patrick Mahomes III—Foles was expendable, again. He hit free agency. In the summer of 2017, he came back to Doug Pederson, who had met Foles on a recruiting trip in Texas. What impressed Pederson about Foles, who had broken all of Drew Brees' passing records at Westlake High School outside Austin, was not his tools as a passer, but his tools as a person. Like Pederson, Foles used his Christian faith as the foundation for his decisions and how he handled people. "That's what I liked the most about Nick," said Pederson. "He was grounded in his faith. And he could play."

* * *

But how much would Doug Pederson play Nick Foles in *this* game? The Eagles had a short week to prepare for the final game of the year, a New Year's Eve showdown with the Dallas Cowboys that was meaningless in terms of the NFL standings—the Eagles had the No. 1 seed sewn up, the Cowboys had been eliminated. But, in Pederson's mind, the game was one last chance for Foles to find some kind of grounding within the Eagles' up-and-down offense. There wasn't much time to practice. After the Monday night game against the Raiders, the players needed time to heal and rest and study. Practice time was limited. The Cowboys game was just six days away—Sunday afternoon. Certain players—those injured, selected veterans—would sit out the contest. But after much discussion with Frank Reich and John DeFilippo, Pederson decided that Foles would start the game—a huge risk, considering that if he got hurt against the Cowboys, the Eagles' playoff chances would be in even more serious doubt. To many outside observers, including the oddsmakers in Vegas, the Eagles were already considered a long shot to advance in the NFC postseason *with* Foles. Without him? With third-string Nate Sudfeld at the helm? Long shot would go to no shot. But Pederson said he was not going to be a slave to possible injury as the reason to rest his players, including his starting quarterback.

"If that's the approach, then I would have rested him [against the Raiders], quite honestly," he said the morning after the Oakland game. "I can't worry about that. I got to play and get him as many reps as I can, and then be smart about it."

The problem with that reasoning was Foles was not some rookie. He was about to turn 29 years old. It was his sixth year in the league. The risk of him getting injured was not worth the possible reward of him playing a few snaps in a game where most of the players just wanted to get on with the next chapter of their lives. The Cowboys: Stay healthy to work another season. And the Eagles: Stay healthy for the postseason. Foles had playoff experience—with the Eagles at Lincoln Financial Field. He was well aware of how high the stakes were, of how this was his best, and perhaps last, shot at redemption—and that elusive championship ring.

* * *

Nick Foles was born into the game. The family has a baby photo of Foles holding a football. "It's actually pretty funny," he said, "because in that picture I'm using the same grip as I do now."

At Westlake High School, he threw for 5,658 yards. Westlake High, with 2,540 students at the time Foles graduated, was a highly competitive campus that graduated great businessmen and athletes, including Olympic swimmer Scott Spann, major league third baseman Kelly Gruber, the aforementioned Drew Brees, and Justin Tucker, the kicker who won a Super Bowl with the Baltimore Ravens. Tucker and Foles were teammates at Westlake, where Foles was a three-year starter and two-time MVP for the varsity basketball team. He could've played Division I basketball. But football was in his blood.

After a detour—all of life is about getting around the detours, right?—at Michigan State, Foles landed at the University of Arizona in Tucson. His favorite memory from school? Mentoring four brothers from an underprivileged home—Aaron, Jose, Chris, and Anthony. He still talks to them all the time.

In 2012, Foles was one of eight quarterbacks selected in the first four rounds of the NFL draft. Check out this list:

- Andrew Luck, No. 1 overall in the first round, to the Indianapolis Colts.
- Robert Griffin III, No. 2 overall, to the Washington Redskins.
- Ryan Tannehill, No. 8 overall, to the Miami Dolphins.
- Brandon Weeden, No. 22 overall, to the Cleveland Browns.

Four quarterbacks in the first round. Five years later, none of them had made a significant contribution to football: Luck was recovering from shoulder surgery. Griffin, often hurt, was out of the league. Tannehill was recovering from knee surgery. Weeden was a backup in Dallas.

Now, here's the rest of the list of quarterbacks:

- Brock Osweiler, second round, to the Denver Broncos. He has bounced around the NFL.

- Russell Wilson, in the third round, to the Seattle Seahawks. He led them to two Super Bowls and their first title.

- Nick Foles, also in the third round, 13 picks after Wilson.

- Kirk Cousins, in the fourth round, to the Washington Redskins—signed a huge free agent contract with the Minnesota Vikings in 2018.

Who would you take first on that list? Wilson, for sure. But Foles would be a close second.

With Reid gone in 2013, Foles had a career year under Chip Kelly, throwing 27 touchdown passes and just two interceptions. That year, Foles became the first Eagles quarterback to lead the league in passer rating since Tommy Thompson in 1949. His 19 straight touchdown passes without an interception to start a season were second in NFL history behind future Hall of Famer Peyton Manning, who had 20 in the same year. That's how historic his season was. Using the speed of wide receiver DeSean Jackson and the uncanny versatility of running back LeSean McCoy, Foles lead the Eagles to the NFC East title in Kelly's first year—and a home playoff game against the New Orleans Saints. In the fourth quarter of that game, Foles left the field with the lead, but Kelly left too much time on the clock for Saints quarterback Drew Brees, who—aided by an

Eagles special teams penalty on the kick return and a short field—piloted a comeback win. Westlake beat Westlake in South Philly.

Foles got hurt the following year and then he was gone in 2015 to Jeff Fisher and the dysfunctional Rams. After the one-year stop in Kansas City, Pederson jumped at the chance to bring Foles in to provide backup and guidance to his young quarterback Carson Wentz, and the team promptly put Foles' Pro Bowl photo back up on the long wall of honor at NovaCare. That wall is in a corridor between the locker room and the cafeteria—the players walk past it every day. "I see that Pro Bowl picture," said Fletcher Cox. "I know what that dude could do." Foles' teammates had remained confident in him, despite all the outside doubts—and the seriously bad play he was committing to eternity on tape. In the meeting rooms, going over some of those plays on tape, there were plenty of groans and grumbles at what the offense had been doing—or not doing—in the last three weeks. Players—including Foles himself—agreed with Pederson: Their starting quarterback needed all the game experience he could get. So, Pederson made the decision: Foles would start against the Cowboys.

* * *

It was the wrong decision.

Pederson gave Foles four offensive possessions to do something, anything, that suggested he had regained his rhythm. The four possessions ended like this: Turnover on downs (after a Foles incompletion), punt, Foles interception (right after he fumbled), and punt.

Final book on his afternoon: Foles completed just four passes in 11 attempts for 39 yards. Nate Sudfeld relieved him in the second quarter and wasn't much better. The Eagles did not score in the game.

"It's tough," Pederson said after the game. "Am I concerned? I'm not concerned. I've still got a lot of confidence in our offense. Again, it's not one person or guy. There is enough to go around." Pederson had decided to put Foles on the field with most of the starting offense. Only Jay Ajayi, nursing his sore knees, was made inactive. LeGarrette Blount, Alshon Jeffery, Torrey Smith, Zach Ertz, and the entire starting offensive line all played with Foles. All of them were critically vital to the Eagles' postseason plans and success. And Pederson had exposed all of them to injury in what was clearly a misguided attempt to get Foles some more experience and perhaps rebuild his shaky confidence after the Monday night debacle against the Raiders. But after leading his team to 13 wins and through a myriad of challenges, making all the right moves and decisions along the way, Pederson had finally pushed the wrong button. Playing Foles did not help him. It was a setback. Everybody could see it and feel it.

Was Foles having problems with the bad weather? It was the second straight game where the winds were high and the temperatures were low—wind chill on that sunny South Philly afternoon was just three degrees. If that were the case, if Foles was having problems handling the cold and the wind, that was not a good sign. In two weeks, the Eagles were scheduled to play at home in the divisional round of the playoffs. Pederson was asked a direct question about Foles and the weather. His answer wasn't exactly encouraging to those Eagles fans watching his press conference broadcast live.

"It's hard," he said. "I mean, the winds are howling and swirling on the field. It was difficult to throw a tight spiral." The Raiders' Derek Carr and the Cowboys' Dak Prescott had the same issues, he reminded the press corps. But next month,

Carr and Prescott would be lounging at home, watching the playoffs. Nick Foles didn't have that luxury. The quarterback promised that the last two games were an aberration.

"I feel great and I know what I can do," Foles said. "I know the guys are confident in me. We expect to execute better. This wasn't acceptable. We know how talented we can be. We can do special stuff."

Outside NovaCare, the criticism of Foles was harsh, deafening—and a little bit unfair. One writer who regularly covers the team said, "There is zero confidence in Nick Foles right now to lead this team to a playoff win." Another prominent columnist suggested, "Should there be a quarterback controversy? Should we consider Nate Sudfeld at this point?" Another wrote, "This why the Eagles should have explored emergency options as was suggested weeks ago. Howie Roseman is usually really good about being proactive, and while it may not have made a difference either way, bringing in another quarterback couldn't have made things any worse."

The highly respected Rob Ellis, who writes a column, has a radio show, and appears on TV on Comcast NBC Sports, which has a contract with the Eagles, rejected the Sudfeld talk. But he didn't mince words about Foles: "Nick Foles has looked awful the last two games he's played. Let me rephrase that—Nick Foles has looked avert-your-eyes, cover-your-ears, and crawl-up-into-the-fetal-position bad, these last two games. If his play on January 13, 2018 [the date of the playoff game], at 4:35 PM in any way resembles what we saw vs. the Raiders and Cowboys, despite what the Birds' defense may do, the Eagles will be one and done in the postseason."

Pederson was well aware of the chatter. He heard it firsthand on January 2. With his players getting a much needed respite, Pederson met with the Philly media. The third question

221

stunned him: "Just to be clear, Foles is your starting quarterback going forward for the playoff game?"

"Yes," Pederson replied. It needed no elaboration. But there was a pause in the room as if he was going to provide one. It was a silly thought—Sudfeld replacing Foles at the start of the postseason. But it was out there and Pederson was certain that Foles heard it.

Pederson gave Foles and the team a few days off, including New Year's Day, 2018. New year, he told the team. New season, the playoffs start. Get yourselves ready for a different level of football.

During the bye week, Pederson told me about a conversation he had with Foles—they needed a little heart-to-heart. He told him to focus on football, "eliminate the outside clutter and noise." And he told him that no one was comparing him to Carson Wentz.

"You're not Carson Wentz," Pederson said he told Foles. "You can't be Carson Wentz. But you're a very good Nick Foles." So, Doug Pederson's advice to his quarterback: "Just Go Be Nick."

One important statistical note: If the Eagles had beaten the Cowboys and gone 14–2, Doug Pederson would have owned the best single-season record in franchise history. Still, it's critical to remember just what the Eagles accomplished in a franchise-best-tying 13–3 season. They led the NFL in offensive red-zone efficiency, putting the ball in the end zone 65 percent of the time. The defense led the league in rushing defense, keeping opponents to a staggeringly low 79 yards a game. And they were tied for first place in point differential: 162 points for the season, exactly the same point differential as the New England Patriots. The Eagles and Patriots were the two best teams in football. But one had Nick Foles, the other Tom Brady. And that would be the storyline going into the playoffs.

Final score: Cowboys 6, Eagles 0

Postscript: Nick Foles says he used prayer to find his way back to the game. He told YouVersion, "I kept reading scripture, I kept praying, I kept asking God—and so many of us ask God for signs. We ask God, 'Hey, please just put it on the wall, like, I want to know,' but that's not how it works. He's not always going to do that. He was shaping me. He was bringing me down to my knees…At that moment, through that prayer, He said, 'Hey, just take a step of faith. You're either going to stop playing the game of football and you're going to go onto a different area of your life and I'm going to be with you, I'm going to be the most important thing in your life, or you're going to step back into football and you're going to continue to play and I'm going to be with you every step of the way and you're going to play to glorify me."

Chapter 17

The City of Brotherly Shove

The Falcons at the Eagles
Divisional Round of the Playoffs
Saturday, January 13, 2018 • South Philadelphia

After the postseason bye week, the Eagles woke up to this news: The Atlanta Falcons had been installed as the favorites in the divisional playoff game in Philadelphia—a slap in the face to a team that led its division pretty much wire-to-wire, was 7-1 at home on the season, and was the top seed in the conference. Once again, Philly was the underdog city. No problem—it was in the civic historical DNA.

It all started with Andrew Jackson. In the presidential election of 1832, Jackson, the military hero and populist from Tennessee, campaigned against what he called "the monster"—

the Bank of the United States, which was located down the street from Independence Hall along the old waterfront cobblestone alleyways of Philadelphia. The bank was a semi-private institution reviled by Jackson's constituency, the frontier farmers and herdsmen settling deeper and deeper into the Ohio Valley and along the uncharted territories of Missouri and beyond. The settlers loathed the bank's policies, which they claimed favored the wealthy and the well born. In a speech to Congress after getting elected president, Jackson said the U.S. Bank had failed to establish "a sound and uniform currency." But that bank was one of the city of Philadelphia's most important institutions. It anchored the city's place in the nation's growing finances and power, the hub of its federal activity. Without it, the city might become unmoored from the national consideration. Ignoring pleas from friends of Philly in New York and Washington, D.C., President Jackson vetoed rechartering the Bank. He ordered its deposits removed and the Bank of the United States was dead.

Philadelphia went into an uproar. There was rioting in the streets. The city fathers were beginning to get a complex. A nation which had held Philadelphia in high regard during the struggle for independence and the forming of the Constitution was becoming an afterthought. The federal government had already been relocated to New York—then to Washington—ending in 1800 what renowned city historian E. Digby Baltzell called Philadelphia's "Silver Decade." The Pennsylvania state government left, too—gone to Harrisburg, then just a remote farming village. With the removal of the U.S. Bank deposits to the banks in lower Manhattan, New York became the nation's financial mecca. With the completion of the Erie Canal, trade was already becoming concentrated in the Empire State, leaving the ports along the Philadelphia waterfront scrambling for less and less business. Huddled in its endless neighborhoods of rowhomes, Philadelphia in the late 1800s became more parochial and isolated. Political corruption calcified and became intractable, prospering long after reforms swept into other major American cities. The great newspaper commentator of the early 20th century, H.L. Mencken, described Philadelphia as "a well-lit cemetery."

New York had The Babe and Joltin' Joe and Jackie Robinson breaking baseball's color barrier. It had breathtaking skyscrapers and world-class theater. The Philadelphia Phillies were the last team in the National League to integrate and were the only professional sports team in North America to lose its 10,000th game in the 20th century. And the city fathers refused to approve any building that reached higher than Billy Penn's hat atop City Hall. When the federal government built the interstate highway system connecting Florida to Boston, Philadelphia was made a detour. To this day, there is no direct door-to-door highway from Philadelphia to New York. I remember sitting in an editorial board meeting with businessmen from Moscow, trying to explain to them how to drive from Philly to Manhattan, explaining to them they had to drive through state highways in New Jersey, where there would be stoplights and traffic circles. They were aghast. For nearly 175 years, Philadelphia was an afterthought, a blighted mess to urbanites and farmers, forgotten in the citadels of mass media on both coasts.

The city's Quaker tradition also played a part in Philadelphia's lack of national ambition. In *Puritan Boston and Quaker Philadelphia*, his definitive history of American urban roots, Baltzell argued that Philly was suffocated by the egalitarianism of its core Quaker traditions, which often guided the city's leadership—in the board rooms and before the bar. While the Kennedy family bequeathed Boston a president, an ambassador to England, and U.S. senators, in Philadelphia, Mrs.

Kelly threatened to finance her son's opponent if he were even drafted into the campaign for mayor. Oliver Wendell Holmes Jr. of Boston eagerly served in the Civil War, went to Harvard, and served on the U.S. Supreme Court, where he set down many important laws of the land. In Philadelphia, John Graver Johnson, possessing a legal mind equal to Holmes, reluctantly served with the Union Army, turned down two appointments to the high court, shunned the limelight, and died rich but in obscurity. Philadelphia's inferiority complex, Baltzell argued, was created by historical forces, but partly self-induced. But it lingered and fostered a self-fulfilling regionwide psychosis that could best be summed up in one word—"attytood," a feeling of being underappreciated and misunderstood that permeated the city's sports fans and settled into a shopworn cliché. In Philadelphia, the fans threw snowballs at Santa Claus. They mercilessly booed their hometown teams at the slightest indication of poor play—or worse, lack of hustle. Schmidt, Jaworski, McNabb—they all got the same treatment.

The cycle of bad behavior began to break, however, once the Phillies won the World Series in 2008 and the Eagles started a tradition of winning under Andy Reid. And then when Carson Wentz and Doug Pederson arrived in 2016, the love affair was in full bloom. The city's beloved Birds were on top of the world of pro football, and the fans, traveling coast to coast to support them, were as much a part of the flock as the coaches and players. So, when Vegas made the Falcons the favorites, it was time to unleash the hate on the haters. How dare the national cognoscenti disrespect this football team! It was Andrew Jackson all over again. Go ahead, make us underdogs. But remember, Eagles fans said, you may call Philly the City of Brotherly Love. To us, it's also the City of Brotherly *Shove*.

* * *

National television executives thought so little of the potential draw of this matchup that it was slotted to be the first game on the weekend docket, Saturday afternoon, the least desirable time to attract a large audience—truly an astonishing slap at Philadelphia, the No. 4 media market in the country. And it was all because of Nick Foles. If Wentz were the quarterback, Vegas would have had the Eagles favored by six points and playing in prime time. So, in the last few days leading up to the divisional showdown with the visiting Atlanta Falcons, the city that shoves you back celebrated its current status by embracing the only accessory that truly symbolizes— and embraces—being disrespected: The dog mask. German Shepard, poodle, hound, it didn't matter—the dog mask was suddenly in vogue. And leading the charge on social media were two Eagles linemen who could not be more different and yet so insanely on the same page, as football players and people: Lane Johnson and Chris Long. Both were drafted high in the first round. Both had struggled through different challenges of playing in the NFL. Both were tough, big-hearted, and ready to win a championship—no mattered what it took. Even wearing a dog mask.

"We want to be the underdogs," said Johnson. "Bring it on." The knock on Johnson was, in the words of his teammate and fellow offensive lineman Jason Kelce, that the outside world had convicted him of being "on the juice." In 2016, with rookie Carson Wentz and the Eagles rolling, Johnson was suspended for 10 games for using performance-enhancing drugs. Johnson vigorously defended his honor, saying it was not his fault. But it was his second offense. And strike two in the NFL gets you a 10-game suspension—one step from being banned from pro football. It hurt Johnson's reputation, but it killed the Eagles' season. And he took a lot of the blame. So, coming back in 2017, Johnson was looking for redemption—in and out of his locker room.

At 6-foot-6 and about 320 pounds, Johnson was drafted No. 4 overall in 2013—Chip Kelly's first pick. He had a nasty Texas hill country streak and he was slated to take over at left tackle for Jason Peters. But that just motivated Peters, who refused to relinquish his job. Johnson stayed at right tackle and played with violent intent. He played so well that in 2017—a year he was off the so-called juice—Johnson was selected by the Associated Press as a first-team All-Pro. For the first time in his career, he went to the Pro Bowl. "I love being physical, and I love the brotherhood of offensive linemen," Johnson said. His toughness came from his mother, Ray Ann. She has a degree in criminal justice and her chosen profession is working with death-row inmates at a prison in Riverside, Texas. He brought that life approach north with him to Philadelphia, where he fully embraced the city's attytood. He may have grown up in Texas, but not in Dallas. He went to Groveton High School, outside of Houston. So, he also brought with him an intense dislike of all things Dallas Cowboys. "Just pretty much all my family is from Texas and a lot of them say they're Eagles fans, but I think deep down they root [for Dallas]," Johnson said. "Like even last year, going to the playoffs I heard my grandma in there rooting for Dallas. I said, 'If you want to live to see 75 you better shut your [expletive] up.' Just messing with her."

But even messing with grandma over her potential allegiance to the guys with the star on their helmets gave Johnson instant street cred from Hammonton to Harrisburg. So, when Johnson designed a "Home Dogs Gonna Eat" T-shirt, Eagles fans gobbled up the new craze, especially since Johnson and Long, who was in on the new fashion trend from the beginning, pledged all sales proceeds would go toward Philadelphia's cash-starved public school system.

"We have an extraordinary platform at an extraordinary time," said Long.

While Lane Johnson's mother was a social worker in a prison in Texas, Chris Long came from NFL royalty. His father, Howie Long, was the square-jawed pass rusher from the Oakland Raiders who played like Deacon Jones but looked like John Glenn, complete with the brush-cut Marine Corps hairstyle. He was selected to eight Pro Bowls and was Defensive Player of the Year twice, good enough to land in the Pro Football Hall of Fame and a sweet gig as a broadcaster for Fox Television. His distant relation, Gertrude Ederle, became the first woman to swim the English Channel.

Howie Long had three sons: Howie Jr., Chris, and Kyle. They went to the best schools in Virginia. Chris attended the swanky St. Anne's Belfield School and then the University of Virginia. At both levels, he set records for disrupting first the Friday night and then the Saturday afternoon plans of well-meaning young quarterbacks—all of whom hated to see Chris Long on the schedule. He was taken second overall in the NFL draft by the St. Louis Rams in 2008. He labored with the Rams for eight seasons, earning a solid but unspectacular reputation on the field, but a player that other players just loved to be around—just like his father.

In 2016, Bill Belichick—a big Howie Long fan—signed Chris Long, who promptly registered seven sacks, helping the Patriots win the Super Bowl. About six weeks later, Long—a free agent—got a call from the guy fine-tuning the Eagles' roster, Howie Roseman. The Eagles, Roseman told Long, could use a handful of sacks, at just the right time to make a difference late in the game—the Chris Long specialty. But, more important, Philadelphia was missing a key championship ingredient. They had rising stars, especially at quarterback. But they needed to learn how to win, how to close out games. In short, the Eagles needed a little of the Patriot Way infused into their locker room: "Do your job"—at all costs. That's what the Eagles were missing. And Chris Long could help bring that to Philly. He signed a two-year deal just a few days into free agency.

That's when Long started lobbying for LeGarrette Blount, another castoff from the Patriots' championship team. And he also started bringing his larger-than-life personality to a team looking for somebody to offset the intensity of Fletcher Cox and the amiable Brandon Graham. With multi-colored tattoos up and down his right arm and an unparalleled NFL pedigree, Long fit right in, especially when he and his wife established the Chris Long Foundation, announcing he would donate all his game checks—every penny he made in 2017—to programs supporting educational equity in the inner cities of Boston, Philadelphia, and St. Louis in response to the racial violence sweeping the country. Then, he showed up on the sideline with his hand on the shoulder of Malcolm Jenkins, in solidarity with the social justice cause of African American players across the league. "When a guy donates his whole game check like that," said Jenkins, "that's putting your money where your mouth is." Long's leadership deeply resonated throughout the team and the city. "I like Philly," he said. "It's me." The natural next step from the cause of social justice? Put on a dog mask and bark for the cameras. Whatever this team needed for motivation and inspiration. The Eagles believed in Chris Long back in March. Now, it was time for Chris Long to return the favor.

* * *

The Philadelphia Eagles really had no business beating the Atlanta Falcons in this divisional playoff game. The Falcons had Matt Ryan, a Pro Bowl quarterback who led Atlanta to the NFC championship in 2016. Ryan, known as "Matty Ice" for his coolness under pressure, was a native of the Philadelphia region. He attended William Penn Charter School before going to Boston College—East Coast guy all the way. He got Philly. It didn't scare him. And he had just been in the Super Bowl, handing his team a 28–3 lead on Tom Brady and the Patriots in Super Bowl LI, only to see his coaches and his defense conspire to allow Brady to engineer the greatest comeback in Super Bowl history to win his fifth Lombardi Trophy. The Falcons also had Julio Jones, who often played like a man among boys—a tall, long, tough wide receiver who was nearly impossible to cover one-on-one. He occupied space and bodies and caught anything in his area code. The Falcons had just beaten the Cinderella Rams in Los Angeles in the wild card round, holding young Jared Goff's offense to just 22 minutes of possession and only 13 points. So, Atlanta's defense—under fire most of the year for the shameful meltdown against Brady in the Super Bowl—seemed to be all the way back to a high level of concentration and efficiency under Dan Quinn, the Falcons' head coach who came from the Seattle Seahawks, where he had no problem stifling the Eagles over and over again. "Their defense is playing very fast and very aggressive," said Philadelphia offensive coordinator Frank Reich. "It's a middle-of-the-field, close, zone defense. They don't give you a lot of room to breathe. And they will play man coverage on our wide receivers. We will have to win a lot of one-on-one matchups. They are tightening down on their coverage. That comes from confidence. When you are playing fast and loose and confident like that, you can tighten down and not worry about the consequences. That's the Falcons right now."

And that's what the Eagles coaches were worried about. The Falcons were experienced, a team tempered by the fire of a seriously embarrassing Super Bowl loss and a big road win. Ryan, Jones, and Quinn had their team believing it was all the way back from the bombshell that Brady dropped in their laps. They were playing free, unencumbered by the shame they had been carrying around all year. That was a serious problem for the Eagles, a team coming off some of its worst offensive play in years with a quarterback still trying to find his way.

I texted Doug Pederson on Saturday morning and asked him what advice he gave Nick Foles on Friday night in the team hotel. He told me he had a rare one-on-one meeting with Foles and told him three things:

First, "Let the game come to him."

Second, "Be himself. Do what Nick does."

And third, "Relax and enjoy the moment."

Actually, Pederson was expecting a serious improvement from Foles. On the advice of Jenkins, Johnson, and others on his players council, Pederson decided to line up the first-team defense against the first-team offense in practice—a rarity at any point during the season. Rare because you didn't want anybody getting hurt—players tend to ramp up the competitive level and speed when they know they are being tested at that level by their coaches. Coaches are looking for a certain kind of urgent response—that can often lead to irrational exuberance and a pulled hamstring or tweaked ankle, or worse. But Pederson said, "Let's go for it."

"The practices were intense, real intense," Zach Ertz told me. "The most since the beginning of the year. And I thought Nick responded. I thought it helped him, a lot."

Doug Pederson, carrying the game plan for Atlanta under his right arm, visits with me at my ESPN live position outside the NovaCare Complex two days before his first playoff game as a head coach. (Tony Florkowski)

As the first quarter opened, it didn't look like Pederson's move had any positive impact at all. Foles and the offense started sluggishly. On the Eagles' first offensive drive, running back Jay Ajayi hammered right up the middle and got free for 27 yards. But he lost his handle on the football and the Falcons recovered the fumble at their own 33-yard line. Eleven plays later, Atlanta kicked a field goal for a 3–0 lead. The Eagles were shut out in the first quarter. At the top of the second, Foles managed to cobble together an agonizingly long 14-play drive that put the Eagles on Atlanta's one-yard line. Pederson was so desperate to breathe new life into his offense that he rejected the idea of a game-tying field goal on fourth-and-one. Instead, he called for Blount—right up the gut. (Notice he was not about to put his quarterback in harm's way at the goal line, perhaps thinking about what happened to Wentz. You got a hammer. Use it.) Blount scored. But rookie kicker Jake Elliott pulled the extra point to the left and it caromed off the upright—no good. A fumble, a moribund offense, a missed extra point. The sold-out crowd at Lincoln Financial Field moaned and groaned. It looked like the Eagles were about to suffer the same fate as the Rams did the week before—enough defense to win, just enough offense to lose. And then it got worse.

After scoring a touchdown, the Eagles stopped the Falcons' offense in its tracks at midfield, regaining some semblance of momentum in the half. The Falcons were forced to punt for the second time in the half. But as the punt spiraled to the ground, backup defensive end Bryan Braman, a special teams gunner, lost track of the football and it hit him in the rear end, sparking a mad scramble for the loose ball. The Falcons recovered—both the ball and the momentum in the game. Four plays later, not including two penalties on the Eagles secondary, and Matt Ryan had the Falcons in the end zone— 10–6, Atlanta. The Eagles struck back at the end of the half.

Elliott atoned for his missed extra point with a 53-yard field goal. And Philadelphia went into halftime down a point, 10-9.

* * *

In the halftime locker room, you could predict what Pederson would say. The fumbles, the penalties, not paying attention on a punt—these were outrageous errors for the No. 1 seed in the NFC postseason. It was time to start playing like a 13-3 team again. Let's get our heads in the game—in a hurry.

Didn't happen. The offense remained sluggish, even when Pederson ordered Foles to engage in up-tempo rhythm. Luckily, the defense stoned Ryan for the entire third quarter. Defensive coordinator Jim Schwartz dialed up a linebacker blitz from Nigel Bradham on a third-and-five at the Eagles' 44-yard line. Bradham came screaming at Ryan and wrestled him to the ground—a much needed sack and two-yard loss, forcing another Falcons punt. But whatever the Eagles did with the ball proved to be slow and painful. Two yards here, 12 yards there, no gain, 21 yards on a pass to Alshon Jeffery, no gain by Ajayi—then an incomplete pass on a run-pass option to Ajayi. The Falcons' defense was just too quick to the football. In all, the Eagles managed to go 74 yards, but it took 12 plays and only ate up five minutes and 42 seconds of the clock, resulting in just a 37-yard field goal. Elliott gave the lead back to the Eagles, 12-10.

The fourth quarter brought a carbon copy drive: 14 plays, 80 yards, another Elliott field goal, tacking on three more points. With a 15-10 lead, the Eagles had forced the Falcons' hand: Matt Ryan could not settle for a field goal. He had to get his team into the end zone, something he had not done in the second half. But there were more than six minutes left in the game—more than enough time to solve the puzzle of Schwartz's defense.

Ryan went to work. He hit Julio Jones for seven yards and then 12 yards, sprinkling in a few running plays here and there, putting the ball on the Eagles' 26-yard line at the two-minute warning. On the Eagles' sideline, it was stone-cold silent along the field. But behind the bench, the offensive players were waving towels and pleading with the Eagles fans for more and more volume to disrupt Matty Ice. The fans didn't need any exhortation. I was standing on the Eagles' sideline. My ears were ringing from the deafening screams. But Ryan was unaffected. He hit a seven-yard pass, then unleashed running back Tevin Coleman for 10 more. First-and-goal at the Eagles' nine-yard line. Pederson wasn't sure if his defense could stop Ryan, so he called timeout. In case the Falcons scored, Pederson wanted enough time on the clock to mount a comeback.

Ryan looked for Julio Jones. No go—the Eagles secondary was in lockdown mode. It was too late in the game for the referees to call a ticky-tack penalty. A hold here, a push there—it was all good. Nothing too obvious. But these were the final seconds of the fourth quarter with the game on the line—it's let 'em play time. Ryan unleashed a perfect spiral and Jones collected the football at the Eagles' two-yard line. Fourth-and-goal from the two. Pederson called another timeout—65 seconds and two yards were all that stood between the underdogs and victory.

Everybody on the field and in the stadium and in America knew where Ryan was going with the football—Julio Jones. Covered or uncovered, didn't matter: If Ryan didn't go to Jones, he would be second-guessed for all eternity. Ball snapped. Ryan was in the shotgun. He looked right. There was Julio Jones. He wasn't open. Eagles cornerback Jalen Mills was all over him. No shot—pass incomplete. The Eagles erupted on the sideline. The coaches hugged one another, high-fiving anyone in sight. The stadium sounded like the back end of an aircraft carrier.

The city itself—from the corner bar in Northeast Philly to the swanky living rooms of Blue Bell—came unglued. The Eagles get the ball back. The Falcons throw in an encroachment penalty. Corey Clement, the kid from Glassboro, 10 minutes across the Walt Whitman Bridge connecting South Philadelphia to South Jersey, carries for five yards. How about that? Pederson giving the rookie the responsibility to close the deal, hold onto the football, and get the first down in the most important moment in his coaching career. First down—Nick Foles kneels twice and the Eagles are one win away from the Super Bowl.

* * *

After the game, I ran onto the field to find Long. I wanted to interview him for *SportsCenter*. I could see he was carrying a dog mask. I asked him a question, but he really wasn't in a mood to be serious. So, I just said, "Let's see the dog mask." With the camera rolling, Long put on the mask and began barking—and that video went viral around the globe.

Moments later, Pederson talked about the disrespect his team was shown—a No. 1 seed being an underdog to a No. 6 seed for the first time in NFL history. "I love those guys in the locker room and they don't care," he said. "I don't care. Whether we're three-point underdogs or three-point favorites. They really don't listen to that stuff."

That simply was not true. They heard it loud and clear. And beating the Falcons as home dogs was sweet redemption. But it lasted less than 48 hours. On Monday morning, they woke up to another helping of disrespect. The Minnesota Vikings were coming to Philadelphia to play the Eagles in the NFC Championship Game and they were arriving as favorites—the first time in history that a No. 1 seed was playing at home in a championship game as an underdog.

And the Eagles didn't like it one bit.

"They just did us a big fat favor," said Lane Johnson. "We like being underdogs. Home dogs gotta eat."

One important statistical note: It was the first time the Eagles had won a playoff game scoring 15 or fewer points since 1949. In that year, the Eagles won the NFL Championship Game against the Los Angeles Rams, 14–0.

Final score: Eagles 15, Falcons 10

Postscript: The NFL started selling its own Eagles underdog T-shirts. On Twitter, Johnson and Long called the league out on the fact that the NFL was profiting off their idea. Shortly thereafter, the league announced that 100 percent of the proceeds from its T-shirts would be donated to the Philadelphia school system, too.

Chapter 18

The Team from the
Land of 10,000 Lakes
Visits the City with
10,000 Losses

The Vikings at the Eagles
NFC Championship Game
Sunday, January 21, 2018 • South Philadelphia

Frank Reich, the lanky, stoic football lifer who was serving in his second season as Doug Pederson's adjutant, was bleary-eyed after looking at the film of the Eagles' agonizing win over the Atlanta Falcons. But, as he watched Nick Foles' performance gather steam throughout the game, a smile crept across his wrinkled face. He was thinking that Foles was really beginning to get it, that the up-tempo, no-huddle offense (shades of the days of Chip Kelly) and the run-pass option approach was slowly taking shape. Foles, he thought to himself, is really getting into a rhythm here. He's gaining confidence.

"If you're around Nick, you know he's a great basketball player," Reich said. "He's a point guard. If he was playing basketball on the street he's going to wheel and deal the ball. He's that guy out there. He can throw it behind his back with accuracy. He can give you the no-look pass. He can be looking one way and hit a guy. He has that knack and feel and that's a little bit of the run-pass option game. I think he's very comfortable with that."

Finishing up a five-hour session watching film and breaking down Foles throw by throw, Reich thought that the offense was about to break out. He could feel it.

That was five days before the NFC Championship Game and if Reich had expressed that level of optimism publicly, he almost certainly would have been greeted with skepticism—maybe laughed at. His belief that Foles and the offense were going to break out against the Minnesota Vikings would seem, at best, misplaced optimism—at worst, pie-in-the-sky coachspeak. After all, for most of the game against the Falcons, the Eagles' offense looked like an old jalopy heaving down the road, smoke spitting from the tailpipe. It reached its destination, but it wasn't pretty. There were short stretches of a smooth ride. All game, Foles missed only seven throws. What's more, and maybe most important, the offensive line did not allow much pressure on the quarterback. Foles was only sacked once. But the Eagles only put the ball in the end zone once—at home against a Falcons' defense that was, yes, playing well, but was nowhere near as good as the Minnesota Vikings'.

Under head coach Mike Zimmer, another football lifer who was an acolyte of Bill Parcells, the Vikings finished the 2017 regular season first in total defense and points allowed, giving up a paltry 15.8 points per game. They accomplished that feat with a lethal combination of fast, physical play in their secondary and a four-man pass rush complimented by Zimmer's mind-numbing array of blitzes that would give any quarterback nightmares. "This is the best defense we have faced all year," Reich said. "I think one of the reasons why is that they can get pressure with four and cover with seven. That's a winning formula."

It helped that Zimmer's defense featured perhaps the best defensive player either team possessed, pass rusher Everson Griffen. As soon as Pederson gathered the coaches, he emphasized to them Griffen's ability to single-handedly wreck this game, along with the Eagles' chances of going to the Super Bowl. "You've got to know where he's at at all times," said Reich. "He's definitely earned the respect of being called a game wrecker. It's on his résumé." Griffen's blend of power, speed, finesse, and game smarts made him very difficult to block. Reich knows something about those types of players. He played quarterback for the Buffalo Bills when his teammate was Hall of Fame defensive end Bruce Smith. And the Bills at that time were trying to compete—unsuccessfully—against the New York Giants, who had another Hall of Fame pass rusher, Lawrence Taylor. Griffen was not in that class, but close enough. "We got a lot of film study ahead of us," said Foles.

Considering all that, it is a wonder that Reich had so much quiet confidence that the Eagles' offense was poised to do big things against the Vikings. Once again, the Eagles were three-point underdogs. And once again it became an annoying sideshow in the locker room leading up to the game. Reporter after reporter with camera and notebooks went from locker to locker, looking for the right reaction to the underdog question, something that would propel the narrative of horror and resentment. The Vikings were coming to town after narrowly escaping defeat in the divisional round of the playoffs. In the second half of that game, the Vikings' vaunted defense allowed New Orleans Saints quarterback Drew Brees to march up and down the field at U.S. Bank Stadium in Minneapolis and take the lead. It was only a missed tackle by a rookie defensive back in the final seconds of the game that allowed Vikings quarterback Case Keenum to connect with wide receiver Stefon Diggs for a walkoff touchdown pass to advance to the championship game. And now, Keenum, an NFL journeyman, was coming into South Philly as a favorite to beat the Eagles and go to Super Bowl LII. Time for the dog masks. This time, they were in the locker stalls—a featured part of the wardrobe, right next to the helmets, the shoulder pads, and the photos of the kids. It was a running joke among the players—that they would get asked about it, feed into the myth, and allow the resentment storyline to occupy the evening news loop while they prepared to play a football game. But deep down, many of them felt that they were just better than the Vikings and that they had a chance—to use Reich's words—to do "something special." Running backs coach Duce Staley quietly told one of his former Eagles teammates, "This won't be close. We are going to dominate them."

* * *

And that's exactly what happened. The Vikings scored first— their only touchdown of the game. After Keenum hit tight end Kyle Rudolph on a 25-yard touchdown pass, on the very next Vikings drive, Eagles slot cornerback Patrick Robinson picked off Keenum at midfield and weaved his way through traffic for 50 yards and a game-tying touchdown, igniting South Philly like it was the Fourth of July. "You feed off that," said Pederson. "That put the crowd into it and we started to feed off that energy." Keenum's pass landed in Patrick's arms because Chris Long, coming from the left side, crossed right in front of the face of the Vikings quarterback and ripped into his throwing arm just as he let go of the football.

On their next possession, the Vikings went three-and-out, punting back to the Eagles' offense. And that's when Foles started to play point guard, distributing the football to Jay Ajayi and LeGarrette Blount, to Alshon Jeffery and Zach Ertz: Read the linebacker on run-pass options, find the open man when keeping the football. He kept it six times—hitting on five of six passes. And he gave it to the running back six times—finally allowing Blount to seize the moment off right tackle for an 11-yard touchdown run. In all, a perfect 12-play drive that gave the Eagles the lead for good and seemed to demoralize the Vikings' defense.

Now it was breakout time. Pederson could sense that Zimmer had no answer for them. The Eagles just had too many options and the ball was coming out too quickly. The Vikings' four-man rush was neutralized—by the time they got a sniff of Foles, the ball was out. And if Minnesota overplayed the pass, Foles slid the football into the belly of the back and watched the Eagles' offensive line dance to the second level of the defense, looking for linebackers and safeties to pancake. On third-and-10 from the Eagles' 47-yard line, Foles dropped back, avoided the rush, and waited for Jeffery to get open in the middle of the field. He let it fly and Jeffery collected it near the goal line—53-yard touchdown, and the rout was on.

In the halftime locker room, there was a quiet confidence. Pederson knew exactly what he was going to do after the second-half kickoff. The Eagles were going to get the ball first. And Pederson was going to go for the throat. In the third quarter, he wasted no time. He had Foles throwing the football. Foles hit two straight. Then a handoff to Ajayi. Then another

Foles pass. Then Ajayi. After a one-yard loss on a Blount run, Foles connected with Torrey Smith for seven. Foles looked like Magic Johnson. No gain was longer than 10 yards, but every play worked to perfection, overwhelming the Vikings' defense, which seemed locked in a jail cell of its own defensive design. Then, on first down from the Vikings' 41-yard line, Pederson got into Foles ear: "Flea-flicker."

* * *

No coach at any point in Nick Foles' playing career—not in Pop Warner, high school, or college—had ever uttered the words "flea-flicker" to him in a game. And here he was going to try to pull it off on the biggest stage thus far in his life.

Anybody who's ever played football in their backyard knows what a flea-flicker is. But very few know where it came from. The flea-flicker play in American football was invented by Bob Zuppke, the head football coach at the University of Illinois. Zuppke, who won four national titles at Illinois (1914, 1919, 1923, and 1927), was a bit of a Renaissance man. When he wasn't coaching football, he liked to paint and draw. "Football and art are very much alike," Zuppke once said. One day, Zuppke was tinkering with a pad and paper and created the deception of the flea-flicker play. The exact date is unknown, but it was sometime in the 1930s. He called it a flea-flicker, he said, "because the play evokes the quick action of a dog getting rid of fleas."

The flea-flicker is simply designed to fool the defense into thinking the play being executed is a run, not a pass. The ball is snapped to the quarterback, who hands it to the running back, who dives toward the line like he's going to slice up the middle of the defense. But at precisely the moment he nears the line of scrimmage, the running back turns and tosses the ball back to quarterback, who unleashes the football almost immediately down the field. It's important to get rid of it quickly, because if the running back has done a good job of selling his dubious intentions, the defensive backs have been sucked in and allowed a receiver to leak into the deep secondary.

Normally, a defense doesn't suspect that a team leading in the NFC Championship Game is going to unleash a trick play like the flea-flicker, especially on first down. There are many possible bad results. When you have a big lead at home, why take the risk? But remember Pederson's mantra: Stay aggressive. He was hearing his father, Gordon, in his ear. "I actually told myself before the game to maintain the aggressiveness in the ballgame," Pederson said. He was talking to himself? "Yes, stay aggressive," he said. "I told myself that, just to make sure it sunk in. It was, 'You win, you keep playing. You lose, you go home.' I didn't want to go home and regret any decision." So, he called a flea-flicker. Jason Kelce snapped the ball to Foles, who handed it to rookie running back Corey Clement, who lashed toward Kelce's rear end, then turned and tossed it back to Foles, who threw deep down the left sideline. The ball sailed right in front of the Vikings' bench. The look on Zimmer's face was one of horror. Eagles wide receiver Torrey Smith was beyond his defense, angling toward the yellow pylon at the left front edge of the end zone. The ball came down out of the sky like Zeus himself had thrown a perfect thunderbolt. Smith gathered it over his left shoulder and tapped his feet in bounds.

The touchdown catch sparked a range of emotions. Smith knelt in prolonged prayer to honor his brother, Tevin, who died in a motorcycle crash in 2012. Foles was engulfed in teammates. In the owners' box, Jeffrey Lurie hugged his son.

And Lincoln Financial Field sounded like somebody had just tapped a keg party for 69,596 people.

On the sideline, Carson Wentz, his left leg in that bulky brace, was standing next to backup quarterback Nate Sudfeld. During the wild celebration, they just looked at one another in disbelief—almost as if to say that may have been the best pass Foles or any Eagles quarterback had thrown in a generation of football in Philadelphia.

"It was unreal," Wentz told me. "Right away, I looked at Nate and said, 'That's the dime of the year right there.'" A dime is the coin of the realm in football parlance for a perfectly thrown pass for a touchdown. "It was just an unbelievable throw," he said.

Pederson said he had planned to use a flea-flicker at some point in the game against the Vikings. "You just don't pull it out of thin air," he said. "There's got to be a reason for running a gadget play. And I just felt that as I game-planned for the Vikings and studied our formations and some of things that we did, I felt like we'd get an opportunity to at least attempt the play. It was just great execution. The protection was there. Nick did a great job of stepping up, then sliding to his right. And then the catch. Great catch by Torrey." Smith's catch gave the Eagles a 31–7 lead at the outset of the third quarter, breaking the Vikings' will on defense. On Philadelphia's very next possession, Foles cobbled together a 12-play drive that traveled 92 yards, culminating in a five-yard touchdown pass to Jeffery. Foles' final numbers were astounding. He missed on only seven throws—in his first championship game appearance. Think about that for a moment. He completed over 70 percent of his passes against the No. 1 defense in the NFL in the biggest game of his life. His offense converted on 71 percent of its third downs—a number in Tom Brady's neighborhood.

And the Eagles' defense put on a clinic. The battle of wits between Eagles defensive coordinator Jim Schwartz and Vikings offensive guru Pat Shurmur was totally one-sided. The Vikings gained just 5.4 yards per pass play. They were stoned in the running game: Just 70 yards. Keenum was constantly on the run. Schwartz toyed with the Vikings' pass protection like a jungle cat pawing its prey. Keenum was sacked once and picked twice. The second interception came late in the fourth quarter by defensive swingman Corey Graham. And the citywide celebration was on: Philadelphia, the city where the baseball team lost 10,000 games and that had been denied a Lombardi Trophy, was going back to the Super Bowl—with Nick Foles at quarterback.

On the sideline after the game, the coach and the quarterback had a moment to themselves just before time expired. "I just told him I was so proud of him," said Pederson. "The way he played tonight and the way he's played the last couple of weeks. I told him how proud I am of him and I loved him."

For Pederson, the feeling of going to the Super Bowl with this team was surreal. "It's a tremendous feeling but it just hasn't sunk in," he said. "And the thing about this team is all the adversity and negativity and everything that surrounds the team, these guys don't listen to that. I don't listen to that." Pederson knew that the next negative episode would be impossible to ignore: His upstart Eagles team was about to play in the Super Bowl against the New England Patriots, with a coach on his way to the Hall of Fame and a quarterback considered the greatest of all time. "We've got our work cut out for us," he said.

When he gathered the team in the locker room for a wild celebration that featured owner Jeffrey Lurie leading the dance floor, Pederson didn't have much to say. "We're going to the

After winning the NFC Championship Game, Nick Foles is introduced to Eagles fans by Terry Bradshaw as Carson Wentz watches with mixed emotions.

stinkin' Super Bowl," he said. Yes, it's true—Pederson doesn't cuss. And he had one more message for them: "We're not done yet. We still have some unfinished business. We're going to pack our bags and go to Minneapolis."

While Pederson and the rest of the players were getting dressed and talking with reporters in the postgame locker room, Foles snuck out and I followed him. I figured that Foles was the story and I needed to follow it—and him.

We walked together down the long concrete corridor under Lincoln Financial Field that connects the home and visiting locker rooms, weaving our way through hundreds of family members waiting for Eagles players to emerge, ready to go home and celebrate. Foles was going to make two stops: The X-ray room and the Vikings' locker room to see Case Keenum, his former teammate in St. Louis.

He ducked in to get an X-ray on his ribs. It was just a precaution and it later turned out to be nothing. Just sore ribs from a shot he had taken in the second quarter. As he came out of the X-ray room elated that nothing was wrong, Keenum was standing there. I was the only reporter watching these two friends embrace and talk after the biggest game of their lives. Two Jeff Fisher castoffs who had just played in the NFC Championship Game.

Keenum was in awe of what Foles had just pulled off—totally dominating the No. 1 defense in the NFL.

"Nobody's done that to our defense all year long, dude," Keenum said. Foles, humble as always, said it was a team effort. And then he wished his old friend good luck and disappeared into wave after wave of family and friends.

One important statistical note: The most encouraging development of the Eagles' offensive breakout was that Nick Foles finally got the deep ball going. According to ESPN Stats & Information, Foles entered the game with one completion on 12 attempts on throws 20 yards or more downfield—and was 0-of-10 since becoming the Eagles' starter. Against the Vikings, Foles missed on his first two deep throws, but he went 4-of-4 afterward with two touchdown passes.

Final score: Eagles 38, Vikings 7

Postscript I: The Vikings missed out on a chance to become the first team in NFL history to play the Super Bowl in their home stadium. Despite the fact that fans would have to endure a week of festivities leading up to the big game in subzero teamperatures, the NFL put Super Bowl LII in Minneapolis as a reward for building a new home for the Vikings, U.S. Bank Stadium. Now, against the Patriots, the Eagles would represent the NFC. "We would've loved to play in the Super Bowl if it was in China," said Mike Zimmer.

Postscript II: The Eagles were quickly made a six-point underdog to the Patriots. And why wouldn't they be? It was Nick Foles vs. Tom Brady. But on the day after the NFC Championship Game, I got a call from the producer of the Carmen & Jurko *show, a popular talk show on the ESPN affiliate in Chicago. I like to appear on that show because the co-host is John Jurkovic, who is one of my favorite former NFL players—smart, funny, knows the game. And he has a lot of listeners in a big broadcast market.*

As a reporter, I'm loathe to predict games. But Jurko got me at a weak moment. I just blurted it out in the middle of the conversation.

"Hey, John," I said, "the Eagles are going to win the game. They're going to beat the Patriots. They're going to win the Super Bowl."

It was the first time that I made that prediction anywhere on the air. Now, I had to convince myself it was true.

PART V

"NOBODY LIKES US AND WE DON'T CARE"

Chapter 19

"We Got This"

Monday: The Tale of Three Quarterbacks

Carson Wentz hobbled through a long corridor in the Xcel Energy Center, the arena where the Minnesota Wild of the NHL play their home games in downtown St. Paul. He had just arrived on the team bus with the rest of the Philadelphia Eagles for something the NFL calls Opening Night, a nationally televised question-and-answer session starring the two Super Bowl participants and the 4,000 members of the international media credentialed to cover the biggest sporting event on the planet. It was a frozen tundra outside, so the NFL wisely decided Opening Night would happen indoors.

While the Patriots went first, answering questions on the floor of the arena, Wentz had agreed to do his only one-on-one interview of Super Bowl week with me on ESPN in a suite on a second floor. So, I was getting an exclusive opportunity to find out what has been really going on inside the mind of Carson Wentz as he watched Nick Foles moondance into the national spotlight and finish the job Wentz had started: Taking his football team to the brink of its first Super Bowl title.

Wentz walked with a heavy brace on his surgically repaired left knee. It was a sad sight, really. This guy is a total stallion on the football field. To see him sidelined like this made me feel for him. But Wentz seemed in good spirits. He sat down across from me. But when I looked into his eyes, I got worried. His face quickly revealed that this interview was going to be more obligation than revelation—until I asked him how difficult it has been to "recalibrate" his life in professional football since the injury on December 10. Then, he began to open up.

"Well, it was definitely tough, being hurt and missing time was without a doubt tough for me personally," he said.

"What was tough about it?' I asked.

"It was tough knowing that I won't be running out on the field again with my teammates this year," he said. "It's just tough. I mean, during the week and everything, the preparation, it's all fine. But, you know, really on Sundays when the offense runs out for the first time, and I'm not with them…" His voice trailed off. "It's just tough. They're running out to the field and I'm limping off to the side with a crutch or with crutches or a cane or whatever it may be, it's definitely not easy. I can tell you that."

This was the first time Carson Wentz was expressing this. And the fact that he was doing it on the first day his team was in Minneapolis, meeting the media for Super Bowl week, was very revealing. It was almost like he wanted to get it off his chest, relieve his mind of the pain he'd been keeping bottled up for weeks. He had done an interview session with reporters at his locker before leaving Philadelphia, but this was the first time he had really unburdened his soul. Of course, I tried to be gentle. I had been interviewing him since the day he was drafted. He had always been accessible to me—with time and candor—throughout his short career. When a player gives of his time like that, it's only natural that you wish him success. Seeing him now in this setting, I wanted to make sure that I asked the questions in a way that got him to reveal as much as possible while respecting that he was still a very young man—my children are all older than he is—and something terrible had happened to snuff out a big dream of his. However, I did want to dig deeper into why he made the decision to dive into the end zone in Los Angeles, rather than throw the football away and live for another play. It was only first down, I reminded him.

"There was a lane and I got in," he said. "I made the dive and just kind of got hit kind of fluky in a weird way from both sides and obviously it was a pretty hard hit on my leg."

This was the first time Wentz confirmed that it was the hit on his leg that caused the torn knee ligament and other damage. Previously, it had been suggested that Wentz got hurt before he was hit, while he was scrambling toward the Rams' goal line. "It was tough," he said. "I didn't exactly know at the time until I started walking to the huddle. And I knew something was unstable in there." Wentz finished the drive. But then quickly hobbled to the sideline and decided he needed to get the knee checked out. "Unfortunately, it was what I feared," he said. "But that's what you sign up for when you play this game."

* * *

Tom Brady, playing in his eighth Super Bowl, hopped on stage at the Xcel Energy Center, wearing a glove on his right hand to hide the nasty five-inch gash between his thumb and forefinger that he suffered in practice prior to beating the Jacksonville Jaguars in the AFC Championship Game. It happened during a handoff in practice and Brady was still reluctant to reveal any details about it. He didn't have to. He was Tom Brady, the greatest quarterback to play the game. At this point in his career, Brady is always playing off the sheet music of history. Everything he does goes in the record books. And winning the AFC title with his hand mangled up only added to the myth, putting his name on the list of legends who went to work with a glove on one hand: Tom Brady, Michael Jackson, Luke Skywalker. You look at Brady with that glove and you ask, "Wonder where he's hiding the lightsaber?"

Brady was sitting next to Nick Foles. Sitting opposite the two quarterbacks were the two defensive captains, Malcolm Jenkins of the Eagles and Devin McCourty of the Patriots. Between the players sat Chris Rose of Fox, and me. This little Q&A was happening between the Patriots' interview session and the one for the Eagles—on live TV. And Brady, of course, was the center of attention. He was in full TB12 mode, calm and measured—seen that, done that. I reminded him that the last time the Eagles visited Foxboro, Jenkins intercepted Brady and returned it for a touchdown. I asked him what he learned about the Eagles' defense from that play. He said, "Don't throw it to Malcolm." And the 5,000 or so people watching in the hockey arena had their first collective laugh of the night.

* * *

Nick Foles, sitting just to Brady's right, looked like he had just met the Wizard of Oz. Of the three quarterbacks of the night, he faced the most pressure. And he sounded like it. Afterward I was asked about how Foles did and I replied on a radio show that "he sounded a little nervous." After all, I said, he was sitting next to Brady—the guy with five Super Bowl rings—and this was his first nationally televised Super Bowl event. What's more, when Rose asked Foles a question, his answer was drowned out by boos from the crowd, mostly Vikings fans who just watched their team get waxed by Philly in the NFC Championship Game. (So much for Minnesota Nice.) So, it was perfectly natural for Foles to feel a tad out of sorts. Nevertheless, my use of the word "nervous" went viral on social media and I was asked about it for the next three days. The truth is it was the only time all week that I detected any nerves at all in Foles. As the week progressed and the team returned to the practice field, all I heard from coaches and players was that Foles was calm and confident.

Tuesday: Chasing Super Bowl Ghosts

Donovan McNabb is the all-time leading passer in Eagles franchise history. But in his only appearance in a Super Bowl, he threw three interceptions. The Eagles lost to the Patriots in Super Bowl XXXIX, 24–21. In that game, McNabb completed just 59 percent of his passes. Another would-be interception was nullified by a Patriots penalty and a fumble was overturned on replay challenge by his head coach Andy Reid. It was classic McNabb—moments of brilliance overshadowed by insurmountable mistakes. After the game, the Eagles would be suspicious that the Patriots had been spying on their defensive signals during the game—a charge that would get fresh legs after the late U.S. senator Arlen Specter of Pennsylvania made a federal case of it. The Patriots would be later fined for illegally videotaping the New York Jets' defensive coaches on the sideline during a game at old Giants Stadium. The controversy was known as Spygate. There were further unfounded charges that the Patriots spied on the St. Louis Rams during their Saturday night walkthrough at the Superdome in New Orleans prior to Super Bowl XXXVI.

At the Radisson Blu hotel at the Mall of America, the Eagles' home during Super Bowl LII, the level of security was suffocating. Federal uniformed troops with assault rifles guarded the entrance—as a counterterrorism measure. But it went way beyond that. Federal, state, and municipal police—uniformed and in plain clothes—were layered on top of mall security, hotel security, NFL security, and the Eagles' own security led by the incomparable Dom DiSandro, who suffered no fools—gladly or otherwise. The Patriots' hotel, the JW Marriott, was on the opposite end of the mall. Their security was just as tight. It was the first time anyone could remember the two Super Bowl teams staying in the same connected building. Both teams were extraordinarily cautious: No prying eyes.

The second-leading passer in Eagles history is Ron Jaworski. In the Eagles' first appearance in a Super Bowl, Jaworski also threw three interceptions. The Eagles lost to the Raiders in Super Bowl XV, 27-10. That Philly team was coached by the legendary Dick Vermeil, who would later guide the St. Louis Rams with Kurt Warner to a Super Bowl title. But after losing Super Bowl XV, Vermeil would admit that he had his Eagles team too tight, too overworked.

And the McNabb team that lost to the Patriots in the Super Bowl seemed to suffer the same fate. "That team was tight," said Eagles insider Dave Spadaro, who started working for *Eagles Digest* almost the day he left college about 30 years ago. "This team? Loose. That's the major difference between the two teams."

But, for this team against the Patriots, it all came down to the Eagles' quarterback. Foles needed to have faith in himself. He needed to be comfortable with his own ability and the game plan, believe and trust those around him—and protect the football, at all costs. That's a big ask for any quarterback, but especially a guy playing in his first Super Bowl against a guy playing in his eighth. If Foles threw three interceptions like Jaws and McNabb had, the rest of the team might as well not bother showing up—the Eagles would lose their third Super Bowl. No team had beaten the Patriots under Belichick in the playoffs while losing the turnover battle—he was 16-0.

On my weekly segment with Mike Missanelli on his drive-time radio show on the ESPN affiliate, 97.5 FM The Fanatic in Philly—it's called "Tuesdays with Sal"—I was asked to give my prediction for Super Bowl LII.

"If Nick Foles doesn't throw an interception," I said to Mike, "the Eagles will beat the Patriots."

Wednesday: Happy Birthday to the Guy Who Should Have Been NFL Coach of the Year

Jeannie Pederson was with her husband, Doug, all day—she wanted to make sure she was there to help him celebrate his 50th birthday. I asked him what he wanted to do on his birthday. "Coach practice," he said. Wednesday during the Super Bowl week is always the first day the two teams get their first full day of practice. The Eagles' practice at the University of Minnesota was spirited and up-tempo. Foles was a little rusty. That's to be expected. It was a new venue and the team had not put in a full practice in six days. During that time, the routine of media availabilities, of attending meetings, of being sequestered in a hotel for most of the day (or wandering around the Mall of America because it was just too cold to venture outside) is mind-numbing. The practice field is a refuge—especially for the coaches. "Practice is where we feel like we're doing what we like to do," said Pederson. It's just the nature of the game and the men who play it and coach it. They fall into their routine, speak a language to one another that only they understand, react to each other on a visceral level that is both challenging and rewarding. And there is the promise of ice cream.

During the season, on the Saturday nights before the game, Pederson would always end his speech to the team with a video highlight reel and say, "We got some ice cream." There may be a variety for the players, but always Häagen-Dazs vanilla for him. "One time, we didn't have his favorite ice cream and he got really pissed," said Brandon Graham. "I'm not kidding. He doesn't get mad at much of anything. But he was not happy that they didn't have his favorite vanilla ice cream."

So, to the celebrate the 50th birthday of Douglas Irving Pederson, his players gave him Häagen-Dazs vanilla ice cream.

What they should have done was demanded a recount of the Coach of the Year balloting done by the media. The final tally was 35 votes for Sean McVay of the Los Angeles Rams; 11 for Mike Zimmer of the Vikings; two for Doug Marrone of Jacksonville; and one each for the two Super Bowl coaches, Belichick and Pederson. (I don't have a vote.)

The vote was taken before the postseason—a policy that is absurd and should be changed. But even given that fact, McVay getting 35 votes and Pederson getting one is silly. Pederson went to Los Angeles on December 10 and beat McVay's Rams—without Carson Wentz in the fourth quarter. And, during the regular season, there was no significant statistical category in which the Rams were that much better than the Eagles, who finished with the best record in the NFC—after losing their two special teams captains, starting left tackle, starting middle linebacker, and starting quarterback to injury.

The insult of that lopsided vote annoyed the Eagles players and further fueled their resentment—no one gave them respect. "I don't know how that vote could come out like that," said Fletcher Cox. "It's a joke. Nobody takes Doug seriously. We do. In here, we do. And that's all that counts."

Pederson could not care less. I showed him the final vote tally and he blew it off. "I'm in the Super Bowl," he said. "That's all that matters. I'm with these players in this game. That's all I care about."

Several weeks later, NFL head coaches were asked to vote for their Coach of the Year. Pederson voted for McVay—that's the type of guy he is.

Thursday: Scouting the Super Bowl Referees

On the last day the players were available to reporters, I found out that the Eagles coaches had made a special point of emphasis of scouting the referee team for Super Bowl LII, which would be led by Gene Steratore, one of the most respected referees in the history of pro football.

"I don't want to give everything away," Eagles linebacker Nigel Bradham told me, "but obviously we have to play clean. We are looking at what they like to call, what they are looking for, and help us play a cleaner game—so we know what to expect from them and what they expect from us."

The extra emphasis on studying the referees came after the AFC Championship Game in Foxboro. The Patriots were penalized just 10 yards. The Jaguars were victimized by 98 penalty yards, including two pass interference calls on the Jacksonville secondary that flipped the field into the Patriots' favor. During the regular season, the Jaguars were flagged for a league-low five pass interference calls. This is not to suggest there was any conspiracy. It's just that Belichick and Brady understand the role that penalties play in all games, but especially in the postseason. Penalties can instantly change field position as quickly as a muffed punt, a big special teams return, or a long pass play. Coming into the Super Bowl, in nine playoff losses under Belichick, the Patriots' opponents won the battle of field position seven times, according to ESPN Stats & Information. "Brady will take five or six shots down the field and see if he can connect on the throw or get a flag," said one retired defensive back who faced Brady many times in his career. "We were always taught not to get baited into a bad call when Brady puts it up for grabs deep. That's just smart football on his part."

Eagles rookie defensive back Rasul Douglas said that secondary coach Corey Undlin "definitely emphasized PI [pass interference] and defensive holding. So, we just want to get our head back, play the ball, not the man, because the referee lets you play if you are looking at the ball."

During the regular season, Steratore's crews called 43 penalties for either defensive pass interference, defensive holding, or illegal contact—fifth-highest in the league. Four of the other six on his all-star referee crew for Super Bowl LII were on regular season crews that were in the top half of the league in those kinds of penalties.

Linebacker Mychal Kendricks said that the Eagles were shown video clips of calls by all the Super Bowl referees, but also clips of what happened to Jacksonville in the AFC Championship Game.

"Some of those were questionable," he told me. "Some of those were blatant. Sometimes the refs will let you get away with that. Sometimes refs will let you play. Sometimes they will call a tight game. So, we will have to assess as we go. But it's always good to be prepared, know what we're going to be up against."

* * *

When the team took the practice field at the University of Minnesota, Foles looked completely at ease. The early week jitters and rustiness were gone. The ball came out his right hand like it was on a string. "I wish you could see how Carson and Nick are working together in the quarterback room," Frank Reich said. "It's really something. Like they're two brothers. I've really never seen anything like it in all my days of football. It's special. It's something I will always remember. Carson is so invested in Nick's success. And Nick is really benefitting from that confidence in him. Remember, they are really two different guys. Wired different. Nick is all cool. Carson's wound tight. He wants to know what's in the game plan at all times. Wants to have input. 'Put this in, put that in.' Nick's just, 'What you got for me this week?' So, they have played off one another's personalities perfectly this week."

Wentz said he and Foles get along because they are both "faith-based individuals." They like to put a Bible verse on the wall in the quarterback room to help them find a theme for the week. The most recent one, he said, was Luke 2:11, which reads, "Today in the town of David a Savior has been born to you; he is the Messiah, the Lord."

"It's about Jesus coming, about Jesus' birth in Bethlehem," Wentz said.

"So," I replied, "St. Nick to the rescue? Nick Foles coming to the rescue? Is that what you're telling me?"

"Uh, no, man." He laughed. "You're reaching there. You're reaching there."

In attendance at Friday's practice was Pederson's old coach in Green Bay, Mike Holmgren. "The team loves Doug, you can see that," Holmgren said. "He's not like me. He's much more laid back. More like Brett." That would be Brett Favre, who won Super Bowl XXXI with the Packers. Holmgren was the head coach. Pederson was the backup quarterback. Favre was going to be in Minneapolis on Saturday for a speaking engagement. Pederson invited him to address the team on Saturday morning.

Friday: What Patriots Mystique?

Malcolm Jenkins put it best. "We're not playing against mystique, we're playing against the New England Patriots," he said. "There's no need for us to talk about who they are. If I make this game about them, I'm in trouble."

LeGarrette Blount, who won the Super Bowl with New England the previous season, told his new teammates how to act. "Ain't no friends," he said. "Ain't no homies. None of that." Chris Long, who was on that Patriots championship team with Blount, said, "It's got nothing to do with history, one way or the other."

During Super Bowl week, the players were seen at night having dinner together or with their families at Manny's, the most popular steakhouse in downtown Minneapolis. On Friday night, Deion Sanders was there. So were Archie, Peyton, and Eli Manning—in a private room. The Eagles' defensive backs had their own room for a quiet get-together. As I walked through the main dining room, I stopped to say hello to Mychal

Kendricks, who was sitting with a family member having a private dinner. I shook his hand and said, "Hey, Mychal, good luck." He said, "Don't worry. We good. We got this."

Saturday: Faking the Super Bowl

On the day before the Super Bowl, the Eagles were in fact worried about the New England Patriots. Remember, as part of the mystery surrounding Belichick, there was always the concern that he had somebody watching, somebody "spying" on your plays, your players, your intentions. Spying in football goes back decades—football coaches are among the most suspicious people in any profession. One tenet of game preparation is to keep it secret from the opponent. Practices are closed. Players are told to keep reporters at bay and answer in pablum-laced platitudes. "Loose lips sink ships"—and all that. But the Patriots were actually caught illegally "spying" on the Jets and punished by the league. And there was that unfounded allegation of taping the Rams at a Super Bowl 17 years ago that remained an unresolved spooky episode in Patriots lore.

So, at the Radisson Blu hotel on Saturday morning, in their usual morning meeting, Doug Pederson told Frank Reich to fake it. That's right—he told him to run dummy plays. He was worried about the Patriots spying. Pederson instructed Reich not to have Sunday's game plan a part of the walkthrough when they got to U.S. Bank Stadium.

Reich told me, "He just said to me, 'Just make it up.' I said, 'Just make it up?' 'Yeah,' he said. 'Just make it up.' So, that's what I did. I just made up any play I wanted to. And it's funny, too, because when we got to the stadium, our security guys were looking around and we couldn't identify a random guy sitting up in the stands. So, they went after him, yelling at him, and he just disappeared."

One important statistical note: Going into Super Bowl LII against the Patriots, Nick Foles had completed 75 percent of his pass attempts in his first three postseason games, with five touchdown passes and no interceptions. He is the only player in NFL history to record a quarterback rating of 100 or more in each of his first three career postseason games.

Postscript: Both Jeffrey Lurie and Robert Kraft, two Boston Brahmins, wanted to buy the New England Patriots in 1994. Kraft beat Lurie to it, purchasing the Patriots on January 21, 1994, for $175 million. Less than four months later, Lurie bought the Philadelphia Eagles for $185 million.

According to Forbes, *the Eagles are now worth $2.65 billion. The Patriots are worth $3.7 billion.*

Since 1994, the Patriots rank first in the NFL in winning percentage; the Eagles are sixth. The Patriots ranked first in playoff appearances; the Eagles are fifth. The Patriots had five Super Bowl titles. The Eagles had none.

Chapter 20

In the Nick of Time

The Eagles at the Patriots
Super Bowl LII
Sunday, February 4, 2018 • Minneapolis, Minnesota

The Eagles coaches weren't lying. Nick Foles was sharp. In the opening drive of his first Super Bowl, with Tom Brady sitting on the Patriots' bench watching on the state-of-the-art video screen above, Foles connected on his first three passes and five of his first six. Doug Pederson said he was going to dial up some easy throws for Foles right at the beginning of the game to get him some confidence and establish a rhythm. It worked perfectly. He sprinkled in four runs by LeGarrette Blount and Jay Ajayi, giving the left side of the Patriots' defensive line a steady mouthful of right tackle Lane Johnson's brutish intentions. After 12 plays, the Eagles had the ball on the New England seven-yard line. But then Foles missed on two short throws and the Eagles had to settle for a 25-yard field goal from Jake Elliott to take a 3–0 lead. Still, the message had been sent and heard—Foles was for real.

"I had normal nerves," said Foles. "I had butterflies. But I felt calm at the beginning of the game. I think the big thing that helped me is that I knew I didn't have to be Superman."

Superman was already playing for the other team. And he answered quickly. Brady connected on five of his first seven passes and faced a third-and-four on the Eagles' eight-yard line. He could not cash in, either. And the Patriots settled for a game-tying field goal. Though it was a 3–3 score, the results of the two drives were alarming for the two defensive coordinators, Matt Patricia of the Patriots and Jim Schwartz of the Eagles: If they didn't find a way to ramp up the pressure, this game was going to belong to the two quarterbacks. Of course, any sane coach going into a big game like this would never think that trading punches with the greatest quarterback of all time, a guy who had five championship rings, was the best way to win his first Super Bowl title. "To get into a shootout with that guy from the other team," said Eagles tight end Zach Ertz, "is probably not ideal for anyone, ever."

* * *

On the night before the Super Bowl, I met with head coach Doug Pederson in the lobby of the Eagles' team hotel. Security was extremely tight. I was the only reporter allowed in the hotel that night. Indeed, I was the only reporter allowed in the Eagles' hotel all week long. But even I had been kicked out on Friday morning—it was time to batten down the hatches, and I was out. So, asking to go back into the team hotel, to interview Pederson the night before the game, was a major request. When Pederson said yes, I decided to bring him a little gift—for all the time and exclusive access he had granted me and my ESPN crews all season long. As luck would have it, there was a shop in the Mall of America—near the Patriots' hotel—that only sold Häagen-Dazs ice cream. I walked down to the shop and bought a pint of vanilla. While Brian Franey set up the camera crew for the interview, we had no place to put the ice cream in the lobby of the hotel. So, Brian came up with the idea of just placing it outside near the valet stand. It was five degrees outside—perfect, as long as we cleared it with the bomb squad securing the perimeter of the hotel.

Pederson loved the gesture. His wife, Jeannie, told me later that he immediately went back to his room and ate the ice cream. "He didn't share any with you?" I asked. "Not one spoonful," she said, laughing.

On Saturday night, Pederson talked to the team—just him. He asked Brett Favre to address the team on Saturday morning, but not Saturday night. "That time is for me," he said. "I like to be in front of the team, give them my final thoughts on the game. We show a video of the highlights of the last week's game and then it's just me and the team." It's how his father, Gordon, did it. No gimmicks, no guests, just the coach and his players.

Pederson reminded his team of how they got to the Super Bowl, the struggle through injuries, the resilience, the love for one another. He used the word "love" freely. There was real love between these men. Foles said it all the time, too. "I think it's important that we understand the journey," Pederson said. "Just kind of reflect on it a little bit." He also reminded them to just go out and have fun. He wanted them to approach the game with a looseness that had allowed them to brush off the criticism and naysayers that had made the Eagles underdogs throughout the postseason. If resentment is the rocket fuel of American success, as Frank Sinatra once said, then the hallmark of this team was resisting the dark side of that resentment. "I want them to enjoy the moment," Pederson said. "I am."

What about Foles? What would he tell his quarterback?

"Emotions are gonna run high," Pederson told him. "I know that." He told Foles he wanted him to "start fast, relax, and just get into the game plan a little bit right from the start. Just start managing the team and you'll be all right. Just manage and control the emotions."

Pederson was thinking about his late father on Saturday night. "I wish he was here," he said. But Gordon Pederson *was* there, a voice inside his son's head: "Stay aggressive."

* * *

On the Eagles' next drive of the first quarter, Blount beat a path free of the line of scrimmage and ran for 36 yards on his old team. I was watching Blount the whole way on his run. You could see his smile through the facemask. He was enjoying the contact, savoring the moment and the irony of what he was accomplishing against his former teammates. He gave Foles a nice cushion of field position. Philadelphia had first-and-10 on the Patriots' 34-yard line. Conventional wisdom says the Eagles should continue running the ball. The Eagles' offensive line was pushing the Patriots' front seven all over the field. The hole Blount rambled through was big enough for a pack of rhinos. Besides, if the Eagles continued to run the ball and ate up the clock, that would keep Brady on the bench—the only place he could not beat them.

Instead, Pederson ordered up a bomb to Alshon Jeffery. Right before kickoff, Bill Belichick had benched one of his best defensive backs, Malcolm Butler. Butler, who played nearly every snap in the AFC Championship Game, was near tears on the sideline. But that's where the Eagles wanted him—on the sideline. And Pederson decided to try to make the Patriots pay. Foles unleashed a perfect parabola that traveled 34 yards. Jeffery twisted his body behind two defenders and caught the game's first touchdown.

"They had a good design and kept us off balance," said Belichick.

The Patriots' offensive coordinator, Josh McDaniels, also had a good design. On most downs, McDaniels knew that Schwartz was only prepared to commit four rushers to attacking Brady in the pocket. That would give Brady enough time to unleash those trademark quick crossing routes in the middle of the field—the same passes that Eli Manning threw on December 17 at MetLife Stadium, lighting up the Eagles' defense. Of course, Brady and McDaniels reviewed what Manning did on that Sunday afternoon. But they didn't have to study it for very long. Brady already had a history of success against Schwartz and his brand of defense. There were three games over the last 10 seasons where Brady faced Jim Schwartz, while Schwartz was with the Lions and Bills. Twice Brady threw for at least 300 yards with four touchdown passes and no interceptions, according to ESPN Stats & Information. In all, Brady faced a Schwartz defense seven times and encountered very little turbulence. In those games, he threw 11 touchdown passes and only one pick—and that interception came when Schwartz was the Tennessee Titans' defensive coordinator in 2002. Translation: Schwartz had not forced Brady to throw an interception for 15 years. Most NFL careers last less than four years.

On Super Bowl Sunday, it was definitely a pick-your-poison situation. "The coaching staff made a decision that we were not going to blitz Brady, because he's seen everything and that could have really opened the field up for big plays," one defensive player said after the game. But Brady was hitting on the big plays anyway. He hit running back James White for 15 yards. He hit wide receiver Chris Hogan for 28 yards. Then he cashed in on a 50-yard catch and run to wide receiver Danny Amendola, who was chased by cornerback Ronald Darby to no avail. The Eagles were getting two servings of poison—they were not getting to Brady and their secondary could not handle the shifty, angling, smallish backs and wide receivers that Brady had in his arsenal. Hogan and Amendola are not exactly Jerry Rice and Randy Moss—but they were being made to look like it. It's a good thing for the Eagles that Patriots kicker Stephen Gostkowski, who is usually Mr. Automatic, hit the left upright with a 26-yard field-goal attempt (the snap was mishandled) or they would have been in real trouble early in the game.

Then the Eagles' defense finally made a play. Brady connected with wide receiver Brandin Cooks on his first big-yardage crossing route. The ball and Cooks and Eagles safety Malcolm Jenkins arrived pretty much at the same time 23 yards down the field. Cooks caught the football, but by the time he saw Jenkins, it was too late. Jenkins leveled Cooks—a clean knockout. Cooks was sprawled on the turf for a long time. The play-by-play of the game simply states: "NE-B.Cooks was injured during the play. He is Out." Cooks never returned—not even to the sideline to watch. "It was tough," said Brady. "Very disappointing to lose him. He was a great player for us. But that's football."

"Turning point for our defense, no doubt," said Brandon Graham. "Now it was our job to get to Brady."

With Cooks out, McDaniels tried to switch it up. On a third-and-five on the Eagles' 35-yard-line, he called a reverse pass to Brady, who was wide open in the right flat. But Amendola, who had executed the play perfectly earlier in the year by dropping the ball right into Brady's arms, tossed the football a little too high. It bounced off the tips of Brady's gloved hands, an embarrassing moment for the legendary quarterback. But it really wasn't his fault. It was a catchable ball, certainly. But Brady runs like, well, a 40-year-old man. And his right hand was still healing. If the ball had been two feet lower, Brady could have used his body to gather the pass and run through the open field for a huge gain. Instead, the Patriots were forced to go for it on fourth down. And Brady's pass to tight end Rob Gronkowski, who would finish the first half with just one catch, was broken up by Jalen Mills and Corey Graham.

"We just missed a lot of opportunities in the first half," Belichick said.

After Danny Amendola's pass slides off his fingertips, Tom Brady gets a sarcastic grin and an earful from Eagles safety Malcolm Jenkins.

Immediately, Foles and Pederson went to work on the shorter field. After Foles connected with Ertz and Jeffery, he handed the ball to Blount, who bull-rushed for 21 yards and a touchdown. The two-point conversion was no good. But the Eagles already had a 15–3 lead. Since 2012, when Patricia became defensive coordinator of the Patriots, New England has led the league during those six seasons by allowing just 12 points on average in the first half. The Eagles had already eclipsed that.

They would need much, much more. Brady put together a quick five-play drive that resulted in a field goal. And then the only interception by either quarterback was thrown by Foles. Still eschewing the running game, which was working effectively and could have kept Brady off the field, Pederson had Foles in the shotgun, throwing the football late in the second quarter, up 15–6. Foles heaved the football down the sideline in front of the Eagles' bench and it caromed off Jeffery and into the arms of Patriots defensive back Duron Harmon. Brady had the ball back on his own 10-yard line. A defensive holding call on Mills on a third-and-six from the Patriots' 14-yard line kept the New England drive alive. It was the first penalty on the Eagles secondary. They had learned their lessons from the coaching staff. But this flag came at the worst possible time. No flag, and the Patriots have to punt. No flag, and the Eagles get the ball back with a 12-point lead and a chance to tack on more points before halftime. No flag, and perhaps Pederson does not call for The Philly Special—the boldest play-call in Super Bowl history.

But there was a penalty and Brady still had the football in his hands. Four plays later, he threw a dart to Hogan, who beat Mills on a 43-yard run to the Eagles' 26-yard line. The field and the momentum had been flipped.

What's more, the Eagles' defense was not laying a finger on Brady. "We had no answer for the guy," said Jenkins. "After Cooks went out, I thought there was a shot we would have the upper hand. No way. Dude's too good." Brady could sense the Eagles were looking for another pass play—and why not? He couldn't miss. So, he handed the ball to running back James White, who sliced his way 26 yards. It was the longest run from scrimmage the Patriots would have all game. White settled into the end zone and it was 15-12 with two minutes and four seconds left in the half.

The real problem, one the entire worldwide audience could see, was the Eagles were not getting any kind of pressure on Brady. All across the country, chat rooms of Eagles fans were lit up complaining that Schwartz was not blitzing enough, not finding a way to get to Brady. The New York Giants did it in their two Super Bowl wins over Brady. Why can't the Eagles? If Philly lost, Schwartz might have to check himself into the Federal Witness Protection Program.

And it wasn't like the problem of getting to Brady was some kind of big secret or inside baseball. It had been widely discussed and dissected leading up to the game—from coaches and players to every football writer breaking down the matchup. Consider this, from *Sports Illustrated:* "Schwartz must operate under the assumption that his defensive line, which has been the NFL's best all season long, can disrupt Brady on its own. If it doesn't, Philly's chances of success shrink significantly." The magazine's prediction for the game: Patriots 27, Eagles 16.

The only way to really explain this is to dig deep into the football analysis of how to get to Brady. Put simply, you can't attack him from the edges. It must come up the middle, in his face. And quickly. A breakdown compiled by ESPN Stats & Information found that in the two previous postseasons, Brady completed only 26 percent of his passes when the pressure on him came from the interior of the defensive line. When the pressure is exerted on him from outside the tackles, his completion percentage more than doubles, to 59 percent. Schwartz was well aware of this. That's why he hoped to get pressure on Brady with his best interior defensive lineman, Fletcher Cox, the Pro Bowl tackle who was the highest-paid player on the team for a reason. But the Patriots' sage offensive line coach, Dante Scarnecchia, was determined to nullify Cox at all costs. Schwartz had a countermove—put the team's top sack producer, defensive end Brandon Graham, inside at left defensive tackle, alongside Chris Long. So, from left to right, it would look like this: Long, Graham, Cox, and rookie Derek Barnett. It was Schwartz's so called NASCAR look, mimicking what Giants defensive coordinator Steve Spagnuolo did against Brady when New York beat New England in Super Bowl XLII. In that game, Brady was pressured 14 times and sacked five times. But that Giants team had defensive end Michael Strahan, the future Hall of Famer and all-time single-season NFL sack leader. The Eagles did not have that kind of pass-rushing talent. Thus, the Eagles were getting close to Brady but not close enough—a development that was painfully obvious to everybody watching the game in the stands, at home, in the press box, and both sidelines.

It is against this backdrop that the Eagles got the ball back on their own 30-yard line with one more chance to score before halftime. Foles hit Ertz for seven yards. After an incompletion came the biggest play of the game, a 55-yard catch and run by rookie running back Corey Clement. Patriots safety Patrick Chung, a former Eagle, hunted Clement down on the eight-yard line. If he doesn't, Clement would have sliced into the end zone. Pederson left Clement on the field for two more runs—but he didn't get in. Why Pederson didn't use Blount in this spot to ram his way through the Patriots' defense is a decision that gets lost in the history of what happened next.

Foles and Jeffery could not connect on third down. It was fourth-and-one. Pederson could have easily called for the field-goal unit to run onto the field. Three more points and the Eagles would have had a six-point lead, 18–12—something Brady could quickly erase with a touchdown. And the Eagles were not doing anything to stop Brady. Pederson had to go for it on fourth down, do or die, right now, with 38 seconds left on the clock.

It was time to dial up the play the Eagles had been practicing, the play they had been dying to use, the play they had never had the temerity to try in a game, a play they thought would work, a play that could be a monumental embarrassment, a play that if it failed on fourth down, the Eagles would get no points and Tom Brady would start the second half with the football and the momentum in a close game, a play that if it failed would be considered the reason why the Eagles lost the Super Bowl, a play that if it worked would assign Doug Pederson, Nick Foles, and the Eagles to a place in football history that would have no equal.

It was time for The Philly Special.

One important statistical note: The Eagles knew they were going to be in a close game against the Patriots in this Super Bowl. According to ESPN Stats & Information, each of the Patriots' previous seven Super Bowls under Belichick and Brady were decided by six points or fewer. In fact, the total margin of victory in those seven games was just 25 points. There have been eight individual Super Bowls decided by *more* than 26 points.

Postscript: After the game, Bill Belichick was asked if Malcolm Butler was benched for disciplinary reasons. "No," he replied. "We put the best players out there and the game plan out there because we thought it'd be the best to win." The Patriots players were told of Butler's benching just moments before taking the field.

Philly Special

"You want to know what was going through my mind?" Doug Pederson said. "I'll either be the biggest genius or the biggest goat."

It was fourth down. The Eagles had the ball on the one-yard line—38 seconds to go in the first half of Super Bowl LII. Doug Pederson called his team's last timeout. Foles knew that Pederson was going to do something that nobody does on fourth down on the one-yard line in the Super Bowl in the first half: Go for it.

Listening to Pederson on the other end of his headset were his offensive assistant coaches up in the booth and Foles, whose helmet is equipped with a tiny earphone so the quarterback can hear the play-call. As he jogged over to the sideline to meet with Pederson, Foles could hear his coach decide right then and there that the Eagles would defy conventional wisdom. Pederson was not going to send in the field-goal unit. He was not going to settle for three points.

"We're going for it right here," Pederson said into his headset. "We're going for it right here."

Before the game, both Pederson and Foles had been wired with hidden microphones by NFL Films, which has been recording for posterity all 52 Super Bowls. Putting microphones on NFL coaches and players was the brainchild of the founders of NFL Films, Ed Sabol and his son, Steve, who was also a painter and abstract artist. He liked to quote the French impressionist painter Cezanne, who said, "All art is selected detail." Steve Sabol once said to me, "All journalism is selected detail." Finding those details in a game—"the moment where poetry happens," he said—is what Sabol was looking for. For decades, his films helped promote and mythologize pro football, allowing the sport to overtake baseball as America's national obsession. The moment of poetry in this game turned out to be one of the most shocking and pivotal in any game in pro football history. And it was all caught on an open mic.

As Foles makes his way to Pederson, the coach is staring at his laminated play-call sheet, the so-called Denny's Menu, because it's so big it looks like the supersized menu the waitress hands you at Denny's. In other words, you could order anything you want—a veritable smorgasbord of items from eggs to pancakes or any combination of both. Same for Pederson—he had a half-dozen fourth-and-one plays he could have called in this instance: A dive up the middle by LeGarrette Blount, a jump pass to tight end Zach Ertz, a quarterback rollout known as "sprint right option," the play that resulted in the famous fingertip catch by San Francisco 49ers wide receiver

Dwight Clark on a pass from Joe Montana to beat the Dallas Cowboys on January 10, 1982, at Candlestick Park—a moment of poetry that the Sabols immortalized and seared into the collective consciousness of American sports fans. Any of those plays on fourth-and-goal from the one-yard line would have been perfectly acceptable. Maybe not an immortal moment, but certainly a workable option. But Foles and Pederson were thinking big. To erase history, you gotta make a little history, right?

Foles said four words to Pederson: "You want Philly Philly?"

For a split second, Pederson responded with a puzzled look on his face. That was not the name of any play he remembered or the team had practiced. But then he knew exactly what Foles meant. Pederson stared at his quarterback, as if to say to himself, "Did I just hear that right? Did I just hear him call for that play in his first Super Bowl, on the goal line? On fourth down? Against the New England stinkin' Patriots and their head coach, who has seen just about everything there is to see on a football field—the guy who was playing chess while everybody else was playing checkers?" But Pederson knew his defense was doing very little to stonewall Tom Brady and his team needed a touchdown, not a field goal, to keep pace. And if you're going to be the best, you gotta beat the best, right?

So, Pederson said just four words back to Foles, four words that set his team on a course for football immortality: "Yeah, let's do it."

The trick play was actually called "Philly Special." But it's a play that did not originate anywhere near the city of Philadelphia. The play that was about to unfold and shock a worldwide television audience was actually invented at a small military academy in rural South Carolina.

* * *

The play that eventually became The Philly Special was invented by Hunter Spivey. In the fall of 2011, Spivey was the head football coach at Gray Military Academy, a Christian prep school that specializes in giving troubled kids a second chance. Spivey, a tightly wired, tough-talking coach, cared deeply about his mission at Gray. The main tenet of the school: "In order to succeed in life, a structured process is necessary and in the same way the students in Gray Military Academy are guided under professionals that help them to be physically and mentally strong to clear any kind of teenage problems and learn life skills to face future challenges." Football played a major role in that learning process. Hunter Spivey fit right in. He was caring, but he was not afraid to coach up his players real hard. What's more, because he was a teacher at heart, Spivey liked to tinker with plays. It was his way to challenge his young student-athletes to focus on the game, which, of course, was a way of getting them to focus on life—the Gray mission at its core.

He called the play the Spivey Special. Initially, it was a two-point conversion designed to deceive the defense: A direct snap to a running back, who moved to his left and tossed the ball on a reverse to a tight end or wide receiver, who would look for the quarterback wandering aimlessly but cleverly as a decoy into the end zone. If timed right, the quarterback would be wide open.

Spivey—who played quarterback at tiny Newberry College in South Carolina and married his college sweetheart, Amy, a cheerleader and tennis player—ran the play a handful of times in the fall of 2011 at Gray. It worked every time. On one try, however, his quarterback, Cameron Cox, dropped the football in the end zone. "It was the perfect little play,"

Spivey said. "The quarterback was always open." Spivey liked to say to anyone who would listen. And why not? It was his play and it worked. And like all high school coaches, Spivey was looking for a job at the next level. He liked the Friday night lights of high school football. But he wanted to take that next step: Coach on Saturday afternoons. He wanted to be a college coach.

The following year, Spivey was attending a clinic for high school and college coaches in Greenville, South Carolina. One morning, he tracked down Chad Morris, then the offensive coordinator at Clemson University. Spivey is a big Clemson fan. He was chasing his dream job. On the mezzanine level of the conference center at a high-top cocktail table out in the hallway, the two coaches talked football. The conversation quickly pivoted to his pet project, The Spivey Special. At the time, Morris was coaching the multi-talented quarterback Tajh Boyd at Clemson. Morris was intrigued by Spivey's play. It was perfect for Boyd, who could pass, run, and catch the football with explosiveness and grace. Spivey pulled a pen out of his pocket. "We are sitting at one of those tables outside a conference room and I just grabbed a paper napkin on the table and started drawing it," said Spivey. "And he said, 'I like that one.'"

The conversation lasted all of 10 minutes. Morris grabbed the napkin with Spivey's play drawn on it and put it in his pocket and was gone. There is an old saying: "Amateurs borrow. Professionals steal."

At Clemson, Tajh Boyd ran the play like he'd been practicing it since he was eight years old. In 2012, leading Georgia Tech by five points in the fourth quarter, Morris called for the Spivey Special. The ball went on a direct snap to the Clemson running back, who tossed it to a receiver, who threw it to

Boyd, who was wide open in the end zone. The successful two-point conversion put the Clemson Tigers up by seven.

At the time, Spivey was tailgating at another college football game, South Carolina against Georgia. But being a Clemson fan, he was watching television in the parking lot when Boyd caught the pass on the play he created. "Boyd was wide open," he said. "Just like I drew it up."

Against Ohio State in the Orange Bowl, Morris called the play again. Now, on the national stage, it was renamed "The Clemson Special."

Patriots offensive coordinator Josh McDaniels, the son of a legendary football coach who won state high school championships in Ohio, has always been an astute follower of the game at every level and he picked up the Clemson Special from watching tape of Ohio State. One of the great ironies of the history of the play is that the Patriots ran it against the Eagles in 2015—in Foxboro—resulting in a 36-yard gain. On that play, wide receiver Danny Amendola, after getting the reverse toss from running back James White, dropped the pass right in Brady's arms. Brady caught it easily and ran free in the open field.

But most of the Eagles' current coaching staff was not involved in that 2015 game. It did not resurface in Philadelphia until one of the team's offensive assistants, Taylor Press, mentioned that he was on the Chicago Bears' staff when that team ran the Clemson Special against the Minnesota Vikings in 2017. But that was a Week 17 play, at a time when the Bears were going nowhere. The quarterback who was wide open and grabbed the pass for a touchdown was Matt Barkley, as it turns out, who once played for the Eagles. As far as anyone can tell, the play had only been run those two times at the professional level. And it had never been tried on fourth down. On the goal line. In the Super Bowl.

The Eagles had thought of using the play, which they now called The Philly Special, against the Minnesota Vikings at Lincoln Financial Field two weeks earlier in the NFC Championship Game. But Reich thought that since the Bears had just run it against Minnesota, Vikings defensive coordinator George Edwards would easily decode the Eagles' intentions and decipher the play pretty quickly—as soon as Corey Clement lined up behind center and Foles slid to his right.

Pederson and Reich were so suspicious of giving the play away that they only practiced it in the hotel ballroom in Minneapolis. The practices at the University of Minnesota stadium during the week had too many observers—the pool reporters, the national broadcasters, family members, visiting coaches, and guests. And even though the pool report disseminated to the international media every day had to be approved by Pederson himself, he didn't want to take a chance. Better to keep it a secret. Pederson said he knew the play would work. "I trust my instincts," he said. "And I trust my players."

Frank Reich could not believe that Pederson called the play. "We all just looked at each other like, 'Did he just call that?'" Reich said.

Before Foles and the Eagles ran back onto the field, Patriots running back Dion Lewis, who was also mic'd up by NFL Films, said, "That's a no-brainer. He ain't gonna go for it." Scott Zolak, the former Patriots quarterback who does color commentary on the team's radio broadcast, said on the air, "You gotta take the three here, right?"

* * *

Foles went into the huddle and told his teammates, "Philly Special. Philly Special, ready?"

This breakdown of the play was written by Ryan Doyal, a film study assistant working on the *NFL Matchup* show. It is technical but brilliant. I thought it should be committed to history in this book:

> From the Patriots' one-yard line, the Eagles lined up in a three-by-one "Tight Bunch" formation in "12" personnel: Coachspeak for one running back, two tight ends (hence the name "12"), and two wide receivers. Nick Foles was in a pistol formation, which calls for the quarterback to line up in front of the running back, in this case Corey Clement. As Foles gestured and called out dummy audibles, moving down the right side of the line of scrimmage, center Jason Kelce snapped the ball directly to Clement. Foles, trying to appear as though this was just a Wildcat run by Clement, stood up straight at the snap and assumed the position of a player trying to get out of the way and let the play happen. (Foles yelled "Kill, kill," to further try to confuse the Patriots.) After this pause, which caused Patriots pass rusher Eric Lee to ignore Foles and run right by him, Foles suddenly slid out into the flat, completely uncovered and wide open.

> The reason this worked so well is that Clement and the Eagles' offensive line all showed outside zone or "stretch" technique in the opposite direction, forcing the defense to defend that play, moving to its right. It is one of the Eagles' most common running plays, with the only wrinkle here being that it was a direct

snap. Tight end Trey Burton was aligned widest in the three-man bunch tight to the formation. At the snap, he pivoted and ran behind Clement in the opposite direction, commonly done by teams who are running an option play. Clement flipped the ball to Burton as they passed one another. After a few steps, Burton lobbed up an easy pass to a wide-open Foles in the end zone, who calmly caught the fourth-and-goal pass like it was in practice on a Wednesday in Week 4 of the regular season.

The result: A simple bootleg play, one of the oldest and most widely used plays in the NFL, with the added spice of the direct snap and run from Clement creating the misdirection and Burton coming back the other way, instead of the quarterback keeping the ball the entire time and creating the misdirection by faking it to the running back. In the NFL, most of the trick play-calls are rooted in something that's more commonly run, and this is no exception.

The Patriots were in their short yardage or "goal line" defense. On the field were their five best run-stopping players: Five defensive linemen (Malcolm Brown, Lawrence Guy, Adam Butler, Ricky-Jean Francois, and Trey Flowers); two linebackers (Eric Lee and Kyle Van Noy); and four defensive backs (Patrick Chung, Devin McCourty, Eric Rowe, and Stephon Gilmore). They were in man-to-man coverage, which was distorted immediately at the direct snap to Clement, because every single player at the line of scrimmage read the play as a run and played their run gaps aggressively. No one picked up Nick Foles, and the backfield misdirection worked as planned, causing the

Patriots to think the play was a run and thus garbling their man-coverage responsibilities.

"We worked on it many, many times," said Foles. "For me, the defensive end was a little wider than I anticipated and we practiced. So, I really needed to sell that I'm not doing anything, not involved in the play."

The sales job by Foles makes the play work—otherwise, the Patriots might have abandoned their total sellout to Clement running with the football directly up the middle. It was also critical that Clement's toss to Burton happen quickly. That meant the Patriots' defenders, who were all moving slightly

Eagles quarterback Nick Foles collects tight end Trey Burton's Philly Special pass and waltzes into the end zone and pro football immortality.

to their right because the Eagles' offensive line was moving left as if to block for Clement, did not have enough to time to go back the other way. Still, once Foles moved alone beyond the line of scrimmage and across the goal line and into the end zone, somebody from the Patriots' defense should have picked him up. So, even though the Eagles did everything they could to make the play successful, it only worked in the end because the Patriots were complicit. An assignment was blown. Somebody should have covered Foles. Making matters more complicated was that Philadelphia wide receivers Torrey Smith and Alshon Jeffery were crossing deep in the middle of the end zone, occupying space and the attention of the Patriots secondary. Perhaps if the experienced and shifty Malcolm Butler had been on the field, the play would have been deciphered in time and foiled. We will never know.

Burton's pass on the run worked because he played quarterback at Venice High School in Florida, throwing for 18 touchdowns and only one interception. His first football jersey as a kid was the Miami Dolphins' No. 13 for Hall of Fame quarterback Dan Marino. Burton prays at the same Connect Church with Wentz and Ertz. His connection with Foles was a pass and catch heard from Minneapolis to Manhattan.

"I was so excited—quarterback going out on a route," said Foles. "Trey's pass was just so on-the-money perfect. I just had to look it in. Catch it. That's what I'm thinking right there. Catch the football. That's probably better than it looked any time we practiced it."

Hunter Spivey, who now coaches high school football in Valdosta, Georgia, was at home, watching Super Bowl LII with his wife, Amy, and their three sons, Zion, Jagger, and Levi. "It was kind of surreal, watching that happen on TV—that's my play," he said. "Looking at where it came from, on a dadgum little practice field in South Carolina. It's just a blessing for me to be part of it. I've been playing and coaching ball my whole life. It maybe hasn't hit me as hard as it should. I can't tell you how many texts I've gotten. How many calls. And everyone keeps telling me, 'Hey, they just ran your play in the Super Bowl, you should probably be jacked up about it.' Well, I've got more plays, too. Funny thing is, that's not the best play I've got."

One important statistical note: The Eagles wound up 2-of-2 on fourth down against the Patriots in Super Bowl LII. Including the playoffs, Doug Pederson would end the 2017–18 season converting 20-of-29 on fourth-down calls, 3-of-3 in the postseason. Unheard of.

Postscript: It was the first time in Super Bowl history that a tight end had thrown a touchdown pass and a quarterback had caught one.

Chapter 22

The Road to Victory Goes Through Tom Brady

The Eagles at the Patriots
Super Bowl LII
Sunday, February 4, 2018 • Minneapolis, Minnesota

The shock and awe of The Philly Special swept through social media, sports blogs, talk shows coast to coast, and beyond, and nearly extinguished any excitement about Justin Timberlake, whose halftime choreography was brilliant and mesmerizing—but not nearly as brilliant and mesmerizing as the football choreography Tom Brady was about to unleash on the unsuspecting Philadelphia Eagles.

Down 10 points as he jogged onto the U.S. Bank Stadium field at the beginning of the third quarter, Brady was practicing his own brand of mindfulness, breathing easy, staying in the moment, the moment he had trained for all year and conquered many times before. There is a reason why Bill Belichick ends every training camp practice with a sprint drill up and down a long hill behind Gillette Stadium: So his team will be in shape to fight to the last tick on the clock. In his career, Brady had authored 58 second-half comeback wins—including the greatest of all, erasing Atlanta's 25-point lead in the final minutes of Super Bowl LI. In that game, Brady was 21-of-27 and generated 336 yards of offense in the second half alone. In this game, Brady knew he was getting the football to start the second half—the Eagles were kicking off. And he knew that he had all but ignored his most lethal option, tight end Rob Gronkowski. Brady had thrown 23 passes in the first half and only targeted Gronk five times—for one catch and nine harmless yards. Jim Schwartz had decided that Gronkowski was not going to be the reason why the Eagles lost Super Bowl LII, so he blanketed him with a combination of double and bracket coverages. Jalen Mills, the rangy cornerback in his second season, got a few shots at Gronk. Ronald Darby was thrown into the mix, but it was clear he was overmatched— mentally and physically on this day. So, Schwartz got safety Rodney McLeod into the act. McLeod was smart and tough, but not quick enough to hang with Gronk full time. Nevertheless, it was all hands on deck—stop Gronk, who at 6-foot-6 and 265 pounds, rumbles through the secondary like a runaway grizzly but has the balance of a ballerina and the soft, reliable hands of a fireman catching a baby from a burning building. Make no mistake, there will be a bronze bust of Gronk in Canton one day. So, the instructions all week from Schwartz were simple: Grab and pull, push and hold—do anything you could get away with. Keep the flags to a minimum, but keep Gronk out of the end zone, at all costs.

That lasted all of two minutes and 45 seconds into the second half.

Brady saw that Schwartz had another body on Gronkowski to start the third quarter—backup safety Corey Graham. The switch was odd, considering that Gronkowski had been neutralized in the first half. Brady decided to put the new guy to the test. Graham failed, miserably. On second-and-10 from the Patriots' 25-yard line, Brady hit Gronk near midfield—25-yard gain. Next play, Brady to Gronk and 24 more yards. Three plays later on a third-and-six, Brady found his tight end again for 14 yards. Then, all that remained was a touchdown—a simple five-yarder to Gronkowski that cut the Eagles' lead to three points, 22–19. Good-bye to feeling special about The Philly Special. Hello to the horror of being sliced up by Tom Brady. Someone in the press box said, "Hey, the Falcons had a 25-point lead. The Eagles only led by 10. Not enough against Tommy Boy." Forget boy. Brady had just put the Eagles on notice: Time to man up.

That man remained Nick Foles. At some point, Philadelphia's defense knew it would have to stop Brady. But, for now, Foles had to find a way to keep pace with No. 12. The Eagles' offensive coaches had been telling themselves that they had enough talent to match up with the Patriots secondary. Without Malcolm Butler on the field, the Eagles thought they could continue to find open seams deep down the middle. "There's nobody on that defense that scares us," Eagles running backs coach Duce Staley said earlier in the week to his friends. "We will have success." There was no greater time for that confidence to bubble to the surface than right now. It was time for a little run-pass option, again. And it kept the Patriots' defense on its heels. Foles handed it to Blount for four yards. After two pass attempts, Blount again, for five, then 10. Another incompletion, then Jay Ajayi for nine more. Foles hit Zach Ertz on the right side of the New England defense—a nice chunk of 14 yards. After an incomplete pass intended for Trey Burton, it was third-and-six on the Patriots' 22-yard line. No way the Eagles wanted to settle for a field goal here. Pederson feared Brady would quickly erase the lead and take the momentum, perhaps for good. So, he put Foles in the shotgun and called for Clement to run a flag route to the left corner of the end zone. But the Patriots secondary had the boundary side of the pass route choked off. Clement had no choice but to slice right down the middle of the end zone. Foles just let the football fly, a kind of sidearm throw. The ball landed right in Clement's arms, like somebody tossed a loaf of bread across the grocery aisle into your checkout basket. Clement tapped his feet, one down, two down. Gene Steratore reviewed the catch. After consulting with the league's vice president of officiating, Al Riveron, up in the referees' booth, Steratore ruled that Clement never lost control of the football. The ball moved but—both Riveron and Steratore ruled—Clement maintained control: Touchdown. Foles went back to the sideline and on his NFL Films mic can be heard saying to Pederson, "Not how we drew it up, but it worked." Clement had to adjust the route to the inside. Foles had to read his subtle movement and deliver a perfect pass on a near line drive, putting it beyond the Patriots' defenders, right into Clement's belly. You could easily make the argument that Foles' throw was one of the most astonishing—and difficult—in Super Bowl history. Clement said adjusting the route was "just a natural instinct." On the sideline, the coaches marveled at Clement's intuitive behavior for a rookie in such a big moment. "That kid amazes me," said Staley.

Foles said one thing he refused to do was succumb to the pressure of the game as it was unfolding. That would have doomed him, he said. "I wasn't worrying about the scoreboard," Foles said. "I wasn't trying to worry about what Brady was doing. Or the time in the game. I just tried to stay relaxed and play our game, execute the game plan. Relax and execute the game plan. I was just playing ball."

Problem is, so was Tom Brady.

* * *

I've known Tom Brady his whole career. I was there in the lobby of the Patriots' team hotel in New Orleans in January 2002, when Brady came down from a meeting with Bill Belichick, who had just decided that veteran Drew Bledsoe would be benched in favor of Brady in Super Bowl XXXVI. Bledsoe had been hurt on a hit by Jets linebacker Mo Lewis earlier in the season. In relief, Brady was brilliant. But Bledsoe was on the mend, forcing Belichick to choose. The decision to start Brady over Bledsoe was fraught with danger—Belichick risked losing his locker room. Veterans are not supposed to lose their jobs to injury. But Brady's uncanny leadership and toughness had impressed Belichick. When Brady came down from the meeting first, I knew that he was the choice to take on the St. Louis Rams in that Super Bowl, the first one after the horrible tragedy of 9/11. Belichick's decision paid off: Brady led a drive in the final minutes and the Patriots won, 20–17, inspiring owner Bob Kraft to say on national television, "Today, we are all Patriots." I still get chills thinking about that moment. For me personally, I had made an emotional connection to Brady and the Patriots because I had lost many close friends in the South Tower of the World Trade Center, including a childhood buddy who lived down the block from me, David Leistman. David and I spent many, many hours playing football together. He perished along with many of his colleagues at Cantor Fitzgerald. But that game stuck with me for another reason: As a professional, the Patriots' win taught me a valuable lesson about Tom Brady—never, ever count him out. Ever.

With about seven minutes left in the third quarter, the Patriots' offense went back to work. They quickly got a gift. On a second-and-nine play, the Eagles committed their second defensive penalty, holding on linebacker Mychal Kendricks. Brady put the offense into machine mode. Scat back Dion Lewis, also a former Eagle, kept the Philadelphia defense close to the line of scrimmage with three runs. As soon as the Eagles secondary got too close, Brady backed them off, hitting Hogan, Amendola, and then Hogan again. Brady took the offense on a little 75-yard walkabout in seven plays, taking just three minutes and 55 seconds. It was masterful. And painful. New England was back within three points, down only 29–26. What Foles accomplished in a minor miracle of timing and intuition, Brady answered with matter-of-fact precision. On the football field, he seems to possess an awareness beyond the rational mind. Brady's movements, decisions, and anticipation are in total sync with the rest of his offensive teammates, like he's the leader of a jazz quartet, listening for the bass player and drummer as he tries to find the cracks in the diatonic scale— like Charlie Parker or Thelonious Monk. That kind of ability is to be cherished for the ages. And sometimes, that's what happens to defensive players. Facing Brady, they get lulled into the moment of history and start watching him instead of trying to stop him. "You can't get caught up in watching him too much," Jenkins said. "It's like Peyton Manning. It's all manipulation. And then when you react, it's too late. You got to rely on your own preparation."

Jenkins was heard on the NFL Films replay telling his teammates not to panic. "Hey, we good," Jenkins said. "We're just searching for one stop. That's it. Don't let it frustrate you. We're searching for one stop."

The record-setting third quarter of Super Bowl LII was in the books. Together, the Eagles and the Patriots had kept up a dizzying pace that had a national audience riveted and Al Michaels and Chris Collinsworth in the NBC booth trying to keep pace with the action. In three quarters of play, the two teams had combined for 962 total yards of offense, already the most in any *full* game in Super Bowl history.

* * *

Eagles tight end Zach Ertz came to the sideline and said to Nick Foles, "They cannot stop us." Foles replied, "No, they can't."

But the Patriots did stop the Eagles' offense. On the seventh play of the ensuing Philadelphia offensive possession, Foles could not convert on a third-and-three pass to Nelson Agholor, who was the only Eagles receiver who had been overmatched by the undermanned Patriots secondary. It was a poor choice to throw it to Agholor, who lost eight yards. Elliott's 42-yard field goal was the consolation prize.

And Brady made the Eagles pay immediately. He had already engineered scoring drives of 67, 48, 90, 75, and 75 yards against the Eagles. So, when he lined up with 75 yards in front of him to try to take the lead at the outset of the fourth quarter, it seemed like no big deal—just another day at the office. Josh McDaniels substituted one scat back for another. Dion Lewis was out. Rex Burkhead was in, giving Brady a fresh set of legs to work with. Burkhead went off right guard for five yards. He slid off the left side for nine more, then four more. Then Brady tossed four straight passes like he was playing in his backyard with a bunch of friends. And before the Eagles' defense could catch its breath, the Patriots were on the Philadelphia four-yard line, where Brady found Gronk for an easy score. A 10-play march covering 75 yards in under five minutes. And the Patriots had a one-point lead, 33–32—their first lead of the game.

To the Eagles fans watching in the stands and at home, Gronkowski's touchdown catch had the demoralizing impact of watching a car accident that you cannot stop. This is what Tom Brady does. In all his Super Bowl wins, no team had been able to do the one thing needed to win—make a fourth-quarter stop. The Rams couldn't do it. The Panthers failed to do it. The Eagles, the Seahawks, the Falcons—they were all previously victims of Brady's heroics in the final 15 minutes of the game. Nobody could get to him. The ball came out too quickly. The short passing routes were diabolically precise, his receivers maddeningly reliable. It was all falling into place—another Brady comeback. And this Eagles team seemed powerless to do anything about it.

But Pederson and Foles refused to go down without a fight. The Eagles' final touchdown drive that gave the franchise the lead for good in Super Bowl LII started on their own 25-yard line. Pederson and Foles would have to go 75 yards against the greatest dynasty in modern professional football history, outsmarting perhaps the most driven, prepared defensive coach of his generation, and his loyal lieutenants. Put simply, to retake the lead at this juncture of the game against this opponent was not going to be easy. The Eagles would have to grind it out. So, that's exactly what they did.

The Eagles' drive started not with a bang, but a whimper: Ajayi on a four-yard run, then a Foles incompletion. After a Patriots timeout, Foles found tight end Zach Ertz, who saved his quarterback again—a seven-yard gain for a first down. The Patriots' defense was dug in deep, refusing to yield territory, making sure that nothing went long at the same time each yard gained underneath was agonizing and painful. Blount carried for two more yards. The Patriots just decided that Ajayi and

Blount were not going to get any traction. Foles hit Clement for seven yards, but then his pass to Torrey Smith resulted in no gain, setting up a fourth-and-one at the Eagles' 45-yard line.

Now, it's one thing to call for a pass play on a fourth-and-goal at the end of the first half. If The Philly Special had failed, it would not have been the end of the world. There were still 30 minutes of football to recover. Now, with just over five minutes to go in the Super Bowl, Pederson was calling for a pass play on fourth down. Failure here pretty much meant game, set, match. But the modern analytics of the game screamed, go for it. Play four downs here. Don't punt. And Pederson's analytics adviser in the coaches' booth told him exactly that.

Foles was in the shotgun. He was under heavy pressure, released the football, and found Ertz one yard beyond the line to gain. The Eagles got the first down with just 36 inches to spare.

"That's the greatest play in Eagles history," said Frank Reich. "That pass under those circumstances. I know Philly Special gets all the publicity. It was a touchdown on a pass to the quarterback. I get it. But that pass by Foles—that's the greatest play he makes in the game." Eagles owner Jeffrey Lurie agreed with Reich: Greatest play in team history.

It also gave the Patriots something to think about, opening up the field for the Eagles' offense. Foles hit Nelson Agholor for 10 yards. Then he found Agholor for 18 more yards. Then Agholor again for 10 more. After a three-yard Ajayi run, Belichick—perhaps concerned the Eagles would score—called a timeout. He wanted the ball back in time to let Brady go to work. He was right. Foles found Ertz again open over the middle. Without Butler on the field, safety Devin McCourty was on Ertz and he fell as Ertz crossed over the middle. Ertz stumbled into the end zone, and the Eagles had the lead.

Now it was time to do something only one team—the New York Giants—had ever done in the fourth quarter of any Super Bowl: Get to Tom Brady.

Here's what defensive line coach Chris Wilson said on the sideline on the NFL Films mic: "We have to have more physical rushers. We have to have more power rushers. Or this guy is going to have all day to [expletive] throw the ball, and he's gonna wear our ass out. I'm just telling you."

As Brady gathered his offense on first-and-10 at the New England 25-yard line, here is what Jenkins said on his mic: "See, the funny thing is, somebody on defense is about to be a superhero. Whoever makes the play. Somebody gonna be a hero…Hey, look where we at, bro. Look where we at. We're gonna need one stop, man. It ain't gotta be pretty. We searching for one stop. Let's go. We searching for one stop."

That superhero turned out to be defensive end Brandon Graham. Howie Roseman predicted Graham was made for such a moment about nine years earlier.

* * *

It was the fall of 2009. Howie Roseman, then already an employee in Philadelphia's front office for nine years, was just 34 years old. He was on the road, scouting college players, looking specifically for a pass rusher, a player who could be transformative at one of the most difficult positions in the NFL, somebody who could handle the pressures of the job but also have a big enough personality to deal with the rigors and demands of being a big star in a big city like Philadelphia. He was looking at Brandon Graham. At the time, Graham was playing defensive line at Michigan—Tom Brady's alma mater. Roseman was up in the stands of The Big House, the home stadium of the Michigan Wolverines in Ann Arbor, Michigan.

It's called The Big House because that's exactly what it is—the largest stadium in the United States. It was built in 1927 and has a capacity of 107,601. On this fall afternoon, Roseman was one of those paying customers. He was watching a Michigan home game and he was on the phone with Eagles head coach Andy Reid.

"I think I found our first-round pick," Roseman said to Reid. The Eagles wanted to move up in the first round of the 2010 NFL draft and they needed a good reason. Roseman lobbied Reid that Graham was that reason. Others disagreed. Some scouts argued that at 6-foot-2 and 265 pounds, Graham was too squat and too light to be an effective every-down defensive end. He would not hold up for the long haul. There was an argument that the Eagles needed a safety and that Earl Thomas of Texas was the player they should target. Reid had just promoted Roseman to the post of general manager—at just 34 years old, he was the youngest to be named to such an NFL job in 30 years.

Reid went with Roseman's instincts. And for the next five years, both men suffered ridicule and second-guessing for choosing Graham over Thomas. Graham's rookie year was cut short by a knee injury, which set him back for the better part of two seasons. Meanwhile, Thomas turned into a vicious tackler who had a natural instinct to find the football wherever it was on the field. He played center field for the "Legion of Boom," the nickname given to the record-setting defense of the Seattle Seahawks that beat Peyton Manning and the Denver Broncos in the Super Bowl in 2013. That year, Graham started all 16 games for the Philadelphia Eagles and had just three sacks. The following year, Reid was finally fired.

But under Chip Kelly and Doug Pederson, Graham's career was revived, culminating in his performance in 2017, when he recorded 9.5 sacks, a career high that led the team in that category. The reason was simple: The Eagles got Graham some help. In 2017, Roseman drafted pass rusher Derek Barnett out of Tennessee and signed Chris Long. The No. 1 thing on Graham's bucket list is to drive a NASCAR car. Eagles defensive coordinator Jim Schwartz gave Graham the next best thing: He designed a NASCAR pass-rushing lineup to get after the quarterback in the fourth quarter. Before the Super Bowl, Jon Gruden said the reason the Eagles had a shot to beat the Patriots where the Falcons did not was plain to see: "The Eagles have a fourth-quarter pass rush to close you out, unlike Atlanta did last year." Gruden was right.

On first-and-10 at the 25-yard line, Brady tossed an eight-yard pass to Gronkowski, who was pushed out of bounds by linebacker Nigel Bradham. Too easy. Brady had a second-and-two and the Patriots had stopped the clock. Then Schwartz went NASCAR. It wasn't third down, but Schwartz knew it was a passing down for Brady. Belichick had only one timeout remaining. Brady was in the shotgun. He looked at the line of scrimmage. Right to left, he saw Chris Long at right defensive end, then Brandon Graham at right defensive tackle. At left defensive tackle was Fletcher Cox, with rookie Derek Barnett at left end. With Cox aligned right next to Graham, Brady's center, David Andrews, wearing No. 60, had a choice to make: Help left guard Joe Thuney by double-teaming Cox, or help right guard Shaq Mason by double-teaming Graham. "No. 60's got a problem here," said one of the Eagles coaches prior to the snap. No. 60 slid to his left, choosing to help on Cox, the Pro Bowl tackle who Matt Patricia had vowed before the game was not going to be the one to wreck the Patriots' plans to win their sixth Super Bowl title. He chose wrong. Graham, with a power rush inside, slid his right arm into the pocket and knocked the football loose from Brady's grip. The football rolled on the turf like a lopsided melon on the floor of a grocery store until it found Barnett, who recovered it.

Graham had just performed the toughest job there is on a football field. He had beaten his man, one-on-one, in the fourth quarter of the Super Bowl and violently removed the football from the golden throwing arm of Tom Brady. In short, Graham had stripped the football from the greatest quarterback in the history of the game at the most important time in Eagles franchise history. In my view, this play—not Philly Special, not Nick Foles' fourth-down pass to Zach Ertz earlier in the fourth quarter—is the greatest play in team history. Indeed,

A moment few Eagles fans thought possible back in December: Carson Wentz handing the Lombardi Trophy to Super Bowl LII MVP Nick Foles.

Graham's sack and takeaway must go down as one of the greatest plays in all of Super Bowl history—right up there with David Tyree's helmet catch (also against the Patriots) and Ben Roethlisberger's touchdown pass to Santonio Holmes in the back of the end zone, catapulting the Pittsburgh Steelers over the Arizona Cardinals in Super Bowl XLIII in 2009. Same degree of difficulty. Same critical moment of the game. Same result—pulling off an impossible win against improbable odds.

The Eagles got the ball back on the New England 31-yard line. Four plays later, Jake Elliott kicked a 46-yard field goal, giving the Eagles an important eight-point lead, 41–33, meaning that Brady would have to drive his team the length of the field and make a two-point conversion just to tie the game. Didn't happen. Brady got as far as midfield. But he ran out of time and tried a Hail Mary pass to Gronkowski that was batted around the end zone and finally fell to the ground, sending generations of Philadelphians spilling into the streets: It had happened. The Philadelphia Eagles had won their first Super Bowl title.

One important statistical note: The Eagles and Patriots combined for 1,151 total yards of offense in Super Bowl LII, the most in any game in NFL history—*ever*, in the regular season or the playoffs.

Final score: Eagles 41, Patriots 33

Postscript: Philadelphia joined New York, Boston, Chicago, and Los Angeles as the only cities with a team to win the World Series, the Stanley Cup, the NBA Finals, and the Super Bowl.

Epilogue

M. Night Shyamalan, the movie director known for nasty plot twists and surprise endings, walked into the Marquette Hotel lobby in downtown Minneapolis. It was about 1:30 AM, Monday, February 5, 2018, the early morning after the Philadelphia Eagles won their first Super Bowl title.

I was sitting with a bunch of Eagles fans, eating a slice of cold pizza, sipping a warm beer, enjoying a quiet moment, trying to comprehend what just happened. Shyamalan's appearance abruptly interrupted our stillness. We all began to look at one another as if we were caught in some kind of dream, or worse—that we were all part of one his movies and that Shyamalan was here to announce a cruel ending, that the Eagles had in fact lost Super Bowl LII.

I got up from the lobby couch to introduce myself.

"Do they call you 'M' or 'Night'?" I asked.

He looked at me with a short silent stare. "Night," he said. He delivered the word like it was a line from one of his movies.

Then it dawned on me: Shyamalan grew up in Philadelphia and was a lifelong Eagles fan. He had probably just attended the team's victory party and was calling it a night.

Still, his presence at that precise moment shook us. He turned slowly and walked toward the elevator. Some of us followed him. He pushed the button for the top floor. I thought for sure that if I went up to that floor with him, the elevator doors would slide open and Tom Brady and Bill Belichick would appear, like ghosts of Super Bowls past. And Shaymalan would laugh like Vincent Price at the end of Michael Jackson's video for "Thriller" and tell us that the Patriots had won the Super Bowl. So, I got off on my floor and as I did, I turned to him and said, "Winning the Super Bowl changes a lot of things."

He replied, "It changes everything."

Allen Iverson, who brought the Philadelphia 76ers to the brink of an NBA championship with his unique brand of schoolyard pyrotechnics, was sitting alone at home, watching Super Bowl LII. When the Eagles won, Iverson was overcome with a strange mix of joy and regret.

"I was thinking about my guys on the team, Chris Long and Malcolm Jenkins, and how they were feeling something I never got to feel, win a championship for myself and the city of Philadelphia," he said. "I just thought, 'I'm happy for them,' but I was sad a little for myself. I wanted that feeling so bad. But I was happy for my city."

Dick Vermeil, the godfather of Eagles Nation, the man who single-handedly revived a moribund franchise in the 1970s and took a city to its first Super Bowl, was watching Super Bowl LII with his wife, Carol, his brother Al, and his sister-in-law at his daughter's home in Key West. As the game crossed into the second half, Vermeil admired the sheer relentlessness of Doug Pederson's offensive game plan. "He went after it," said Vermeil. "There isn't a person in the world who would have said the Eagles would win the Super Bowl if Tom Brady set a passing record. But they did. Doug just got after it. Foles was accurate with the football and they kept throwing it."

Vermeil knew it was coming. Before the game, he had advised Pederson about one particular tactic: Don't play it safe in the second half, even if you have the lead. "The history of Brady coming back in the second half—everybody knows it," Vermeil told Pederson. "The fans know it. The media will not stop talking about it. So, the opponents know it. It has an impact. The inevitability of the Patriots coming back has an impact. Your team will feel it. Talk about it. Tell your team about it. And in the second half, you can't play it safe."

As Pederson lifted the Lombardi Trophy over his head, Vermeil got emotional—he had wanted to be the one who did that for the Eagles organization and the city of Philadelphia. Carol looked over at her husband. Dick Vermeil was crying.

Vince Papale, Mr. Invincible, sitting with his wife, Janet; daughter, Gabby; and son, Vinny, in the corner of the end zone at U.S. Bank Stadium, also had tears in his eyes.

"I wasn't sure we were going to win until the freak— Gronk—didn't catch the ball at the end of the game," said Papale. His life as a walk-on hero for Vermeil's Eagles in the 1970s was portrayed by Mark Wahlberg in the movie *Invincible* in 2006. Now, the art of his life collided with the dream of his youth. "After Brady's pass hit the ground, my wife and kids were jumping around with all the Eagles fans," he said. "And I just put my head in my hands and started crying."

More than 48 hours after Super Bowl LII, **Brandon Graham** still had the football he stripped from Tom Brady. Graham was walking around the hallways of the Eagles' practice facility, showing off his personal trophy, what the NFL calls "The Duke," the official game ball with the Patriots' team logo stamped on the nose (to signify it was approved for play when Brady was on the field—that's a book somebody else will have to write sometime).

"This ball gonna be right here," Graham said, tucking it under his arm, "all day, all week, all year. We got the trophy home here in Philly. I got this ball."

Doug Pederson was down the hall, addressing reporters and television cameras. **Jamie Apody**, a sports anchor for Channel 6 in Philadelphia, had this exchange with the head coach:

> **Apody:** You see the smiles around the entire city. People can't wipe the smiles off their faces...
> **Pederson:** Even on all of your faces.

Jason Kelce decided that his team and his city needed one last act of defiance before putting this championship season to rest. What better way to express that defiance than dressing up as a mummer for Philadelphia's official Super Bowl parade? In jolly old England, mummery was practiced by farm workers and townsfolk, who went from manor to manor dressed in jester's clothes and masks, demanding food and drink at Christmas. It was outlawed in many places because, when the Mummers were turned away without sustenance, their behavior was more rebellious than revelry. Philadelphia, not surprisingly, is the only city in America with a full-blown Mummers Parade (on New Year's Day) and it's home to the Mummers Museum, which is located less than a mile from Lincoln Financial Field in South Philadelphia. Kelce dressed as a leprechaun, an outfit supplied by the Avalon String Band, which has been marching in the Mummers Parade since before World War II. After the parade traveled north up Broad Street, wound its way around City Hall, past 1.6 million people, and finished at the Philadelphia Art Museum, all anybody could remember was Kelce, in that

Mummers costume, and the speech he gave at the top of the steps where Rocky Balboa finished his training run through South Philly and into celluloid history.

"I'm going to take a second to talk to you about underdogs," Kelce began. His voice was hoarse with passion and pride. And then he delivered an epic rant that was full of the venomous resentment that has beguiled a city and its sports fans, who were now ready to put an exclamation point on a riotous celebration of a championship that no one predicted, no one thought possible. His speech was passionate. It was profane. It was, in short, all Philly.

Afterword: Almost Special Again

Eleven months after they won their first Super Bowl title in the sparkling new climate-controlled dome in Minneapolis, the Philadelphia Eagles found themselves in the ancient concrete monument built to America's fallen heroes: Soldier Field in Chicago.

Eagles at Bears, wild card playoff game on the evening of January 6, 2019. The wind whipped off Lake Michigan through a wild and anxious crowd, slid down onto the field and swirled around the players like a menacing ghost laughing at their resolve.

I was on the Eagles' sideline, my snow boots caked in mud, my face chapped and red. Chris Long and Fletcher Cox were five yards away from me, standing on the white plastic molded team bench. Their teammates stood shoulder to shoulder along the sideline. We were all transfixed by Nick Foles, who was about to find one last special moment.

Foles, starting in his first playoff game since being named MVP of Super Bowl LII, had taken over for an injured Carson Wentz for a second straight season—rescuing the Eagles from oblivion for a second time. And here he was again, facing yet another postseason fourth down on the doorstep of the opponent's goal line, almost a carbon copy of the one that inspired Philly Special—with one important twist. This time, the game was on the line. Sixty-one seconds left. Make a play or go home.

Foles collected Jason Kelce's snap. The Bears' defensive linemen came at him like they were shot out of a cannon. He shuffled a half step to his right. Tiny veteran running back Darren Sproles tried to knife his helmet into the thighs of Leonard Floyd, who plays defensive end like LeBron James on roller skates. It was no match. Floyd's 33$\frac{1}{8}$-inch arms formed a 10-foot high fence, blocking Foles' view and exit.

But with a flick of the wrist, Foles sidearmed the football like John Stockton finding Karl Malone in the low post amid a dancing herd of Chicago Bulls. His pass landed softly in the hands of Eagles wide receiver Golden Tate, who tiptoed past the yellow pylon, giving the Eagles a 16–15 lead—which would hold up after Chicago's kicker, Cody Parkey, double-doinked a possible game winning field goal off the upright and crossbar, sending 62,462 angry Bears fans spilling onto Michigan Avenue for the long slog home.

Afterward, on the field, I caught up with Foles at about the 50-yard line, with an ESPN camera rolling. He was in the moment—his eyes were calm and clear. But what he *said* revealed other emotions. He knew that despite any more heroics, he was in NFL purgatory. Wentz may have been injured in December for the second straight season, but the future ultimately belonged to the kid from North Dakota.

I put my left hand on his right shoulder. "I just cherish every moment I have out there with my teammates," he said, foreshadowing what would happen next.

* * *

In New Orleans, the following Sunday night, the Eagles' historic ride rolled to the last stop.

Up 14-0 against the Saints, driving for another score, Foles leaned off his back foot and tossed a wobbly pass down the sideline right in front of the Eagles' bench. It was horribly underthrown. Foles knew it from the moment he let it go. His shoulders slumped just as Saints cornerback Marshon Lattimore snatched the easiest interception of his brilliant young career.

Much later in the game, wide receiver Alshon Jeffrey took his eyes off a pass over the middle and the ball slipped through

Nick Foles speaks with me near midfield at Soldier Field in Chicago, minutes after leading the Eagles to a playoff victory over the Bears on January 6, 2019. (Brian Franey)

his hands right into Lattimore's lap: Interception No. 2. But the first interception was the momentum killer. It provided the moment when fate is no longer enough to propel history. After that first pick, the Eagles never scored again, losing 20–14.

After the game, Foles was the last one to step to the podium to address the inevitable question: What was left for him in Philadelphia? It wasn't fair, really. By winning the Eagles' first Super Bowl, St. Nick had moved into the neighborhood reserved for just a few sports legends known by just one name: Namath, Montana, Bradshaw, Unitas.

In the visiting locker room, Pederson and Foles huddled after the game—one-on-one, the coach and quarterback who wrote the most improbable history together. Both of them knew how this was going to end. No need to pretend otherwise. So, Pederson did what he had to do. He said good-bye.

"I just told him that I appreciate everything he has done, to come in and step in the way that he has," Pederson said. "I just told him that I loved him."

One important statistical note: With his one-yard touchdown run in the first quarter against the Saints, Nick Foles became just the third player in NFL history to record a passing touchdown, rushing touchdown, and receiving touchdown (Philly Special) in his postseason career, joining Kordell Stewart and Freeman McNeil. Of the three, only Foles won a Super Bowl.

Postscript: A very wise man once told me, "If you set out to make money, that's all you'll make. If you set out to make history, you'll make both." In March 2019, Nick Foles signed a four-year, $88 million contract with the Jacksonville Jaguars. If he reaches certain incentives, Foles will pocket $102 million.

Acknowledgments

This book represents a 25-year journey. Many, many people helped me along the way. Please indulge me while I try to thank each one of them.

Thank you, Brian Franey. When you are on the road, trying to gather new information in real time in a highly competitive environment for a national television network for 25 straight Sundays, you need somebody you can trust to make sure you're getting it right—all the time. I like to say to my journalism students, you're playing in the big leagues at ESPN. If you get it wrong, they don't let you play. Brian Franey made sure I got it right. And he has one other special skill. He knows every line of every scene in *Goodfellas*. Thank you, Brian, for carefully reading much of this manuscript.

Same goes for Charlie Moynihan. Thank you, Charlie, for always being on the front line with me. Thank you, Tony Florkowski. Felicia's right. We are the same person. Thank you, Andrea Pelkey, Shari Greenberg, Malinda Adams, Eric

Lundsten, Shawn Fitzgerald, Jim Witalka, and Willie Weinbaum, for being road partners and an inspiration.

At the headquarters of the Worldwide Leader, where I arrived in July of 1995, there are so many people who have supported my career, my work, and this book.

I have to start with Seth Markman, the godfather of all things pro football at ESPN. Thank you, Seth, for always believing in what I do and how I do it. You're a great leader: Tough, smart, caring, and you have a big heart.

Thank you to Norby Williamson, Mark Gross, Mike Shiffman, Stephanie Druley, and Mike McQuade. Nobody knows the NFL better than Mike Cambareri. Thank you, Camby. Thank you, Greg Jewell, Matthew Garrett, Chad Minutillo, and Todd Snyder.

Thank you to the BMT management group, especially Tim McHugh and Jon Wolf. Thank you to the crews at *Sunday NFL Countdown*, *NFL Live*, and *Fantasy Football Now*. Thank you everybody at *SportsCenter*, particularly Steve Levy, Linda Cohn, Kevin Negandhi, and Hannah Storm. Thank you to three long-time mentors: David Brofsky, Jim Cohen, and Chuck Salituro.

A very special thank-you to the indispensable crew at ESPN Stats & Information, particularly Vincent J. Masi and Evan Kaplan. Without your help, I don't go on the air and this book does not get written. A special thanks to Elida Witthoeft and the ESPN news desk.

Thank you to everyone at ESPN radio, particularly Mike Golic, Trey Wingo, Beth Faber, Adam Amin, and the Hall of Famer Bill Polian. Giving me the assignment of radio sideline reporter helped shape this book.

The Philadelphia Eagles franchise has been so helpful to me since I started covering the team on January 25, 1993. Imagine being let in their home in South Philadelphia for 25 years! The team has always been welcoming and supportive.

Thank you, first and foremost, Doug Pederson. You promised to take me along for the whole ride and you did. Thank you for the front row seat. Thank you, Jeffrey Lurie, Howie Roseman, Don Smolenski, and the entire public relations team: Brett Strohsacker, Zach Groen, Anthony Bonagura, John Gonoude, and Allison Waddington. Big Dom, you're the best in the business.

In the locker room, there are dozens and dozens of players to thank over more than two decades. Thank you, Carson Wentz, Nick Foles, Donovan McNabb, Michael Vick, and Randall Cunningham. Thank you, Fletcher Cox, Jason Kelce, Brandon Graham, Malcolm Jenkins, Zach Ertz, Brent Celek, Alshon Jeffery, LeGarrette Blount, Jay Ajayi, Chris Maragos, Duce Staley, Frank Reich, John DeFilippo, Jim Schwartz, and Jordan Hicks. Thank you to the long list of Eagles alums: Jeremiah Trotter, Jon Runyan, Brian Westbrook, Brian Dawkins, Mike Quick, Harold Carmichael, Tommy McDonald, Vince Papale, Seth Joyner, and Eric Allen. Thank you, coach Dick Vermeil. Jim Solano, Bob LaMonte, and Tony Agnone, thank you for answering my questions about the business of football.

At the NFL, thank you, commissioner Roger Goodell, for always looking out for me. Thank you, former commissioner Paul Tagliabue. Thank you, Joe Browne, Greg Aiello, Brian McCarthy, Michael Signora, Tom Adden, and the dedicated men and women of NFL security who always make sure that I'm in the right place at the right time.

At NFL Films, thank you, Greg Cosell, the king of the *NFL Matchup* show, which I have hosted for 16 years. Thank you to my colleagues on the show over the years: Ron Jaworski, Merrill Hoge, and Louis Riddick, and the great staff, including Darrell Campbell, Bob Angelo, and Steve Silver. A special thank-you to Ryan Doyal for his brilliant work on The Philly Special.

Thank you, Howard Katz, Ross Ketover, and Chris Willis for your support, insights, and friendship.

At the Pro Football Hall of Fame, where I proudly serve as one of the 46 selectors, thank you, David Baker, Joe Horrigan, Pete Fierle, and Chris Schilling for all your research help and support.

The NFL public relations family has been extraordinarily helpful to me over the years. When I call, they pick up the phone to answer my questions, even when—as Chad Steele of the Baltimore Ravens says—I'm in "full Sal mode." Thank you, Kevin Byrne, Dan Edwards, Derek Boyko, Pat Hanlon, Peter John-Baptiste, Corry Rush, Avis Roper, Ted Crews, Burt Lauten, Stacey James, Aaron Salkin, Amy Palcic, Patrick Smyth, and Bruce Speight.

There are people behind the camera who have gone above and beyond the call of duty for me, routinely enduring 20-hour days, sometimes in brutal cold, snow, and rain, and always making me look good, which is not easy. Thank you, Dominic Orlando and all the men and women at Orlando Video: Kimberly Orlando, Bob Hartman, Steve Barcy, Chuck Calhoun, and Paul Alfe. The DGA crew in Boston has shared special moments with me. Thank you, Jan, Aaron, Dan, and the boys. Jimmy Amperiadis, Dimitri Lagos, and the Interface Communications family in New York—no one works harder than you guys.

At 97.5 FM The Fanatic in Philadelphia, thank you, Anthony Gargano, Mike Missanelli, Eric Johnson, Coach Camille, and Joe Bell.

At *SJ Magazine*, thank you, Marianne Aleardi and photographer David Howarth. And thank you to Maria Esche and all the professional and helpful staff at the Moorestown Public Library for their graciousness and time.

Thank you to my brothers in South Jersey, who have supported this and many other projects of mine: Big George, Frankie Smiles, The Senator, Brother Vince, and The Coach. Thank you, Don Sico, for your sage advice on this project and your invaluable friendship.

Finally, a special big thank-you to my family for supporting me for 25 years on the road. This book has my name on it, but it belongs to them. Thank you, Lynn, Zoe, Kyle, Sarah, Dre, Justin, and Ben, and my three grandchildren, Kira, Etta, and Audrey. This book is dedicated to our collective sacrifice and our shared celebration.